Saints and Sinners
in Queen Victoria's Courts

Saints and Sinners in Queen Victoria's Courts
Ten Scandalous Trials

Tom Zaniello

McFarland & Company, Inc., Publishers
Jefferson, North Carolina

LIBRARY OF CONGRESS CATALOGUING-IN-PUBLICATION DATA

Names: Zaniello, Tom, 1943– author.
Title: Saints and sinners in Queen Victoria's courts : ten scandalous trials / Tom Zaniello.
Description: Jefferson, North Carolina : McFarland & Company, Inc., Publishers, 2021 | Includes bibliographical references and index.
Identifiers: LCCN 2020058692 | ISBN 9781476680811 (paperback : acid free paper) ∞
ISBN 9781476640952 (ebook)
Subjects: LCSH: Trials—England—History—19th century. | England—Social conditions—19th century. | Law—England—Social aspects—History—19th century.
Classification: LCC KD378 .Z36 2021 | DDC 345.42/0709034—dc23
LC record available at https://lccn.loc.gov/2020058692

BRITISH LIBRARY CATALOGUING DATA ARE AVAILABLE

ISBN (print) 978-1-4766-8081-1
ISBN (ebook) 978-1-4766-4095-2

© 2021 Tom Zaniello. All rights reserved

No part of this book may be reproduced or transmitted in any form or by any means, electronic or mechanical, including photocopying or recording, or by any information storage and retrieval system, without permission in writing from the publisher.

On the cover: London and Big Ben © 2021 livepixx.de/Shutterstock

Printed in the United States of America

McFarland & Company, Inc., Publishers
Box 611, Jefferson, North Carolina 28640
www.mcfarlandpub.com

For Mike Silverman,
who loves London as much as I do.

I was now ... to have access to every part of the [Convent], even to the cellar, where two of the sisters were imprisoned for causes that [the other nuns] did not mention. I must be informed that one of my great duties was to obey the priests on all things; and thus I soon learnt, to my utter astonishment and horror, that I was to live in the practice of criminal intercourse with them.
—*Awful Disclosures of Maria Monk* (c. 1836)

Table of Contents

Acknowledgments   ix
Preface   1

Part I—A Crisis of Victorian Culture

1. The Specter   6
2. Outside the Law   10
3. The Court of Lost Causes   21
4. The Family Tree and Genealogical Puzzles   25
5. The Victorian Intellectual Aristocracy   32
6. Architects on the Defensive   44

Part II—Ten Scandalous Court Cases

7. The Ex-Priest and the Nun Who Was His Former Wife: *Connelly v. Connelly*, 1849–1851   52
8. The Defrocked Dominican Priest and the Future Cardinal Whose Brothers Were Atheists: *Regina v. J.H. Newman*, 1851–53   64
9. The Royal By-Blow, the Wandering Statue, and the Religiously Divided Church: *FitzClarence v. Blount*, 1851–1852   88
10. The Medieval Architectural Folly, the Tenth Cousin, and the Earl Who Was a Jesuit: *Talbot v. Earl of Shrewsbury*, 1857–1867   99
11. The Convent Scandal, Fatty Mutton, and the Goosebury Fool: *Saurin v. Star and Kennedy*, 1869   113

12. The Twenty-Six-Stone Claimant and the Invisible Stonyhurst College Quadrangle: *Tichborne v. Lushington*, 1872–1873, and *Regina v. Tom Castro*, 1873–1874   125

13. The Catholic Lord and the Protestant Vicar in the Valley of Martyrs and Queens: *The Duke of Norfolk v. Arbuthnot*, 1879   152

14. The Archbishop and the Jesuit College Building Fund: *Eyre-Eyre v. Eyre*, 1883   165

15. The Lord Chief Justice and His Anti-Vivisectionist Son-in-Law: *Adams v. Coleridge*, 1885–1886   171

16. The Deathbed Letter and the Secret Codicil of the Perfidious Jesuit: *Jerningham v. Caddell*, 1888   187

Part III—The Unbuilt Victorian Church

17. Divided Churches, Divided Souls   194

Chapter Notes   207
Bibliography   217
Index   229

Acknowledgments

Emily Taylor has earned my gratitude and admiration for her line drawings created for the book. The Family Echo website has facilitated the creation of the genealogical charts. The staff of the Jesuit archives in London have been very generous in their hospitality and advice. Librarians too numerous to thank individually have also earned my gratitude.

Some passages in this book appeared earlier in different form in the following essays: "Another Link Between Hopkins and Newman" and "The Coleridges: Notes on a Family Associated with Hopkins," both from the *Hopkins Quarterly*, and "The Divided Victorian Church: Butterfield and the Anglo-Catholic Compromise" from *Religion and the Arts*. (Details of their publication are in the bibliography.)

I would also like to thank the pastors, priests, and staff at all of the religious and other distinctive buildings I have visited while doing the research for this book. The research and writing of this book have also benefited significantly from the support and camaraderie of the Honors Program at Northern Kentucky University as well as the National Labor College (AFL-CIO) and Capitol Hill Village, both located in Washington, D.C.

Preface

Not long after I published *Hopkins in the Age of Darwin* (1988), about the Victorian poet and priest Gerard Manley Hopkins and his interests in nature, science, and related philosophical issues, I realized I had undervalued his obsession with one of the most idiosyncratic and successful architects of the Victorian age, William Butterfield. From that moment, I began to visit many of the churches in England designed by Butterfield that Hopkins himself visited and admired.

In terms of social standing and career the two men could not have been more different. Butterfield was a nationally celebrated architect with numerous ecclesiastical commissions to his credit, not to mention the substantial acknowledgment of his status and expertise in the *London Times* as well as his standing as an expert witness in the courts. He had a long friendship with the Lord Chief Justice John Duke Coleridge and many members of the latter's illustrious family.

Hopkins, on the other hand, was an obscure Jesuit priest and an even more obscure poet. And while Hopkins had close friendships with a number of well-known poets—especially Robert Bridges, who became poet laureate and published Hopkins's poetry only many years after his death—it was science, not poetry, the public could associate with Hopkins because of the four scientific letters about dramatic solar phenomenon he had contributed to *Nature* magazine.

Butterfield's contribution to Victorian aesthetics was considerably more significant than his name recognition today would indicate, because it has been W.E.M. Pugin or John Ruskin that have dominated discussions of Victorian church architecture for most of the twentieth century.

It turned out that Butterfield was the architect of choice of the prominent Coleridge family, who were descended from both poet Samuel Taylor Coleridge and his brother. Descendants included John Duke Coleridge, lord chief justice; Ernest Hartley Coleridge, a close friend of Hopkins; and Henry James Coleridge, a Jesuit priest, who became known as the editor who did *not* publish Hopkins's now quite famous poem *The Wreck of the Deutschland* (1875–6) when it was submitted to the Jesuit journal Coleridge edited.

John Henry Cardinal Newman, Hopkin's spiritual mentor, was also closely associated with the Coleridges. In addition to having a friendship with a number of members of the family, when he was in legal jeopardy Newman relied on a close friend, later a nun, Maria Rosina Giberne, a member of Hopkins's extended family, to rally witnesses for him.

Gradually, then, the genealogical, architectural, and religious patterns of these members of the Victorian intellectual aristocracy began to cohere for me to pursue. I soon discovered that almost all of these figures were involved in some of the most contentious and scandalous trials of the Victorian era.

Given the subject matter, an interdisciplinary approach was inevitable. My training in literary criticism enabled me to include and analyze a number of relevant novels and poems. My earlier study of Hopkins provided me with an understanding of Catholic theology as it interacted with the scientific controversies of the age, especially involving matters of biological inheritance and genealogical descent, both promulgated in the work of Charles Darwin and his cousin Francis Galton. My extensive travels throughout England allowed me to visit the buildings—and assess the church plans and architectural proposals—of competing architects and their patrons, both religious and secular.

The ten scandalous trials provided the entrée into an early- and mid-Victorian "structure of feeling," to use the important concept pioneered for a previous generation of scholars by Raymond Williams in *Marxism and Literature* (1977) to connote a culture of both institutions and social relationships that actively define personal (informal) and institutional (formal) experiences. The "structure of feeling" in this book draws on Catholic–Protestant struggles, architectural extravagances, genealogical obsessions, and inheritance anxiety of the day. The Victorian courts provided the perhaps unexpected but inevitable arena for all of these.

Why were there ten scandalous trials (more precisely, eight trials and two legal actions non-suited or settled out of court), a number of which were patently absurd if not devilishly strange, the others driven by both real and faux-religious zeal or avarice, all populated by so many of the same important intellectual and public figures who were often contesting inheritances or pieces of church property?

The trial of the "Tichborne Imposter" (chapter 12) was so absurd that Arthur Sullivan of the famous comic opera writing duo Gilbert and

Sullivan, who at one point sat with his friend, Chief Justice Alexander Cockburn, at the judge's bench during the trial, soon after launched the duo's very first comic opera, *Trial by Jury* (1875), inspired in part by the case.

Readers should take note that every inch of contested religious property in London and in British villages that I discuss may still be easily visited today, as I myself have done, except Alton Towers, where one may have to put up with thousands of children beside themselves with excitement, as one of England's premiere amusement parks was built on the Tower's grounds (see chapter 10). With the exception of the latter, then, visiting these sites will bring to life the "structure of feeling" of competing religious experiences and architectural preferences that I explore.

But I do not think it's likely that even peripatetic readers of *Saints and Sinners* will encounter the specter that was haunting the streets of early Victorian London…

Part I

A Crisis of Victorian Culture

1

The Specter

> One of the most disgusting penances we had ever to submit to, was that of drinking the water in which the [Mother] Superior had washed her feet.
>
> ❖❖❖
>
> Infants were sometimes born in the Convent, but they were always baptized, and immediately strangled.
> —*Awful Disclosures of Maria Monk* (c. 1836).

A specter was haunting the streets of early Victorian London: a runaway Roman Catholic nun, clutching an infant, recently escaped from a convent that was in reality a house of horrors, sexual license, and infanticide. The nun's name was changeable, and she escaped her convent not once but twice. No matter that Maria Monk's original story was set in Montreal, because many Protestant Londoners believed that she could easily have been in a British convent too. In the public imagination she soon morphed into similar wayward figures, under other names but with just as unlikely back stories of abuse, lifted indiscriminately from the pages of the *Awful Disclosures of Maria Monk* by legions of fanatical or frightened Protestants who believed Catholics were hiding behind every Anglican altar.

She appeared in cities across the Atlantic as well: New York City, Montreal, Charleston, sometimes as Maria Monk, sometimes as Rebecca Theresa Reed, "author" of *The Thrilling Mysteries of a Convent Exposed*, and sometimes as Sister Mary Agnes of *Six Months' Residence in a Convent*, Mary Agnes being a thirteen-year-old student who was being groomed as a nun at the Charleston, Massachusetts, Ursuline Convent, one of the religious houses that was in fact attacked by an anti–Catholic mob in 1834 and burned to the ground after she had escaped.

She felt escape was necessary because she knew too much: one of her friends in the convent was allowed to waste away and die, another who was considered "insane" was "disappeared," presumably to Canada. Mary Agnes was obsessed with the petty religiosity of the Mother Superior and the fairly unpleasant—and unhygienic—practices of convent life. The nuns were forever kissing the floor as a sign of their obedience, but the overuse of the spittle of the father confessor of the convent was truly disturbing to her and inevitably to all her readers. When Mary Agnes was baptized, for example, a piece of salt was placed in her mouth, the priest breathed on her three times, and touched "her eyes, ears, and nose with spittle." Later Mary Agnes was taught that a blind woman recovered her sight when the priest touched her eyes "with spittle and holy oil." Just before her escape, Mary Agnes faced a final and perhaps tragic/comic moment of humiliation when the Mother Superior sent from her table "a plate of apple parings, the remnant of her dessert" for Mary Agnes to eat.[1]

The only problem with Maria Monk—and her sisters who supposedly participated, willing or not, in immoral activities behind convent walls—is that she did not exist. She was the greatest fake news story of the era, so successful that American historian Richard Hofstadter in *The Paranoid Style in American Politics* was moved to call the anti–Catholicism her story generated "pornography for Puritans" because "the anti–Catholics invented an immense lore about libertine priests, the confessional as an opportunity for seduction, licentious convents and monasteries."[2] In the end Maria Monk's memoir was outsold in the United States only by a different kind of horror story, Harriet Beecher Stowe's *Uncle Tom's Cabin* (1852), but Maria Monk was already a best-seller in London as well, to John Henry (later Cardinal) Newman's dismay.

Maria Monk's *Awful Disclosures* was followed by numerous other published books and pamphlets that a credulous public seemed to crave: there were alternative versions of her original story and sequels and prequels and even entirely different Maria Monks using her or another fictitious nun's name. Ministers who knew probably less than nothing about convents had their own "exposés" co-published with Maria Monk's memoir: T.B. Peterson, one of the self-styled "most celebrated Methodist preachers now living"—and conveniently his own publisher as well—wrote in his *Thrilling Mysteries of a Convent Revealed!* that it was routine for a mother superior to conspire with off-site confederates to inflate tuition and fees for students attending convent schools and, even more disturbing, encourage—albeit with grotesque jealousy—a priest to groom a "beautiful" young and naïve nun as a kind of concubine.[3] The convent also conspired to send a young nun to impersonate the legatee of an estate whose lawyers would be ignorant of the appearance of the real, now deceased, legatee.[4] Other entrepreneurs even flogged photos showing "Maria Monk" with her baby.

Nonetheless, our consensus must be: all fake news, almost every last titillating bit. Real convents were not immune to scandal, of course: chapter 11, "The Convent Scandal...," indicates some basis to suspect that certain aspects—especially concerning food—of convent life were unacceptable to public morals if not common sense. Even the Earl of Shrewsbury, one of the most celebrated Catholic lords in the land, was accused in 1847 of forcing a niece into a convent in order to control her inheritance. The Court of Chancery dismissed the case as having no merit.[5]

Often the stories Maria Monk told were straight out of a Gothic or sensation novel saturated with anti-convent pornography: the nuns were told always to be sexually accessible to priests who came secretly visiting the convent back door at night, announcing their arrival—and readiness for sex—with what could only have been the most annoying toothy "whistle" known to man or woman.[6] Should a pregnancy arise, the baby at birth was immediately baptized, smothered, and thrown into a lime pit conveniently located inside the convent walls for such purposes.[7]

When nuns were disobedient, they were imprisoned, usually beaten, and in one particularly horrific instance, a nun was tied to a bed while other nuns and even a priest took turns jumping on her until she was crushed to death.[8]

Even the not-so-salacious stories were unlikely. At one point, Maria Monk tires of convent life, leaves, and gets married for about three weeks! Mistake: her man is unsuitable, but she now wants to get re-admitted to her old convent, although she knows that her marriage would not be considered a suitable furlong for a virginal nun. Instead she concocts a tale of being under the "protection" of a woman with whom she had taken a temporary teaching position. Too busy with unpleasant deeds, the leadership of her old convent readily takes her back in.[9]

The popular obsession with Maria Monk fueled the anti–Catholic campaigns throughout the country and in a sense provided the popular context for the scandalous trials with religious emphases featured in this book. These stories of ten scandalous trials from Victorian England tell of an ongoing struggle against Roman Catholicism that many Anglican Protestants would not—many of them believed, would never—relinquish. It is also the story of competing architectural visions for houses of worship for these contending faiths. And finally it is the story of numerous saints and sinners from every social class in London, high and low, from the street vagrants and "sturdy rogues" Henry Mayhew catalogued in his encyclopedic *London Labour and the London Poor* (1861–2) to the jurists, landlords, businessmen, and skilled operatives who would sit on the bench or in the jury box to give judgment on those persons both pathetic and well-born who found themselves in the dock.

2

Outside the Law

> I cannot help thinking that while the Pope continues to be an Italian ecclesiastic, clear insight into the character and circumstances of John Bull will never be among his gifts, either human or divine. ... The sight of a Cardinal's hat will, for some time to come, perhaps, make him as dangerous as a scarlet rag makes the four-footed sovereign of the meadow.
> —Sara Coleridge, *Memoir and Letters* (1874)

At mid-century John Bull believed that the invasion his countrymen had predicted—and feared—ever since the sixteenth century was imminent: the pope and his cardinals would take back the Roman Catholic Church properties Henry VIII had seized 300 years earlier and re-establish sovereignty over both Anglican property *and* clergy. Wilkie Collins' novel *The Black Robe* (1881) explained the mechanism for this retrieval: monks, just before Henry VIII's henchmen seized their properties and drove them from their religious houses, secreted the original deeds of their Catholic properties in marble statues that they tossed into the monastery's ponds. Three hundred years later, their order would retrieve the statues and the deeds that "proved" their ownership.

This Roman Catholic "invasion" was popularly known as the Papal Aggression. Unfortunately both sides of this struggle often resorted to violence in the streets to defend their version of absolute truth.

The Roman Catholic side was clearly a minority movement. Not many bishops were needed at first to lead the country's three distinct subgroups of Catholics. The "old" or Recusant Catholics were descendants of wealthy families whose Catholicism predated the Reformation; after the Reformation, according to Lawrence Stone's history of the period, they were virtually "a quietist sect of aristocratic and upper-gentry families" who "retreated into self-imposed isolation." It is possible that their somewhat parochial approach to

2. Outside the Law

wealth—concentrating on houses, land, and mercantile pursuits, as opposed to investing, military pursuits, or other grand schemes of the aristocracy involving monasteries or bishoprics, protected them from extreme confiscations of wealth and forfeiture of life.[1]

There were also many more recent English converts from middle- and upper-class Protestant families, of whom John Henry (later Cardinal) Newman was the most notorious and Gerard Manley Hopkins, Newman's earnest Oxford convert, the most poetic. And finally there appeared—as they always do—the great pathetic mass of poor working-class Irish immigrants, fleeing starvation in their homeland.

The second group, who were, after all, drawn from the nation's leading religious, public service, and aristocratic ranks, disturbed the establishment the most. *The Whithall Review* in 1878 named more than 1,900 men and women they titled *Rome's Recruits: A List of Protestants Who Have Become Roman Catholics*. This was their collection of "the names of the elite," now members of the Catholic intellectual aristocracy, many of whom who had held positions of great responsibility, formerly as part of the Protestant establishment.

This extraordinary act of investigative journalism attracted the attention of W.E. Gladstone, who had just completed his first term (1868–74) as prime minister under Queen Victoria and who would go on to three more terms. Although Gladstone's own sister and cousin were on the list, he asserted in 1874 that a Roman Catholic could not be a loyal subject of the United Kingdom. The same year Newman published a pamphlet, *A Letter Addressed to His Grace the Duke of Norfolk on Occasion of Mr. Gladstone's Recent Expostulation*, rebutting this commonly held belief.

Gladstone thought it would be of great help for the *Review* to analyze the recruits according to this scheme: "1. The number of peers. 2. Of members of titled families. 3. Of clergy. 4. Of Oxford men. 5. Of ladies." The categories speak for themselves, of course, but they reflect the anxiety of influence their numbers—and their social status—surely projected. Gladstone also wanted to know if these recruits appeared before 1840, between 1840 and 1860, and since 1860; that is, he attempted to create a possible metric to determine the influence of the Oxford Movement (approximately 1830 to 1850) among other current religious moments.[2] The new clergymen on the list were drawn almost exclusively from the ranks of the Jesuits and the Oratorians, the two groups that rankled anti–Catholics the most, the former because of their supposed stealth methods of recruitment and obsession with securing inheritances for their church, the latter because of Cardinal Newman's leadership. Very rarely was the name of the order of the nuns who converted, however, identified. Oxford men, as Gladstone surmised, were the largest group of university men identified.

With the exception of Catholics from Recusant families who, after all, had medieval roots, virtually every single middle- and upper-class British Catholic convert discussed in this book is on this list.

Sara Coleridge, the daughter of the Romantic poet Samuel Taylor Coleridge, had in fact accurately assessed some of the potential violence of her fellow Protestants, for the third quarter of the nineteenth century marked the high tide of mutual religious and civic intolerance among British Protestants, Roman Catholics, and Anglo-Catholics.[3] The attacks of Protestant mobs on Catholic churches and some retaliatory raids on Protestant churches by Catholics were the most flagrant examples of street-fighting, even as scandalous religious and civic strife found its way into the austere British courtroom as well. Often church services were disrupted, as well.

St. Barnabas Church, in a poor district in Pimlico—although an established Anglican parish—was suspected of having been a target of Roman Catholic "aggression." Its Anglo-Catholic services were described as the "very Popery itself under the thinnest guise of the Protestant name."[4] W.J.E. Bennett, its vicar, had by 1850 been accused of a number of Romish practices, including having lighted candles on the altar, facing eastwards during the celebration of communion, and allowing parishioners to take the host directly into their mouths.[5]

St. Barnabas had been built by Thomas Cundy with support from the most distinguished architect of the Anglo-Catholic movement, William

Sara Coleridge, daughter of Samuel Taylor Coleridge and editor of his biographical writings, from *Harper's New Monthly Magazine,* June–November 1873 (author's collection).

Butterfield, complete with a beautiful ceiling by Pre-Raphaelite painters. Sir Charles Eastlake's contemporary account of the church in his *History of the Gothic Revival* (1872) makes it easy to see why dedicated mainstream Anglican parishioners were suspicious of what Cundy and Butterfield had wrought, complaining that a Butterfield church was considered "proof positive of Popery." Why? The "chancel was separated from the rest of the building by a screen," a Gothic feature that was a design obsession of the Roman Catholic architect Pugin to create more mystery at the altar but was also typical of Butterfield's work. Even more to the latter's taste were the encaustic (glazed) tiles, colored diapering on the walls, and the "corona of beaten metal; and glass bosses depended from the paneled roof." The marble pulpit, stained-glass windows, and Latin texts carved into the arches made this a church like few others. Eastlake pointed out that even the parsonage and the school had "narrow and pointed" windows, suspiciously resembling a neo–Gothic convent. And, Eastlake concluded, "the St. Barnabas Parsonage was probably the first instance in which a Victorian drawing-room received its light from a lancet window," one of the defining features of the Gothic style.[6]

Bennett threatened to resign from this magnificent church and convert to Roman Catholicism in the summer of 1850. After demonstrations of parishioners hissing, "That is popery!" during a particularly Catholic moment in the services and the gathering of a hostile crowd outside the church in November, the church was closed by the Anglican bishop's authority just before Christmas, and although the judge, John Duke Coleridge, ruled that his decision could not stand, he was overruled upon appeal.[7] When the services were resumed—without Bennett—the candles were unlit and the services proceeded undisturbed.[8] John Duke Coleridge wrote that "Puritan intolerance" was the guiding force in one of the legal decisions in 1857 that forbade "lace on the white cloths" on the altar even if the appeal to the Privy Council "legalized" the cross.[9]

In another London district, Protestants campaigned against Alexander Mackonochie, the vicar of St. Alban the Martyr parish church on Brooke Street in Holborn, designed by William Butterfield in 1859 with his characteristic alternating bands of colored brick. Just three years later, closure of the rebellious church seemed imminent, the *London Times* opined, when the judge "performed the remarkable feat of turning people out of a church to which they had never come," as "the district ... can scarcely be described as a church-going neighborhood."

Mackonochie had been so bold as to even include in his parish Roman Catholics, in particular the poor Irish immigrants[10] whose

St. Alban's Holborn, London. Architect: William Butterfield. Vicar: Alexander Mackonochie (photograph by the author).

allegiance was of particular concern of competing Anglo- and Roman Catholics.

Mackonochie imagined himself to be a Jesuit without portfolio: he used the *Spiritual Exercises* of St. Ignatius and other Jesuit manuals as the basis for his sermons and other church-work.[11] His commemorative plaque at the church to this day bears the Latin abbreviation AMDG ("For the Greater Glory of God") that is a virtually exclusive Jesuit sememe.

Mackonochie's decade of persecution began in 1867 when he was accused of elevating the host at communion, excessive kneeling, and using incense and lighted candles, among other things. His first Court of Arches trial the following year declared everything but kneeling and lighted candles legal. Mackonochie, characteristically, began genuflecting instead of kneeling.[12]

Mackonochie became synonymous with "the enemy within." Even the Presbyterians enjoyed attacking him: the Rev. J. Cumming of the Scotch National Church on Russell Street in Covent Garden (the church attended by the Duke of Norfolk, a rare Protestant convert of this Catholic clan), criticized St. Alban's in particular and the "ritualists" in general:

> I believe the Papal Aggression of 1850 was bold and perilous, but it was open. The Papal Aggression of 1867 is the Pope in the garb of a Protestant minister, and within a Protestant place of worship. ... That in 1850 was the artillery of the Vatican laid and leveled at the fortress of Protestantism; the Aggression of 1866 and 1867 is the action of poisoners within the citadel, poisoning the springs of water, corrupting the living bread, extinguishing the lights of heaven and giving to deceived people the candles of the priests instead.[13]

Ten years later Mackonochie was back at the Court of Arches facing more or less the same list of charges. Convicted once more and suspended for three years, he eventually resigned his Anglican living. Exhausted from his losing campaigns, he perished in a snowstorm in 1887 while hiking in Scotland. It may not have been an accident. At his funeral, Newman's hymn "Lead, Kindly Light" was sung.[14]

Gerard Manley Hopkins' fellow Jesuit and friend, Richard F. Clarke, reviewed Mackonochie's career in the Jesuit journal *The Month* three years after his death, arguing that Mackonochie's approach to his poor parishioners involved teaching them "spiritual realities" using "outward symbols," obviously too close to Roman Catholic practices for his Anglican masters. And although he spent years "living on such crooked lines,"[15] he nonetheless occupied a William Butterfield church.

Victorians may have had the reputation for piety, but nasty doctrinal divisions among Christians were widespread. Not only was there the historical split between the Anglican Church—as established by Henry VIII during the Reformation—and Roman Catholicism—as symbolized by the papacy, but within the ranks of British Protestantism the High Church or Tractarian party was still a suspicious cohort to be feared by the Low Church forces. The Anglo-Catholics, the highest of the high, as it were, within the Anglican church, seemed to be adopting every attribute of Romanism except papal authority itself. Even within the ranks of Roman Catholicism, a major fissure existed between the Old Catholics, families who had held on for centuries during periods of anti–Catholic persecution, and the native English converts who with recent Irish immigrants looked to Rome for leadership.

At this time those who identified with a "Catholic" position within the Anglican Church but who refused to leave that church became the enemy within. Although Queen Victoria believed that the threat of Roman Catholicism was exaggerated, she listened approvingly when her prime minister quoted Tom Arnold, headmaster of the Rugby School: "I look upon a Roman Catholic as an enemy in his uniform; I look upon a Tractarian as an enemy disguised as a spy."[16] Although the Anglo-Catholics did not wish to dwell on the Tractarian Wars of the 1830s, they still believed they could "Catholicize" the Anglican Church: one of their weapons was the innovative architecture of William Butterfield. Anglo-Catholicism dreamed of a Pre-Raphaelite medieval Catholic facade on an Anglican foundation, hoping to reduce the hostility to Catholic ideas and practices within the Anglican Church, win the Catholic masses (the Irish and other poor folk) away from the papists, and re-establish the church building as an aesthetic object in itself. On the first two fronts they were generally unsuccessful, but the Butterfield churches of London and elsewhere are the dramatic—and even to this day spectacular—monuments of their aesthetic of compromise.

The year 1850 marked the most significant deterioration in the relationship of Protestants and Catholics in centuries. Superficially, civil rights for Catholics had mostly been restored in the Emancipation Act of 1829 and Parliament had repealed a number of restrictive acts: Jesuits did not have to post bonds merely because they were Jesuits, for example, and public funerals for Catholics were no longer banned. What was won in the political realm, however, could be lost in the court of public opinion, as the success of the best-selling scandalous "memoir," *Awful Disclosures of Maria Monk*, first published in 1836, was ready-made to fan anti–Roman Catholic sentiment. John Henry (later Cardinal) Newman was shocked to discover in 1851 that the book had sold in England (at least) a quarter of a million copies. In less hysterical times, perhaps, the author's outrageous name alone would have convinced many of the book's status as a piece of fiction, a literary cousin to the popular Gothic romances of the previous quarter century. But Maria Monk revealed a life of incredible danger and horror, as she witnessed—and recounted in gruesome detail—numerous infants and one adult nun murdered by nuns and priests inside a Montreal, Canada, convent.

2. Outside the Law

Unfortunately, *Saurin v. Star and Kennedy*, a notorious public trial in 1869 involving abusive and demeaning activities in a convent, discussed in chapter 11, made some of Maria Monk's tales seem all too plausible.

But other forms of anti–Catholic sentiment were common. Carlyle fumed about the manifestations of "Jesuitism" in his successful *Latter-Day Pamphlets* in 1850. In 1857 Pre-Raphaelite painter John Everett Millais exhibited a deliberately sensationalist painting, *The Escape of a Heretic*, in which we see a Roman Catholic priest gagged and tied up with his own vestments and rosary, while a gentleman disguised as a monk rescues a distraught young woman whose apron has the image of a hideously contorted devil, remarkably like Maria Monk's description, that Newman knew well, of "a picture of an infernal pit" with a "wretch who was biting at the bars of hell, with a serpent gnawing her hand, with chains and padlocks on."

After 1829 Roman Catholics had claimed their civil liberties, led by the 12th Duke of Norfolk, who sat in the House of Lords as the first Roman Catholic to take such a seat since the sixteenth century. The freedom was potentially short-lived as a result of the announcement in 1851 by the Vatican—through Nicholas (later Cardinal) Wiseman—that the Roman Catholic hierarchy was being restored in England with the appointment of Wiseman himself as the archbishop of a newly reconstituted "see" or ecclesiastical zone of Westminster. *If,* by Roman Catholic definition, the Church of England was schismatic, this appointment gave the pope, many Protestants argued, some kind of vague and mysterious power over their queen.

Intellectuals and members of the upper classes for their part concentrated on the threat of Puseyism within their own ranks, monitoring whenever Anglican ministers seemed to be succumbing to one form of "ritualist practice" or another: raising the host during communion, for example, or genuflecting at the altar. Londoners and other provincial Protestants, on the other hand, kept their eyes peeled for the real enemy—the popish invasion of priests they felt was inevitable once Wiseman tried to take over the Church of England.

The London *Times* dutifully reported all of the enemy's movements, not only within the ranks of the established church but also on the skirmish lines in the streets. An all-out war in a colonial outpost could hardly compete. Given the nature of relatively free economic enterprise, it was hard to control the border, and security breakdowns were inevitable. A scout observed a French ship disgorging "21,000 crucifixes of different sizes, from one inch to two feet, several thousand figures of the Virgin Mary, and a large quantity of bleeding hearts."[17]

Three weeks later, the *Times* confirmed what would come of having a priest-ridden society, when it reported the Abbe Gothland's murder of his servant, "the widow Deguisal." This exemplar of "the priesthood in France" had an intimate sexual relationship with Madame du Savlon, the wife of a doctor and the priest's neighbor. Madame Deguisal had "enlarged a hole which happened to be in the ceiling of the cure's bedroom and placed herself in the garret above. Peeping through the hole, she distinctly saw the parties on the bed." When she made the mistake of telling the cure to his face what she knew, he and his lover poisoned her.[18]

The *Times* was barely a genteel improvement on the culmination of the street-life of the "No Popery!" movement which came on the anniversary of the most significant anti–Catholic event of the early seventeenth century—November 5, Guy Fawkes Day, the "almost forgotten celebration," as the London *Times* stated, "of the anniversary of the Gunpowder Plot." While child- and adult-sized effigies were always common on this populist "street" holiday, effigies of "Guido" Fawkes turned into an extravaganza "*got up* by some zealous anti–Romanists regardless of cost." A procession of fourteen figures, "animate and inanimate," led by a Guy (now a Guido) sixteen feet in height on a carriage drawn by two horses arrived at Fleet Street at mid-day. In addition to effigies, live actors impersonated Cardinal Wiseman, a lusty monk, and a nun, while still another monkish figure held a brush with a pail of whitewash labeled "Holy Water for the Penitent!" Accompanied by police, the procession toured central London all afternoon, gathering forces but apparently caused no violence.[19]

Less fortunate was Newman's own Oratory in Birmingham ten days later, when police had to be called out to control a crowd of Protestants who had gathered outside the doors of the chapel in response to an open-coffin funeral of a recently deceased Oratorian. After struggles between funeral-goers inside the chapel and outsiders pushing their way in, in part to marvel at Roman Catholic funeral rites and in part to cause mischief, Newman himself called out the police to protect, as the *Times* noted, the funeral of the only Oratorian who had *not* been a former Anglican.[20] On another occasion Newman himself was hit by a bag of flour[21] and he noted that during excavations for a cellar, quite a few people passed by to take a look at the possible secret cells under construction.[22]

A very close second to the anti–Catholic rumors and half-truths were the scandals developing around "the enemy within," those Anglicans who were (and remained) Anglo-Catholics and those Anglicans who were "going over to Rome." There were a number of notorious cases, often cited by Protestant intellectuals and rabble-rousers alike: it would not be easy to estimate to what extent such bad publicity helped to bring the crowds into the street.

The "perversion" in 1850 of Rudolph Feilding, later the 8th Earl of Denbigh, reinforced the Protestant view of a conniving Catholic clergy. Louisa Pennant, Lady Feilding, had promised to build an Anglican church in Pantasaph, a poor rural area of Wales, despite her—and her husband's—developing Roman Catholic sympathies and friendship with Henry (later Cardinal) Manning. The Privy Council's Gorham Decision, according to the traditions within the Feilding family, had been the last straw for Lord Feilding's faith in the Anglican Church as a part of a universal church independent of the civil state, as that decision meant that a civil court (the Privy Council) had decided on a religious matter (reversing the Court of Arches decision to discipline Gorham). Feilding remained in the Anglican communion even as he chaired an important London meeting protesting the decision.[23]

Louisa Pennant had entered into the early stages of an illness that would soon take her life. When the local minister refused to administer communion to the couple because they were skeptical of the authority of his priesthood, the couple were received into the Roman Catholic Church, and subsequently Feilding's father, the 7th Earl of Denbigh, disinherited his son.[24]

Although construction of the church at Pantasaph had already begun, the couple decided to re-dedicate its foundation as a Roman Catholic church. There was a storm of protest from Anglican quarters, mainly based on the allegation that Feilding had also used a large bequest by Lady Emma Tennant after her death and after the subsequent conversion of her husband to Roman Catholicism to continue construction on the church. In vain did Feilding protest that none of her inheritance was used to build this Catholic church, but his analogy was perhaps ill-chosen: "St. Paul did not, after his conversion, consider himself bound by the promise which he had made to the Jewish synagogue, that he would do the utmost to crush the rising Christian church at Damascus. And why? Because he made it in ignorance."[25]

The culmination of the No Popery campaign of the early 1850s was the Achilli scandal that ensnared the one Roman Catholic leader the militant Protestants hated the most—John Henry Newman. While this trial is the subject of chapter 8, at this point we should note that Newman was baited by the Evangelical Alliance, who had hired Giacinto Achilli, a former Dominican priest, to convert Roman Catholic Italians living in London to the Anglican faith. Newman, following the lead of Wiseman, who had assembled evidence of Achilli's misdeeds, had denounced Achilli in one of his lecture in the series, "The Present

Position of Catholics in England." That Newman survived this trial with his reputation intact is a testament to the complicated currents of religious controversy at the time.

The second major wave of anti–Roman Catholic agitation occurred in the 1860s and, as in the previous decade, both Roman Catholics and Anglo-Catholics were the objects of attack. A new No Popery campaign had started in the provinces, this time led by a charismatic stump speaker, William Murphy, whose supposedly Catholic family from Ulster had been secretly Protestant. His anti–Catholicism was also strongly anti–Irish immigrant: "The way to get rid of Fenianism is to hang the priests," Murphy threatened, according to a *Times* letter-writer (a Unitarian minister). After this suggestion, Murphy's listeners marched down the street four abreast singing, "Britons never shall be slaves!"[26]

The following night, Murphy told his audience the basic rules of Catholicism. Priests were required, he said, to have concubines, easily within reach at every convent, where "wives and daughters ... are betrayed and kidnapped." On the lay side of things, a man could murder his baby or wife if he paid a priest exactly twenty-six pounds, two shillings, and six pence and confessed to the deed. Murphy punctuated his lecture by firing a "ten-chambered revolver" through the window of the hall. Hired by the Evangelical Mission and Electoral Union, he was himself always half-cocked.[27]

On a number of occasions he led the roving mobs as they attempted to sack Roman Catholic chapels. In one village (Oldham, eight miles from Manchester), local men were discovered making pike-heads at a foundry while a number of other youths began to openly sport "orange favors" to show their sympathy with Irish Protestantism. Observers were left with the conviction that these were dedicated Murphyites. Eventually the Irish Catholic workers in the area also began to form up, marching to two chapels—one Baptist and one Independent—where they smashed all the windows.[28] In the end Murphy was in fact done in by an Irish crowd who beat him within an inch of his life. He never really recovered and died in 1872.[29]

Despite Murphy's lament that the authorities in the end no longer protected him from Irish mobs who would not respect his right to free speech, Murphy did have some parliamentary support in the form of an MP, G.H. Whalley, who told the House of Commons, "A more honest, truthful, and he might almost say a more careful man in his statements had never appeared as a public lecturer than Mr. Murphy."[30]

3

The Court of Lost Causes

> London, Michaelmass Term lately over, and the Lord Chancellor sitting in Lincoln's Inn Hall. Implacable November weather. ... Smoke lowering down from chimney-pots, making a black drizzle, with flakes of soot in it as big as full-grown snow-flakes—gone into mourning, one might imagine, for the death of the sun.
>
> —Charles Dickens, *Bleak House* (1853)

The London courts in these pages are filled with a number of outrageous and fascinating Victorian men and women, quite a few upstanding and virtuous, a few of them clearly mad, some of them certainly charlatans and bold-face liars, and a big handful of opportunists of various stripes. Saints or sinners? Neither? Both?

Many of the targets of legal action, innocent or otherwise, survived. That justice of any kind was meted out is a tribute to the Victorian courts, despite their unwieldy and sometimes byzantine rules. Nevertheless, that at least ten of these attempts at justice would meet the definition of scandal in any age should make them provocative and, I hope, rewarding reading.

Charles Dickens, of course, already knew this. His novel *Bleak House* (1853) satirized the High Court of Chancery, perhaps the most notorious of the Victorian law courts, in his dramatization of the characters trapped in *Jarndyce v. Jarndyce*, a "scarecrow of a suit [that] has, in course of time, become so complicated, that no man alive knows what it means." The novel opens with a description of London fog above muddy streets, symbolizing the legal mess the parties of the suit have found themselves: "The dense fog is densest, and the muddy streets are muddiest" near Temple Bar. And "hard by Temple Bar, in Lincoln's Inn Hall, at the very heart of the fog, sits the Lord High Chancellor in his High Court of Chancery."[1]

The fictional *Jarndyce v. Jarndyce* was based on an actual Chancery suit, *Jennens v. Jennens*, that began in 1798 and finally collapsed in 1915. William Jennens died in 1798, possibly the richest man in England. The case contesting his estate had already been running for fifty-five years when *Bleak House* was published. By the end of the novel *Jarndyce v. Jarndyce*, like *Jennens v. Jennens*, just "lapses and melts away" because "the whole estate is found to have been absorbed in costs." In brief, not a pence remains for any heir. On that final day the clerks in Chancery come streaming out of the court carrying reams of paper and laughing, throwing "immense papers of all shapes and no shapes" on the pavement because even they are free of this infernal and seemingly never-ending suit. "It was all up with at last!" shouted "an official-looking person" who "burst out laughing too."[2]

In large part because of Dickens's marvelous prose, Chancery, the first division of Common Law, has become the most famous (notorious) division of the London courts, although there are three other divisions, completely independent of Chancery, that often picked up the cases that resisted Chancery's touch. The second division of Common Law itself also consisted of three courts that directly administered trials or other legal proceedings in three areas: (1) criminal matters were decided by the Queen's Bench, (2) customs and fines were handled by the Exchequer, and (3) personal disputes were placed in the Court of Common Pleas. The official presiding over the first and third of these courts was the lord chief justice, while the chief baron judged matters in the Exchequer. Seven of the ten criminal trials in this book were held before the courts of Common Pleas (one) and the Queen's Bench (six).

A third division of Common Law included four church courts: the most "public" was the Court of Arches, since it adjudicated marital suits. The first of our scandalous trials, a very unusual, long running marital drama, *Connelly v. Connelly* (chapter 7), characterized by cheeky Londoners on the street as the case of an ex–Catholic priest suing an ex–Catholic nun, his ex-wife, for resumption of marital privileges, began in the Court of Arches. Presiding over this court was the Dean of Arches, who also presided over the second Church Court, the Court of Faculties, which settles disputes on "plural livings" or multiple parishes or other religious assignments that a single clergyman could lead and administer. The bishop of London presided over the other two Church Courts: the Consistory Court, which adjudicated controversies of divorces and wills, and the Prerogative Court, which settled disputes involving bishops.

As a world power England needed a separate maritime or fourth division called the High Court of the Admiralty to handle wrecks and

3. The Court of Lost Causes

other "acts on the high seas." This court was called to order by the man simply called "the Judge." The shipwreck that generated the Tichborne Imposter Case (chapter 12) would have come before this court because the real Tichborne heir perished in a shipwreck on his way to Jamaica.

Before 1873, appeals for both the Court of Arches and the High Court of Admiralty were sent to the Privy Council, short for Her (or His) Majesty's Most Honourable Privy Council, whose members were tasked as advisors to the queen or king, and which drew its ranks from senior members of the House of Lords and the House of Commons, as well as leading churchmen, judges, diplomats and military leaders.

Even Parliament recognized that the organization of the principle courts was a muddle and reconfigured them by the Judicature Act of 1873 into four divisions under one High Court of Justice. The act effectively removed religious matters from the civil court system entirely and reduced the multiple avenues of appeal by channeling them into one body, the Court of Appeal.

Four of our ten cases come from before 1873, five from after, and one during the transition (*Talbot v. Talbot-Talbot*). The Judicature Act of 1873 replaced the original ungainly four-part structure of independent divisions with eight divisions: Queen's Bench, Common Pleas, Chancery, Probate, Divorce, Exchequer, Admiralty, and Bankruptcy. They do resemble a number of the earlier divisions by name and function, except for the disappearance of the Court of Arches, and the addition of Probate, Divorce, and Bankruptcy, the last three the former purview of the old Chancery court.

The importance of the Court of Chancery both before and after 1873 is obvious, with four cases—*Talbot v. Talbot-Talbot, Eyre-Eyre v. Eyre, Jerninghamn v. Caddell*, and *Tichborne v. Tichborne*—all launched in that contentious court. The same surnames on both ends of the title of the suits indicate that these are families, generally speaking, even dynasties, that are divided within themselves and in danger of genealogical implosion.

In addition, when a single Court of Appeal was created, the Privy Council no longer served that purpose. The eight divisions of the new High Court of Justice with its own Court of Appeal together formed a system that appears more familiar to us now. Purely religious matters that had come previously to the Court of Arches were now handled by the church, while its traditional docket of divorces and marital suits were now in the civil courts. Re-organizing the courts did not, of course, stop the internecine challenges for inheritances and other family disagreements.

All the significant details of the litigation in each of the ten cases are set out at the end of each chapter as the "Details of the Litigation": name of court, dates of the trials, title of the proceedings, the charge, judge(s), name of plaintiffs or defendants, their attorneys, and the verdict or outcome.

The reader should, if possible, attend one of the sessions of the criminal court now at the Old Bailey (Central Criminal Court) in London to see how little—except perhaps for the crimes charged—legal proceedings and personnel have changed. The year before last, I attended two trials (no cell phones allowed on your person): in the first, the notorious St. Francis Boys' Home case, the accused had already died, but his crimes (abusing children at the home) had to be adjudicated nonetheless to determine the compensation for the children (now adults); in the second the witnesses were boxed in with a makeshift screen in an assault case so that we could not see who was testifying. It may still all be a muddle, as Dickens swore, but it is a compelling muddle, like our ten trials, nonetheless. The muddle becomes more understandable if not crystal clear when one consults a standard law history like William S. Holdsworth's *History of English Law* (1903).[3]

4

The Family Tree and Genealogical Puzzles

> The setting of parents against children, and children against parents, brothers and sisters against each other, both by the horrible Inquisition, and by the monastic system ... seems to me so dreadful a fruit of the Romish system, that nothing in any other religious system of Christianity, at least, is at all to be compared with it in evil.
> —Sara Coleridge, *Memoir* (1850)

> Primogeniture is dreadfully opposed to [natural selection]; suppose the first-born bull was necessarily made by each farmer the begetter of his stock.
> —Charles Darwin, Letter to J.D. Hooker (1862)

While there is no question that family trees signal potential inheritances, it is often more than money that generates anxiety and high feeling in matters related to family genealogy: it is the sense of *who* is part of the family, *who* marries into it, and *who* is of sufficient quality or even legitimacy to deserve to be a branch of the tree.

It is obvious that the religious conversion of a son, for example, could disrupt the family inheritance, not to mention the continuity of the family name, especially when celibacy is an issue in the cases where there may be not only conversion to Catholicism but the attachment to a religious order and a celibate lifestyle. But for many Protestants the very language of Roman Catholicism generated anxiety about perverted violations of the "natural" family. Protestants fulminated against the Catholic usage of such honorifics as *mother superior, father confessor, spiritual father,* and *religious brothers* and *sisters*. Encroaching on the relationships of the natural family provoked violence in the letter columns as well as in the streets.

Like many constructed genealogical images of family and gendered relationships, the family tree seemed on the surface to be the very model of modern stability. The excessively neat schematic model of a metaphorical "tree" itself suggests that laws of *nature* are at work. Family relationships do not just happen—they grow naturally. If families have an organic structure, what need would there be for rules, legal challenges, and other attempts (even parliamentary decisions) at pruning? Indeed, why even have a court of Chancery?

The most common visualizations of Victorian genealogy were the schematic tree and the imitative or natural-appearing tree. They were zealously maintained; indeed, British upper-class culture (not to mention its horse-fanciers) in general is known for its obsession with blood lines. But other forms of genealogical imaging were also quite common: grave markers with genealogical remarks were quite traditional, but memorial plaques on interior church walls were once more in vogue, championed by A.W. Pugin as part of his Gothic Catholicizing of church furnishings. While either gravestones or plaques provide shorthand or truncated genealogies, Cardinal Newman's mother, Jemima Newman, was memorialized as if her leadership in establishing the Church of St. Margaret and St. Nicholas at Littlemore was iconographically equivalent to the Annunciation, with an angel pointing to the future church while Mrs. Newman holds an architectural model.

The Victorian preoccupation with genealogy was not limited to the upper class, with its obsessive titles, entails, and inheritances, but also permeated the middle classes. In the course of analyzing the English novel of the 1840s in *The Long Revolution* (1961), for example, Raymond Williams outlined changes in what he called "the structure of feeling" in the early Victorian period. Using both popular fiction and those novels now generally regarded as literary works of art, he charted the gradual decline of the aristocratic "social character" in which "birth mattered more than money" and the subsequent rise of the social character of the "industrial and commercial middle class" in which "social position is increasingly defined by actual status rather than birth." This major shift is marked in the novels by "unexpected legacies" that cancel crippling debts or track orphans who turn out to be well-connected or follow black sheep like Roger Tichborne who fled to the far ends of the empire—all the fictional props of the novels' "pervasive atmosphere of instability and debt."

The obsession with genealogy may have begun in the pre–Victorian period when new rules defining eligibility for the seats in the House of Lords came into use: "The standard of proof required ... was by now exacting and the claimants were both rich and prepared to spend very

4. The Family Tree and Genealogical Puzzles

large sums for the chance of winning the great prize of an ancient barony." Disraeli satirized the situation in his novel *Sybil* (1845) when an Inner Temple lawyer specializes in creating "heredity" peers, charging aspirants only twenty or thirty thousand pounds for the documentation. Fiction aside, Lord Atlay noted, "The decade between 1830 and 1840 witnessed a very undesirable laxity in the admission of peerage claims."[1]

The great *Peerage* volumes and annuals by Debrett (begun in 1802) and Burke (begun in 1826) appeared in the decades just before Queen Victoria came to the throne but continued throughout her reign, being supplemented by such volumes as Burke's *Landed Gentry* (begun in 1837). The publication of similarly obsessively family histories (a number of which I have used in this study) was the rule from 1830 to 1930.[2]

Various forms of Victorian family trees are the visualization of these and other significant cultural pressures on the "structure of feeling." I would argue that the image of the stable Victorian family tree was in itself a powerful means of cultural regulation but that it showed the stresses of religious, scientific, and legal fracturing. By mid-century dramatically and by the 1870s with even greater emphasis, however, two major developments in British culture challenged Protestant hegemony even in matters of family kinship: (1) the impact of Catholic Emancipation and the numerous conversions associated with the Oxford Movement and afterwards, leading to widespread anxiety about inheritances; and (2) the scientific implications of Darwin's evolutionary tree of the "descent of species" and Francis Galton's "scientific" analysis of genealogy or what he preferred to call "hereditary genius."

Most religious challenges took the form of eliding the sacred and the worldly in an attempt to define the inadequacy of the latter, while the scientific challenges promoted the analysis of kinship (both familial and species) with experimental and (proto)genetic demonstrations. Often the religious challenges had to be settled in the civil courts, while the scientific challenges—at first mightily resisted by the Protestant religious establishment—became themselves, for the most part, a new orthodoxy in some instances contested even to this day. Both in fiction and in court, a challenge to a will was an alternative—even sometimes desperate—way of challenging a religious conversion.

Two famous cousins dominate the scientific exploitation of the family tree from mid-century: Charles Darwin and Francis Galton. There is only *one* illustration in all of *On the Origin of Species* (1859): a schematic tree representing the descent of species. On the tree, A through E represent five species in a genus, while a and m are varieties of species A, and so forth: "After ten thousand generations, species A is supposed to have produced three forms, a, f, and m, which ... will have come to differ largely ... from each other and from their common parent." Howard Gruber's analysis of Darwin's notebooks of the 1840s leads him to conclude that the deployment in his manuscript of the "tree of life" was an essential moment in formulating the "branching model in terms of human survival and descent, as though the ordinary form of the genealogical tree were inherent in his idea from its conception." Or, in Darwin's words: "Organized beings represent a tree, irregularly branched...."[3] The only other "genealogical" tree is Darwin's careful classification of the rock pigeon, showing its descent from "fancy pigeons" in *The Variation of Animals and Plants Under Domestication* (1868): James A. Secord calls it Darwin's only "explicit evolutionary tree, relating a specific group of organisms to one another through lines of descent."[4] In this instance Darwin traced the evolution of varieties of fancy pigeons from the ur-species of rock pigeon (the slightly more proper name of the everyday urban pigeon). We can only imagine the indignation of Bishop Wilberforce, Darwin's legendary opponent in debates about evolution, when he saw this chart, proving the importance of natural selection by referring to the kinds of animals forever underfoot in Trafalgar Square. In the famous debate about evolution at the British Association meeting in 1860 with Thomas Huxley, Wilberforce said there was nothing to evolution because rock pigeons were rock pigeons and have always been rock pigeons.

Darwin's tree diagramming the "descent of species" combines the mythic archetypal tree of life with the genealogical family tree, which, for his critics, went a long way in establishing the popular—and often demagogic—view that Darwinism meant that apes were our distant cousins on some branch of the human family tree. Darwin only tried somewhat halfheartedly to support his use of a family tree of species by means of a proto-genetic theory, called *pangenesis*, involving the transmittal of family characteristics through the blood.

Darwin's cousin fairly enthusiastically accepted Darwin's (eventually) doomed theory of *pangenesis*, which nonetheless came fairly close to anticipating Mendel's discoveries of paired genes, one from each parent.[5] *Pangenesis* postulated particles or *gemmules* that originated everywhere in the body but congregated in the gonads. Galton's lasting and most controversial contribution to Victorian science was his theory of the inheritability of talent, and in the end he was less interested in the mechanisms of inheritance than the classification of inheritable types. Nevertheless he concluded his critical discussion of *pangenesis* in a fairly detailed letter to *Nature* (then as now one of the leading scientific journals in English), in 1871 with this line: "In the meantime, *Vive pangenesis*."[6]

4. The Family Tree and Genealogical Puzzles

For many years in our era Galton was persona non grata. I defer to other scholars the racist but perhaps inevitable exploitation of his "eugenic" theories by other commentators, although they are theoretically at one with much of his analysis of inheritability: one cringes, for example, that despite his grudging praise of the Haitian slave-revolt leader, Toussaint L'Ouverture, his assessment of "negroes" in general demeans them in the extraordinarily racist language common to Galton's era.[7]

Galton's purpose in *Hereditary Genius* was clearly to expand and re-invent some core elements of his cousin's science: "I propose to show in this book that a man's natural abilities are derived by inheritance, under exactly the same limitations as are the form and physical features of the whole organic world." Not only that: "As it is easy ... to obtain by careful selection a permanent breed of dogs or horses gifted with peculiar powers of running, or of doing anything else, so it would be quite practicable to produce a highly-gifted race of men by judicious marriages during several consecutive generations."[8] With that sentence alone he would have stopped the hearts of many prominent London families or at the very least caused their pulses to race. These ideas were essentially the early version of eugenics, a term Galton coined that inevitably led him down some racist paths, as clearly—at least for the Negro "races"—he expected that the inheritability of talent was going to be rare if not nonexistent. But Galton would not always pander to his contemporaries' effusive beliefs in national temperaments and abilities. He took obvious pleasure in recalling a gathering of Scottish Highlanders in Holland Park in London who challenged "all England to compete with them in games of strength." The mighty and well-trained "race" of Highlanders were handily defeated in a foot-race "by a youth who was stated to be a pure Cockney, the clerk of a London banker."[9] One must never underestimate, as Henry Higgins once did in *Pygmalion* (1914), the prowess of a Londoner from the East End who was born hearing the bells of St. Mary-le-Bow of Cheapside.

Galton's drive to "scientize" all aspects of Victorian genealogy are obvious in at least three fairly different variants on family trees and genealogies he uses in his book. His first or *prosaic* genealogy for the Brontes discards the actual tree in favor of quasi-algebraic (and patriarchal) symbols: U and *U* stand for uncle and aunt, B and *b* for brother and sister, and so forth.[10] He also uses a second or *traditional tree* for a literary genealogy as in the then-successful scribbling Taylor clan of Norwich,[11] but he virtually drove his argument into the ground by his discussion of Titian's Italian family, with "eight or nine good painters" whose names are carefully recorded on the family tree while all of their parents and grandparents, lawyers every last one of them, are dutifully diagrammed with X's.[12]

In two other charts he schematized a third type or *conceptual* tree, discussing the same two branches of the Coleridge family tree of chapter 5, one emphasizing the judges (whom I call the Ottery St. Mary's branch), and the other emphasizing the literary talents (whom I call the Highgate branch).[13]

Somewhat invisible in all of these genealogical schemas was Galton's suspicion of the value of primogeniture whereby the eldest son received the primary benefits of the family's name and estate. Galton believed that his researches demonstrated that primogeniture "cannot logically be based on the supposed hereditary transmission of ability."[14] Galton's assessment of blood-relationships as only an index to ability rather than a guarantee is summed up in *Hereditary Genius*: "I cannot think of any claim to respect, put forward in modern days, that is so entirely an imposture, as that made by a peer on the ground of descent, who has neither been nobly educated, nor has any eminent kinsman, within three degrees [of kinship, from one's immediate family to one's great-grandparents]."[15]

Even in his support of the strong lines of judicial descent, Galton argued, "Because one or both of a child's parents are able, it does not in the least follow as a matter of necessity, but only one of moderately unfavorable odds, that the child will be also," although he has inherited "an extraordinary mixture of qualities displayed in his grandparent, great-grand-parents, and more remote ancestors, as well as from those of his father and mother." Galton never succumbed to class prejudice: "The most illustrious and so-called 'well-bred' families of the human race, are utter mongrels as regards their natural gifts of intellect and disposition."[16]

Galton was never as objective as he often appeared. His insights were always tempered, for example, by his inevitable suspicion of artistic types. Despite his detailed analysis of the Coleridge clan (and even of Wordsworth's) he still believed that poets were "not the founders of families." They are too susceptible to "the exercise" of their "senses and affections," a combination that is "unstable in inheritance."[17] As we know from the amazing array of Coleridges in this book, the clan, with the exception of the lord chief justice's daughter (discussed in chapter 16), had no problem passing on its prestige and wealth.

Galton's expertise in matters genealogical led him to comment on one of the schemes put forward by Arthur Orton, the Tichborne imposter (or claimant), the subject of chapter 12 below: Orton's publicity machine had seized upon a recent invention, the optical "identiscope,"

4. The Family Tree and Genealogical Puzzles

as a means of demonstrating Orton's physical resemblance to the Tichbornes, whose long-lost son he claimed to be and whose property, immense fortune, and title he wished to inherit. In 1884 in *Nature* Galton dismissed their use of the identiscope—a kind of stereopticon—to compare portraits of Roger Tichborne, the rightful heir who had disappeared, and Arthur Orton. "There would be no difficulty," Galton argued, "in selecting photographs of many different persons that should harmonize with the photograph of the Claimant," including "a distinguished member" of Her Majesty's government.[18] The identiscope, in this instance, was of no value.

The upper-class Victorian obsession about family trees reflects their definition of themselves in terms of aristocratic, occasionally royal, ancestry, and, to put it crudely, making it clear what the lines of inheritance were. Most of the genealogies in this book are of the latter sort, although I have also included two—the Coleridges and the Hopkins's Giberne-Sieveking relationships—that also illustrate the Victorian intellectual aristocracy as well.

5

The Victorian Intellectual Aristocracy

> There were as many Coleridges as there were Herods, and ... it was impossible to remember how they were related to each other.
> —Benjamin Jowett, from Ernest Hartley Coleridge, *The Life and Correspondence of John Duke Lord Coleridge* (1904)

Who were all these Coleridges Galton was so keen to schematize, both as judges and authors? Truth to tell, Galton was much more interested in the judicial Coleridges, having devoted an extensive chapter in *Hereditary Genius* to the "Judges of England, and Other High Legal Officers between 1660 and 1865, Who Were, or Are, Related." "There cannot," he concluded, "then, remain a doubt but that the peculiar type of ability that is necessary to a judge is often transmitted by descent."[1]

Readers will of course expect to hear about the most famous Coleridge of them all, Samuel Taylor Coleridge, the great British Romantic poet who wrote *The Rime of the Ancient Mariner* (1798), *Kubla Khan* (1816*)*, and *Christabel* (1816), but they may be surprised to encounter ten other Coleridges from the poet's family tree in this book, inevitably sucked into trials and scandals rarely of their making. For six of the ten trial chapters, the Coleridge family tree is essential to any understanding of their judicial history.

They seem to be omnipresent, but they were also part of an intensive network of relationships that the British cultural historian Noel Annan called an "intellectual aristocracy" of jurists, religious leaders, architects, titled lords, and even a poet or two, forming a "caucus of power or influence" or a "new intelligentsia" in mid–Victorian England.[2]

The Coleridge family tree had two branches, a Highgate or literary branch, with poet Samuel Taylor as its most prominent member, and

5. The Victorian Intellectual Aristocracy

33

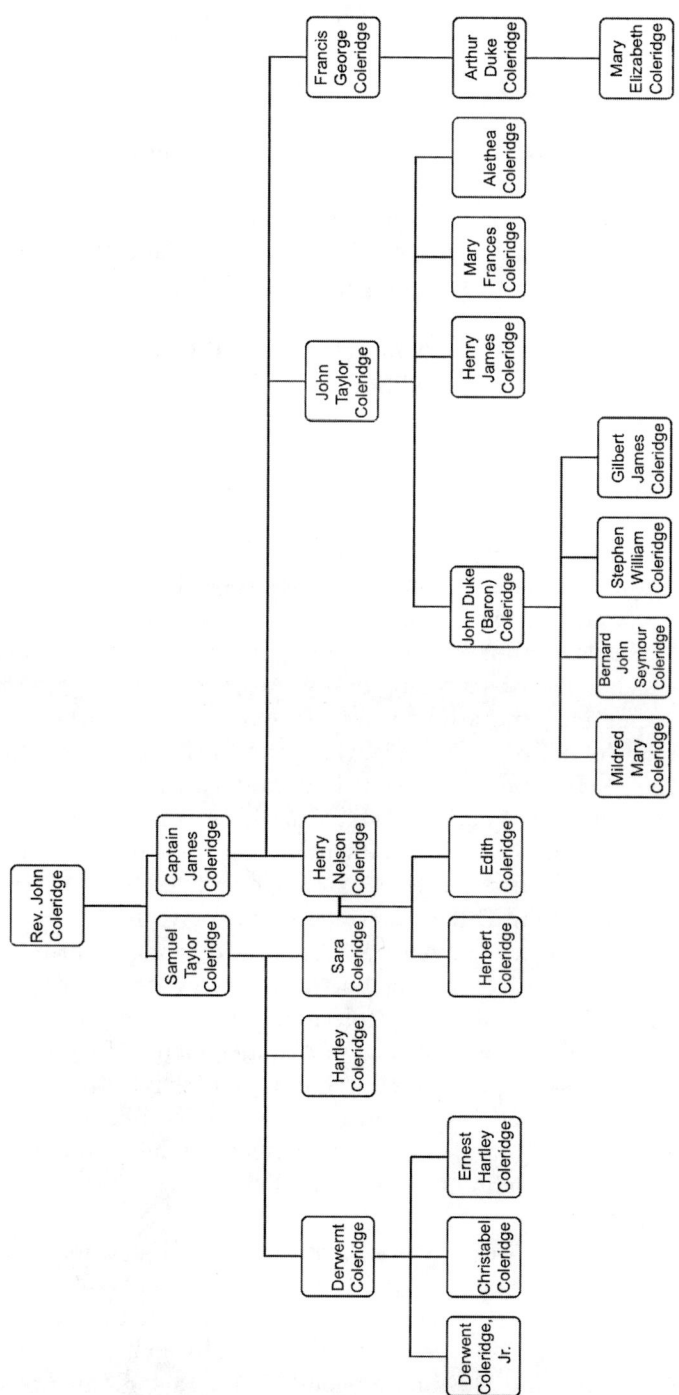

Coleridge family tree (template courtesy Family Echo, http://familyecho.com).

an Ottery St. Mary's or judicial branch, descending from Captain James Coleridge, the poet's brother.

The two brothers plus eight siblings made up the offspring of John Coleridge, the headmaster of Ottery School and the vicar of the church of Ottery St. Mary, the village in Devon that has retained its Coleridge associations for generations and even to this day, as the current Lord Coleridge still lives there. S.T. Coleridge was typically immodest even when praising his brother George: "He was a man of reflective mind and elegant talent. He possesses learning to a greater degree, than any of the family, excepting myself."[3]

Both branches were briefly united when S.T. Coleridge's daughter Sara, who edited the enlarged edition of her father's classic autobiography, *Biographia Literaria* (1817; 1847), married her cousin, Henry Nelson Coleridge, a barrister and classical scholar. One of their children, Herbert, a Balliol College star pupil, was a family legend. He was a lawyer in Chancery and a philologist who died young. When he was told he had only eighteen months to live, he said "it was just long enough to learn Icelandic."[4] His cousin, John Duke Coleridge, believed it was Sanskrit, not Icelandic, he mastered.[5]

The Coleridges labored to undo the knots in various genealogical and religious tangles in their courtrooms. Two of the most noted jurists of their respective generations were descended from Captain James Coleridge: Sir John Taylor Coleridge, judge on the King's Bench, a close friend of John Keble and an occasional rambler with Wordsworth in the Lake District,[6] and his son, John Duke Coleridge, who became the lord chief justice. Sir John Taylor was the sentencing judge in the Achilli trial of John Henry (later Cardinal) Newman that convicted Newman of libel (chapter 8), while John Duke Coleridge vindicated a much-put-upon nun in the *Saurin v. Star* convent case (chapter 11) and also protected a valuable Catholic estate in the Tichborne imposter case (chapter 12). In a bizarre architectural imbroglio, Coleridge ruled in favor of a lord (the Duke of Norfolk) over the local vicar in Arundel, men of different faiths who "shared" the same physical church building (chapter 13). The lord chief justice was himself in court in an ignominious coda to his career as a defendant in the *Adams v. Coleridge* case, when he tried to prevent the marriage of his daughter to a man he believed to be a fortune-hunter (chapter 15).

The Coleridges of the nineteenth century were High Church Anglican, with one major exception, but most of them lionized the Roman Catholic Newman. Their first patriarch, John Taylor Coleridge, was a follower and eventually the biographer of John Francis Keble, the leading Tractarian and Newman's friend.[7] John Taylor was, however, originally so disturbed by the number of Roman "secessions" from the Anglican faith that for a while he considered leaving his judicial career and becoming an Anglican priest. His nephew, John Coleridge Patteson, was murdered while serving as the missionary bishop of Melanesia and was long considered an Anglican martyr.[8]

We see in the letters of Sara Coleridge—from the Highgate wing of the family—her remarkably prescient and somewhat tortured view of Anglo- and Roman Catholicism. "I do believe," she wrote in 1848 during a rash of Romanist secessions, that "the religion of enlightened Romanists ... does not differ materially from Anglicanism," especially if such "enlightened Romanists" had no interest in the Virgin Mary, no truck with the pope, no requests for intercession from the saints in heaven, and certainly no forgiveness from a priest after confession.[9] As she herself must have realized, such "enlightened Romanists" were quite rare. If such Romanists actually existed, they would clearly be Anglo-Catholics and not Roman Catholic. There seemed to be no way for her to resolve this issue: at one point in 1850 (during the country's widespread anti-papal demonstrations) she wrote, "What is called Anglo-Catholicism—vulgarly Tractarianism or Puseyism—is out of place in the Church of England." But a year later she reversed herself: "Anglo-Catholics have as much right to keep their places in our Church as the main body of the Evangelicals or the Philosophicals." The fact of the matter is that she attended Christ Church in Albany Street near her home, fairly High Church in its service, and one that had been restored by William Butterfield, *the* Anglo-Catholic architect of choice. She did not budge, however, from a negative view of Newman, made especially acute from her belief that when Anglicans grew closer to "the Romish system" they "become weaker in their moral perceptions."[10]

The most prominent Coleridge of the nineteenth century was John Duke Coleridge, later Lord Coleridge, chief justice of England. The judge was a follower of Oxford's Nathan Pusey, a controversial leader of the Oxford Movement despite his living "for the sake of preventing conversions to the Catholic Church by any means, fair or foul." In many ways, John Duke Coleridge's initial distaste for Newman was characteristic of his class: he was especially annoyed by Newman's sponsorship of the volume of *Lives of the English Saints* (1844–45) and not simply because the preface to one of the lives was the "most magnificently ultra–Newmanic thing" he had read: "I never beheld the serpent and the dove in such amicable union." What sent him around the inevitable Protestant bend, however, was peasant Catholicism, although he would never call it that—that the *Lives* consisted of "fifty or sixty old woman's tales" considered "as true without a tittle of evidence to the outrage of all decent possibility and common sense." Newman was fortunate Coleridge had not heard about the full range of Newman's beliefs on miracles.[11] The Oratorians, as Eurocentric as they often were, used "translations of authorized foreign works" whose "piety" would not always pass muster among more traditionally minded English Catholics.[12]

Nonetheless it may be a surprise that Coleridge, who always remained a Protestant, became a great friend of this, the most famous Roman Catholic of his generation, in part no doubt because Henry James Coleridge, his brother, had converted to Roman Catholicism: his brother always spoke of Newman as the Lord's instrument of his conversion.[13] He became a prominent Jesuit and editor of the society's magazine, *The Month*. His secretary was Ernest Hartley Coleridge, his second cousin, who was Hopkins's friend at Highgate School.

When Newman wrote to Henry James Coleridge about the influence of Pusey in the 1860s it was the conversion of the poet Gerard Manley Hopkins they discussed. Hopkins was a Newman protégée, a relative of one of Newman's closest friends, Maria Rosina Giberne (later Sister Maria Pia), and one of the greatest poets in the English language and certainly the greatest *Catholic* poet in the English language. Even Hopkins at his conversion by Newman spoke positively of Pusey and "how young men revered him chiefly for his very austere life, and his meekness in controversy."[14]

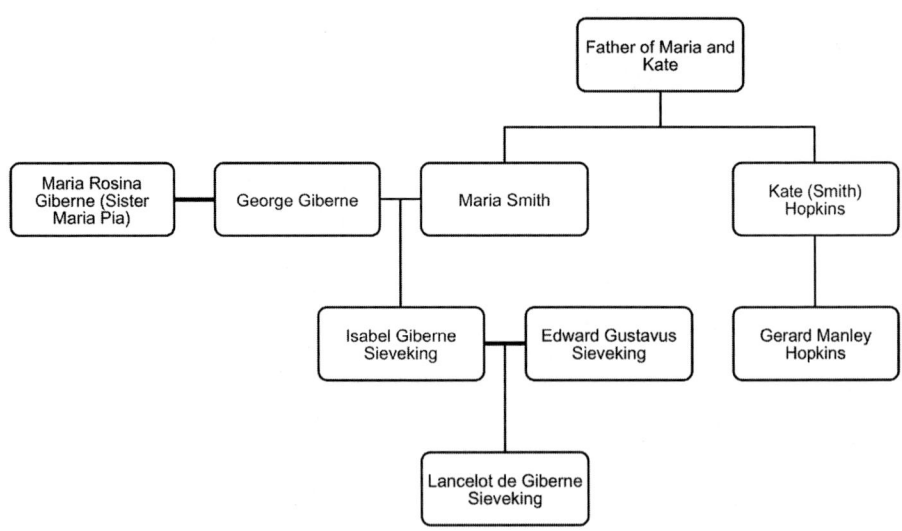

Gerard Manley Hopkins's family tree, with Giberne and Sieveking relatives (template courtesy Family Echo, http://familyecho.com).

5. The Victorian Intellectual Aristocracy

Lord Coleridge became a liberal on matters of Roman Catholicism, and his very public lifelong friendship and support of Newman must have eased his conscience because his father had lectured Newman severely while censuring him for libel in the great Achilli trial of 1853 (chapter 8). Lord Coleridge's speech moving the second reading of his Abolition of Tests Act in 1867, giving non–Anglicans the right to be fellows of Oxford colleges, asserted, "There was a man [Newman] in my time of admirable genius, or rare eloquence, of saintly life, of singular humility and self-denial, who taught us not any peculiar theological dogma, but simple religious truth."[15]

Coleridge kept a painting of Newman in his London house done by Lady Coleridge[16] and entertained him there whenever he was in town, the only residence besides the Duke of Norfolk's that Newman visited when he was in London. Coleridge also led a group who purchased a carriage for Newman emblazoned—"small and so as not to make a blaze of color"—with a cardinal's hat and his motto, "*Cor ad cor loquitur*" ("Heart speaks to heart").[17] Newman often tried to return such generosity, supporting Lord Coleridge when his own daughter, Mildred Mary, became estranged from him because Coleridge did not approve of a suitor. Newman was quite shocked that the disagreement ended up in the courts, and he wrote Henry James Coleridge (who lived in London) to ask him to assist his father, Lord Coleridge, in any possible and to call on Newman for any assistance as well.[18] If Newman did write that particular letter, we have no copy of it, and it was a sad day for all the Coleridges—even Mildred Mary—when her suitor sued Lord Coleridge and his son for libel (see chapter 15). Although neither Coleridge nor Newman could anticipate that the matter would involve six separate trials with daily disturbing news articles in the *London Times*, Newman even before the trials began sending letters to Coleridge's brother, in which Newman expressed his anxiety about the matter. Newman was also quite concerned about the physicality of the exchanged letters themselves, since he didn't want "to destroy carefully written letters, which are to you perhaps formal memoranda without copy." Newman's only consolation was that although the matter was "most strange" he agreed that "as the Providence is strange, so the design, which is involved in it, is strange and good also."[19]

On a less anxious note, Newman mentioned that he was pleased that Henry James Coleridge had shown one of Newman's controversial pamphlets to his brother for his approval. The year before (in 1884), when another Coleridge, Gerard Manley Hopkins's friend Ernest Hartley Coleridge, who was Samuel Taylor Coleridge's posthumous editor, wrote to ask Newman to join a distinguished group of gentlemen such as Matthew Arnold and J.C. Shairp, one of Wordsworth's editors, in writing a letter to support the placement of a bust of Samuel Taylor Coleridge in the Poets' Corner instead of the baptistery, Newman grew testy and refused: "Various reasons," he wrote to Henry James Coleridge, "which it would be too long and irrelevant to do justice to, lead me to view the present state of the Abbey with little satisfaction. I think it no real honor to obtain a memorial there."[20] The Catholic convert, long a target of Anglican invective, was obviously not in a conciliatory mood here.

Newman, however, was more gentle on the issue of second marriages, normally not a subject strict Catholics would have any problem being decisive about. Lord Coleridge married for the second time in 1885 when his wife's first marriage, according to the editors of Newman's letters, had been "declared null by English law." The second Lady Coleridge "was not accepted by those who felt a repugnance to such tampering with matrimony, nor by those who did not admit in the State power to declare invalid a Christian marriage." Newman had written Henry James Coleridge that he "never forgets [his] brother day after day" and hoping that their "great trial" over the second marriage "does not affect" his health.[21]

As understanding as Newman was about the Coleridge family, Newman seemed not, however, to have understood the Tichborne imposter trial (chapter 12), in which Lord Coleridge defended the Tichborne family, because Newman stuttered when he wrote: "The ghost of Orton [the Imposter], or, rather of Tichborne, is, I suppose, at least laid."[22]

Henry James Coleridge has now become known—accurately but perhaps inadequately—as the editor who rejected for publication in the Jesuit magazine, *The Month*, one of Hopkins's most famous—and most difficult—poems, *The Wreck of the Deutschland*, although Hopkins later said Coleridge initially was going to publish it rather than another poem Hopkins had sent him (*The Wreck of the Eurydice*) but changed his mind even though (in Hopkins's words) it "pained" him to do so. Both Henry James Coleridge and Hopkins had been received into the Roman Catholic faith by Newman, whom Coleridge later called the "instrument and the means" of his conversion.[23] His father was so intent on his remaining in the Anglican fold that he commissioned the "family" architect, William Butterfield, to build a church and parsonage for Coleridge in Alphington near the family home in Ottery St. Mary.[24]

Henry James Coleridge was also a novelist whose works dramatize some of the most acute inheritance problems of an era of controversial conversions, contested wills, and other legal struggles. In his *Wafted*

5. The Victorian Intellectual Aristocracy 39

Seeds (1870–71), for example, the death of a Catholic convert in prominent family with Protestant and Catholic relatives sends his mixed relations in a tizzy. Should he be buried in the Catholic family vault within the Anglican parish church but receive no Catholic rites, or in the local Catholic convent chapel cemetery with no proximity to other family burials, or in the private cemetery on the family estate?

In *Anemone* (1877–79), his second novel on related themes and also a curious social-realist novel of the landed gentry, combined aspects of the new literary genre about "perversions"—Anglican slang for "conversions" or "Romanist secessions"—and other contemporary Catholic obsessions—in which a family of divided loyalties buries its dead—all filtered through the lens of a rural setting that resembles the Devonshire area of Ottery St. Mary. Coleridge's characters are afflicted with a massive anxiety about inheritance, legacy, entailing, and primogeniture.

The titular hero, Anemone, has a relatively easier time than her kinswoman, Alice. Anemone is unmarried, with a small fortune, and effortlessly converts to Catholicism and becomes a Carmelite novice. Alice, on the other hand, is married to a vain Anglican clergyman and has to suffer virtual house imprisonment and the denial of access to her newborn babe for her boldness in choosing to convert. Coleridge therefore reverses the hysteria associated with the fictitious and notorious memoir, *The Awful Disclosures of Maria Monk* (1836) about the "horrors" of Canadian convent life, by arguing for a different kind of terror, that of torturing those who give in to "perversion."

But there are so many discussions of property, fortunes large and small, and family trees in *Anemone* that one expects graphs and account ledgers as illustrations. What if, the story asks, a Catholic convert becomes—through the shipwreck of the heir to an immense fortune—the rightful lord of a Protestant estate? (Of course this was exactly the motor of the Tichborne scandal in ch. 12, in reverse, so to speak.) What would he do with such money? Turn it over to the Catholic Church to fund more "perversion" schemes? Perhaps luckily for the Ottery St. Mary Coleridges, author Henry James Coleridge—a second-born son—chose to publish *Anemone* (and *Wafted Seeds*) anonymously.

The novel also has occasional discussions of what both Coleridge and Hopkins really had to promise their fathers during the tense days following their conversions: that they would be allowed to return home only if they promised not to try to convert their siblings, a deal Alice's spiritual advisor (in the novel, himself a second son) says she should not make.[25]

Henry James Coleridge was a remarkable editor (aside from his decision not to publish the greatest Catholic poet of his era) and activist for Catholic theology and history, paradoxically sharing with the Earl of Shrewsbury and other patrician British Catholics an interest in peasant Catholicism. He was witness to at least two major controversies that resulted in widely divergent judgments on his part. In his travels through France in 1852 he stopped at La Salette, where he interviewed Melanie Calvat, an illiterate local girl to whom the Virgin Mary gave a remarkable "secret" that prophesied the destruction of Paris ("this city soiled by all kinds of crimes"), the assassination of the pope, and other apocalyptic goings on.

Coleridge interviewed Melanie while twenty thousand pilgrims gathered at the site. Fellow Jesuit convert Richard F. Clarke wrote in Coleridge's obituary that Coleridge put Melanie "through a searching cross-examination like the hereditary lawyer he was." Clarke concluded, "There was no flaw in the girl's evidence, and the different parts of her story hung together very well." Perhaps inevitably the self-anointed visionary, whose followers were called "Melanists," fell afoul of the church's leadership when variants of her secret messages (perhaps written by ghost writers?) were published by an Italian bishop and her protector in a book that was condemned by the Vatican.[26]

Coleridge was much more skeptical of another visionary, Margaret Anna Cusack, a young Irish woman who became known as the Nun of Kenmare. Influenced by the Oxford Movement, she became an Anglican nun, but soon converted and became a Franciscan nun assigned to depressed Kenmare County. Besides feeding the poor she became a radical Irish nationalist, appalled by tenants' abuses. Her religious and political autobiography eventually sold 200,000 copies, but her instant rise to fame occurred on her self-propelled mission to Knock, where the Virgin Mary appeared to her. The simultaneous leadership of nationalist and visionary followers drove her to leave for England, where a new religious order she established precipitated her de-conversion back to Anglicanism.[27] Besides being suspicious of her role as a political radical, Coleridge doubted her religious fervor and "long before her final defection," Clarke wrote, Coleridge received letters from her that were "most impudent."[28]

Some readers may know of two of Samuel Taylor Coleridge's children and their literary efforts—Hartley as poet and Sara as editor and writer—but less well-known are two other writers, Ernest Hartley Coleridge (his grandson) and Mary Elizabeth Coleridge (his great-grand-niece). Ernest Hartley, the Balliol student who was Hopkins's close friend at Oxford, named one of his own children Gerard. Mary Elizabeth was a member of the loose circle of late Victorian writers associated with Hopkins's friends, Canon R.W. Dixon and Robert

5. The Victorian Intellectual Aristocracy 41

Bridges, the poet laureate who was the first editor of Hopkins's poetry. She taught at the London Working Women's College from 1895 to 1907.[29]

Hopkins may even have come into contact with some of Samuel Taylor Coleridge's unpublished work directly, having visited the home of Coleridge's son (Derwent, Ernest Hartley's father), where Coleridge's numerous manuscripts were stored. In what Henry Nelson Coleridge asserted was Coleridge's last poem, "My Baptismal Birth-Day," we can even hear Hopkins's own cadences:

> God's child in Christ adopted, Christ my all.
> What that earth boasts were not lost cheaply, rather
> Than forfeit that blest name, by which I call
> The Holy One, the Almighty God, my Father?[30]

Hopkins admired Coleridge's Christabel for its use of accentual verse—in which the number of stresses rather than syllables determines line length and rhythm—what Hopkins felt was a forerunner of his personal theory of "sprung rhythm," with its omission of unaccented syllables (in what would normally be iambic pentameter lines) as in one of his most famous poems, "The Windhover" (written 1877, published 1918)—"I caught this morning morning's minion, king- / dom of daylight's dauphin, dapple-dawn-drawn Falcon...."—in which almost all unaccented syllables are dropped to make the accented ones even more emphatic.

Whenever the Coleridges chose to build a church, they commissioned the architect William Butterfield, John Duke Coleridge's close friend and the recipient of his extensive patronage. Butterfield had virtually single-handedly created a whole island of Anglo-Catholic churches. Hopkins admired Butterfield's work and visited his churches and other religious buildings whenever the opportunity arose.

Hopkins and Butterfield had common roots in a Pre-Raphaelite aesthetic that left both of them open to charges of eccentricity and singularity in their respective arts. Hopkins's Catholic and sacramental view of nature was often only satisfied by his detailed verbal sketches and explosive accentual lines, while Butterfield's polychromatic brickwork likewise astounded his contemporaries with its dazzling artifice.[31] Despite the differences in public acceptance—Butterfield had numerous commissions, while Hopkins remained relatively unknown—both received numerous provocative critical reactions from contemporaries unused to their artistic experiments.

Butterfield, like most of the Coleridges, remained an Anglican, but his work exhibited a mass of contradictions typical of the High Church and Ritualist camp of the second half of the century. He turned High Church architecture into a virtually Anglo-Catholic art, he built a number of buildings for new Anglican sisterhoods—a controversial imitation of Roman Catholic practice—without a fee, and his decorative obsessions were more Siennese than Gothic. But he resisted some of the Ritualist practices which seemed too close to Roman Catholicism when he worked with a dozen clergymen at major (and a few minor) churches who had converted.[32] In two instances—West Lavington and Alfington—he built Anglo-Catholic churches in a vain attempt to keep their ministers—Henry James Coleridge and C.J. Laprimaudaye, another Hopkins family connection—within the Anglican fold. They left nonetheless. Although one of the chief patrons of the Anglo-Catholic churches was John Gellibrand Hubbard (first Lord Addington), his family connections included both the Laprimaudayes and the Pollens, two of whose sons became Jesuits.

The Coleridges were an ideal family for Galton's purposes in his book *Hereditary Genius* because they epitomized his theory of the inheritability of genius; indeed, he diagrammed them twice: once, under the rubric of "judges," to demonstrate the ancestors of Sir John Taylor Coleridge, then judge of the Queen's Bench, and secondly, under the rubric of "poets," meaning descent from Samuel Taylor Coleridge. The second chart summarizes virtually all of the Coleridges—and their artistic and intellectual impact—featured in this book:

> Coleridge, Samuel Taylor; poet and metaphysician; was filled with poetry and metaphysics aet. 15; always slothful and imprudent. He had warm friendships, but was singularly regardless of duties, and somewhat querulous; of a peculiarly hesitating disposition; opium eater. Fully eight members of this family—indeed, nearly all of its male representatives—have been gifted with rare abilities.

His three children, especially Hartley and Sara, were the poet's most direct legacy:

> Hartley, poet; a precocious child, who had been a visionary boy. His imaginative and colloquial powers were extraordinary. He was morbidly intemperate.
>
> Sara; had in a remarkable degree the intellectual characteristics of her father. She was authoress and principal editor of her father's works. She married her cousin, H. Nelson Coleridge, and was mother of Herbert.
>
> The Rev. Derwent Coleridge, author, Principal of St. Mark's College, Chelsea; is the remaining child of the poet.

The remaining Coleridges were no less distinctive members of the Victorian intellectual aristocracy, especially Judge Coleridge and Edward Coleridge, who was a noteworthy vicar of St. Margaret's of Mapledurham (see chapter 9):

Sir John Taylor Coleridge, judge; eminent in early life as an accomplished scholar and man of letters.

Edward Coleridge, master at Eton, now fellow.

Henry Nelson Coleridge, scholar; a well-known writer of many articles in periodicals; married his cousin Sara.

Herbert Coleridge, philologist.

Henry, late fellow of Oriel College; now Roman Catholic.

Sir John Duke Coleridge, solicitor-general.[33]

6

Architects on the Defensive

One of the most influential evaluations of the achievements of the Victorian architect William Butterfield (until Paul Thompson's definitive study came along) was the essay "William Butterfield, or the Glory of Ugliness," by John Summerson, former curator of Soane's Museum in London, whose architectural analyses of Victorian culture are so important but who nonetheless misread both Butterfield's and Pugin's importance in the scandals that marked the era. Summerson argued that Butterfield was "a devout adherent of the narrowest Anglicanism" and "hardly a medievalist at all," while Pugin's Roman Catholicism made his personal contribution to Anglican church-building minimal.[1] Both of these mis-assessments will be re-evaluated in this chapter.

In reality, Butterfield and Pugin were the uneasy duo at the heights of High Victorian Gothic architecture, Butterfield seeking an Anglo-Catholic compromise, while Pugin was a Roman Catholic absolutist. The Anglo-Catholics, spiritual descendants of the Tractarians (many of whom remained within the Anglican fold), dreamed of a medieval Catholic facade on an Anglican foundation and hoped to reduce the hostility to Catholic ideas within the Anglican church. They set out to win the Roman Catholic masses (the Irish and other poor folk) away from the papists and to re-establish the church building as an aesthetic (virtually a Pre-Raphaelite) object in itself.

Butterfield was the architect Anglo-Catholics championed—and often hired—for their campaign. What the Victorians called "constructional coloration" was Butterfield's polychromatic obsession and flaunting of Italian Gothic elements, an approach which, to take the line of least contention, paralleled Ruskin's theories.[2] In practice, Butterfield (using different colored bricks, variegated marble and stone courses, stained-glass windows, encaustic floor tiles whose surface pattern was based on colors of the clay, not a glaze—typical of both Butterfield and Pugin to obsess about tiles—and saints' images) almost dared observers to call him a follower of Rome. Nonetheless, Butterfield dissociated himself from any identification with Roman Catholicism, despite the similar ties his chief patron, Lord Chief Justice John Duke Coleridge, maintained with his own brother, Henry James Coleridge (a prominent Jesuit priest), and John Henry Cardinal Newman. Coleridge had always been keen on church architecture, and as late as 1851 in an essay "On the Restoration of the Chancel of St. Mary the Virgin" he celebrated his family's patronage of the Oxford church and its restorer, William Butterfield.[3]

Butterfield's work would always be an ideal compromise for the religious crosscurrents of his age. Butterfield's models for his distinctive facades were usually Italian: Guido Fawkes notwithstanding, these were of course Roman Catholic masterpieces—Sienna or Monza—with their horizontal striping of bricks. Butterfield also supported the Puseyite revival of institutions that smacked of popery, such as sisterhoods, monastic poorhouses and hospitals, and even designed two Anglican convents for free.

Beyond the conspicuous Gothicizing of Pugin's work and the neo-Romanesque architecture of the Oratory, Butterfield's third way was to subsume Roman Catholic excess in a façade of Anglo-Catholic rhetoric. He used geometrical and other variegated patterns on his exteriors and European Roman Catholic excess in his interiors. He would never consciously admit to an admiration of excess, of course, but he seems to have appreciated at least some of the most daring Italian frescoes, such as those at Assisi and Orvieto.[4]

His first major breakthrough in what came to be his distinctive style was the Balliol Chapel (1856–57), with its horizontal bands of colored brick, labeled by critics as "Butterfield's pink obscenity," ignoring its model, Monza Cathedral, with its characteristic brick striping.[5] But a High Church poet like Gerard Manley Hopkins—soon to be a Roman Catholic and an enthusiastic admirer of Butterfield's work—loved it for its "inscape," its unique patterning representing the same impulse that his poems revealed about God's creation, as in "Pied Beauty": "All things counter, original, spare, strange; / Whatever is fickle, freckled (who knows how?)." Hopkins also wrote an enigmatic poem about Butterfield's Balliol Chapel, "To Oxford" (1865), that included these lines:

> The vigorous horizontals, each way fall
> In bows above my head, as falsified
> By visual compulsion, till I hide
> The steep-up roof at last behind the small
> Eclipsing parapet; yet above the wall
> The sumptuous ridge-crest leave to poise and ride.[6]

The "visual compulsion" is an optical illusion that creates the unique experience of what Hopkins called "instress," the natural force creating the inscape of the pitched roof, communicating it to the perceiver. "None besides this bye-ways beauty try," he concludes, "or if they try it, I am happier then." Hopkins intuitively understood Butterfield's goal of creating "extra height of the Chapel above the library," architectural historian Thompson explains.[7] For Hopkins this "irregular new roofline" was a challenge in perspective[8] that should be seen as a triumph of architectural design, not a source of mockery.

Hopkins visited a number of other Butterfield churches and chapels in Oxford, Devon, and London, where he called attention to the cusps (the meeting point of two arches), five-spoked wheels, rosettes (round flower designs), quatrefoils (four over-lapping circles with interior designs), and other distinctive patterning that signal a Butterfield interior. Hopkins also described Butterfield's sumptuous use of numerous varieties of marble and his rich and showy pulpits, baptismal fonts, side chapels, and screens. Hopkins had visited All Saints Babbacombe in Torquay (Devon), where he was fascinated by Butterfield's endless obsession with architectural surprises, such as "seven-foiled blind tracery in the spandrels meant to contain mosaics" and "medallions by [an] east window ... alternate inscapes—all five-spoked wheels or roses." Hopkins's sister Millicent was an Anglican nun in the Society of All Saints Sisters of the Poor at Margaret Street, possibly in residence at one of the adjoining school buildings Butterfield designed. Hopkins never visited her and was in fact quite disdainful of her "ritualist" superiors there, an uncharacteristic harshness for the man known as the "gentle Hop" among his friends.[9]

Hopkins's appreciation of Butterfield's architecture was comfortably in step with the Anglo-Catholic establishment journal *The Ecclesiologist,* the house organ of the Cambridge Camden Society, that urged architects to take the pitch of decoration up more than a few notches to capture the hearts and worship of the poor:

> When the congregation consists mainly of the poorer orders, there we commonly observe a great love of a majestic and even elaborate service. The ornaments of their church—the storied glass—the painted, and, it may be, gilded walls—the table of the Lord elevated above the rest—the chanted psalms—the surpliced choristers—the solemnity of the whole ritual—gladdens while it elevates their minds; they recognize in it their own high privilege as Christians, and rejoice to find themselves equal participants with their richest neighbors in the homage thus paid to the common LORD and FATHER of all.[10]

Although often the discussion of Butterfield's work was polemical, that is, related to contemporary Protestant-Catholic controversies,

Butterfield himself was more interested in the technology of his innovative art. The changes in the industrial manufacture of colored bricks (the uniformity of size and lowered costs) and the re-discovery and deployment of encaustic tiles, for example, were his way of turning architecture away from the Ruskinian orthodoxy of Gothic stone and marble. Nonetheless Ruskin, perhaps somewhat grudgingly, admired Butterfield as being "original and independent."[11]

But how could such "Catholic" mentality of decoration be squared with Butterfield's supposed dedication to the Book of Common Prayer?[12] And this seeming devotion to the plain style of the Anglican Church from a man whose designs (and pieces completed) for church metalwork—lecterns, candlesticks, flagons, and altar vases—have a polychromatic splendor and ornate presence as mini-architectural reflections of the church interiors? The extent of Butterfield's obsession with these richly made objects became obvious when they were last exhibited in 1982, at which time the exhibitors concluded, "Butterfield's work in the 1840s has remained to this day the basis for most of the church-plate in the Church of England."[13]

Butterfield was involved with two London churches in the Ritualist controversies of the third quarter of the century, as the architect of the Reverend Mackonochoe's St. Albans and as the consulting architect of the Reverend Bennett's St. Barnabas of Pimlico, but his masterpiece was clearly All Saints, Margaret Street, in 1859. All Saints replaced the Margaret Chapel on the same street, where Anglo-Catholic ritual had been a way of life for many years, including "complete musical masses."[14]

A visitor to All Saints, Margaret Street, will be dazzled by the polychromatic panorama. "Byzantine" was a common contemporary explanation, as every surface was covered by colored stone, brightly hued marble, patterned encaustic tiles, stained glass windows, and even painted wood with gilding. It is the closest we can imagine a Pre-Raphaelite architect could do in addition to employing—as Butterfield sometimes did—a Pre-Raphaelite for interior decorating.

The interior, which the *British Almanac* in 1860 called "the most gorgeous church interior in the kingdom"[15] employed the Pre-Raphaelite painter William Dyce, who did a fresco ("The Holy Trinity and Saints") for the reredos or retable (the former a decorated screen, the latter a table for religious objects, both behind the altar). What we see today is a copy painted by Ninian Comper in 1909. Dyce, whose most famous painting was actually the non-religious "Pegwell Bay: A Recollection of October 5th, 1858" (now at the Tate Britain), was also an expert on church rituals and music.

Butterfield's usual sounding board—*The Ecclesiologist*—found All

Saints almost *too* Pre-Raphaelite: his deliberate exterior striping and vertical interruptions seemed to one reviewer in 1859 to have "that same dread of beauty, not to mention the same deliberate preference of ugliness, which so characterizes in fuller development the later paintings of Mr. [John Everet] Millais and his followers."[16] Butterfield, it is true, often repeated his effects, even in less showy commissions, such as the Clergy House of St. Michael's, Burleigh Street, which he built in 1859–60 in Convent Garden, London, that became the Rectory of St. Paul's Covent Garden when St. Michael's was demolished.

Butterfield was the Coleridge family's architect of choice; indeed, John Duke Coleridge said of Butterfield's work, "Some of which I have known for forty years, seems as if it would last for ages." He was a close friend of Coleridge and his wife, whose portrait of Butterfield—as well as one of Cardinal Newman—was exhibited at the Royal Academy.

St. Paul's Covent Garden Rectory, formerly St. Michael's Church Clergy House. Architect: William Butterfield (photograph by the author).

6. Architects on the Defensive   49

Butterfield had restored the Coleridge parish church in Ottery St. Mary's, and he had even designed controversial wallpaper for the couple's London home in Sussex Square that he had renovated for them. Judge Coleridge shuddered to think that he would ever get used to the worm-like design his nephew Ernest Hartley Coleridge characterized as part of this "fantastic" Butterfield wallpaper.[17]

Part II

Ten Scandalous Court Cases

7

The Ex-Priest and the Nun Who Was His Former Wife

Connelly v. Connelly, 1849–1851

What British Protestants labeled as the Papal Aggression at mid-century was in part a fantasy of anxious Anglicans in which Roman Catholics conquered their nation by unnatural and dubious stratagems. Curiously, some of their fears were justified: in addition to waves of poor Irish Catholic immigrants fleeing the potato famine, thousands of middle- and upper-class Brits, many of them Anglican ministers and intellectuals of all stripes, were in fact deserting the established church for Rome willy-nilly. A third constituency, really a kind of fifth column, were the Old Catholics, many of them rich aristocrats who had learned to preserve themselves as an obedient minority, sometimes for centuries after suffering as recusants during the Reformation, often penalized with immense fines, occasional prison sentences, and only rarely execution.

Then came the case of an ex-priest who sued a nun who had been his wife for the restoration of his conjugal rights. Known in legal circles as the remarkably intricate and embarrassing conundrum of *Connelly v. Connelly*, it probably drove both Protestants and Catholics around the bend, because its motivating petition called for the restitution of conjugal rights between the priest and a nun! And while Catholics would have been doubly outraged, perhaps, the correct legal course in England for such a "religious" petition was through the Anglican Church's Court of Arches.

Pierce Connelly, an American Episcopal priest, married Cornelia Connelly in a home service officiated by the Protestant Episcopal bishop of Philadelphia in 1831. They may have had a successful early married

7. The Ex-Priest and the Nun Who Was His Former Wife

life, although only three of their five children survived. Not long after the children's deaths, the couple agreed to end their marriage. Cornelia, her husband, and her children were then received into the Catholic Church by the bishops of New Orleans, their exit port for Europe and specifically for Rome.[1] When Pierce finally decided to sell their home in Natchez, Mississippi, he also sold both of their slaves for a substantial profit. Once he arrived in Rome he decided, however, to become a Catholic priest and for a time in Rome was a Jesuit, advancing in the ranks in an aggressive if not unseemly manner. Having agreed to a separation from Cornelia, he celebrated his first mass as a Jesuit in 1845 at the Roman convent where Cordelia was currently residing, not expecting that she would be there for a year because of her unsettled status.[2] Among the attendees were members of the wealthy British Shrewsbury and Arundel clans, but more remarkable perhaps was the presence of the couple's daughter (Adeline), whom Pierce addressed directly during the mass for fifteen minutes, telling her (according to a witness) "to remember this day, and celebrate the anniversary of it, not only here but in Heaven."[3] If anyone needed any evidence of Pierce's stupendous ego and yes, even megalomania, that moment should have sufficed.

When it came time for the couple to part, possibly for an indefinite period of time, after the mass, Cornelia (according to still another witness) "fell on the ground and remained there some time, and on rising there was literally *a pool of tears* on the floor." To be sure, this was a different but equally revealing harbinger of things to come for her, not the least of which was the fact that she was destined, because of Pierce's ego and eventual vindictiveness, to be separated from her daughter Adeline, who was supposed to enter her mother's convent school and perhaps join her mother's order herself when she came of age.[4]

With special papal permission, Cornelia remained in the convent and took a vow of celibacy in 1848 after her ex-husband was ordained: "I, Cornelia, vow to have no future intercourse with my children and their father, beyond which is for the greater glory of God, and is His manifest will known through my director, and in case of doubt on his part through my ... [confessor]."[5]

Very early on, Pierce had delusions of grandeur. When he could not keep to the Jesuit discipline, he campaigned instead to be made a cardinal. His religious zeal nevertheless made a great impression on the English community in Rome, which at that time included numerous important people from the highest British Catholic circles, such as John Talbot, the Earl of Shrewsbury, head of one of the richest Roman Catholic families in the north of England, as well as C.J. Laprimaudaye, Cardinal Henry Manning's assistant, lately in the news because of his own religious vacillation. Pierce's ability to speak Italian, his overweening confidence, and his single-minded zeal to advance in status appealed to many in the Roman hierarchy, including Pope Gregory XVI. When the latter died in 1846, however, the new pope, Pius IX, was not quite as pliable in response to Connelly's entreaties. Whenever Connelly later examined his conscience, only his self-confidence came through. This passage from his *Reasons for Abjuring Allegiance to the See of Rome* (1852) shows his utter lack of introspection: "Though my allegiance to the Church of Rome was a delusion, and a culpable delusion, for it had its origin in carnal-mindedness and pride, it was most sincere."[6]

Earlier, Pope Gregory XVI had already decided that Cornelia had the makings of a mother superior, and he dispatched her to England to found a new order, the Society of the Holy Child of Jesus (SHCJ), with a rule or constitution modeled on the Jesuits, despite Pierce's belief that the Franciscans of St. Francis would have been the better model. His tendency to meddle in his wife's religious vocation was already in full swing.

Pierce himself soon left Rome to become one of the Earl of Shrewsbury's personal chaplains, complementing the other extremist in his retinue, A.W.N. Pugin, the militant medievalist and Catholic architect of the earl's Alton Towers complex (see chapter 10).

Left to her own leadership skills, Cornelia slowly but surely built her order with great competence, at first in Derby in a building Pugin built near his church of St. Mary's, although her tenure there was made difficult by the unsympathetic owner of that building.[7] Upon her arrival Cornelia noted that it was "not Bethlehem," but not much in the surrounding industrial landscape was. Her mission was to teach the children of the poor Irish Catholic immigrants fleeing their homeland's potato famine. Cornelia's model for prayer and discipline was the Jesuit order, facilitated by their chaplain who was in fact a Jesuit. The nuns taught the factory girls at night or on Sundays, the only times they were free, and also ran a school for the poor.[8]

Charles Laprimaudaye, Henry Edward (later Cardinal) Manning's close friend and curate, had two daughters who joined Cornelia's order, while a third became a nun in the Order of the Sacred Heart. His strong support for her order was cut short when he, after joining Manning to found the order of the Oblates of St. Charles, died suddenly in 1858. One of the Laprimaudaye daughters in the convent summed up the adoration English Catholics felt for Cornelia: "Mother Cornelia looks as if she must be obeyed. If she ordered me to kiss her feet or clean her boots, I should have to do it."[9] Other early recruits to the order included Emily Patmore, the daughter of poet Coventry Patmore, known in her order

7. The Ex-Priest and the Nun Who Was His Former Wife

for her remarkable piety and disposition and who died at aged 29,[10] and Emily Bowles, the sister of Frederick Bowles, one of Newman's close comrades at Littlemore in the early years after the Oxford Movement, who joined the order because of Cornelia's charisma. Pierce Connelly had in fact been one of the people in Rome who had encouraged Bowles to convert to Catholicism.[11] Later, the daughter of the prominent lawyer Sergeant Bellasis also joined; many years later she ended up becoming the primary witness to Cornelia's will.

Of course Shaftesbury's favorite megalomaniacs could not get along. Even Pierce couldn't compete with Pugin's grandiose schemes, so he turned instead to an even more unlikely scam—attempting to be named as the founder and supervisor of his wife's religious order. After this absurd quest made some unexpected initial progress in Rome, he decided, quite unhinged at this point, to visit his wife's convent, where he had temper tantrums and crying jags that lasted six hours. It finalized his role of persona non grata everywhere among the Roman Catholic leadership, including with Bishop (later Cardinal) Wiseman, who at first had been one of the Connellys's benefactors. Pierce even abetted the Protestant slur of "Mrs. Wiseman" for Cornelia. His compulsive, irrational letters in 1848 to Lord Shrewsbury make unnerving reading: "The first of my duties is to rescue my blessed wife from the hands of devils." And again later that year when he turned the quest over to his solicitors: "I will now never cease till Mrs. Connelly is placed absolutely and unreservedly under my control."[12]

Although technically British law would support a father's absolute right of control over his children, Pierce more or less kidnapped all of them from the boarding schools in which his wife had placed them, including one son at Stonyhurst College, who later became his father's fiercest advocate against his mother. He treated the children with care, but they were his hostages for his wife's return. His public excuse for taking the children was his belief that there was a Catholic plot to kidnap them from *him*.[13] In fact the exact opposite situation was developing: as related above, Cornelia took the vow in 1848 have no further relations with them.[14] When Pierce's own misdeeds, not to mention his misbegotten ambitions, led to his alienation from the Catholic Church, his reversion to Protestantism was inevitable. He would not be bound by any religious vows whenever ambition called.

Another of Pierce's forays into disequilibrium came in his choice of "conversion" to the Irvingite sect of fanatic Protestants, some of whose members spoke as prophets predicting the second coming of Christ. Lady Shrewsbury, one of Pierce's former supporters, was aghast at his choice of this *"awful* sect."[15] Pierce became a close friend of the sect's leader, Henry Drummond, an MP whose district served as headquarters for the Irvingites. Drummond, himself one of the Chosen of the sect, the Twelve Apostles, hoped to recruit Pierce as another Apostle. Pierce only lasted two years in this Apostolate, but during that time his lawyers suggested Drummond to Bishop Wiseman as a go-between to avoid scandal.[16] In brief, Connelly asked Wiseman to meet with Drummond to arrange the return of Cornelia—since she is "under" his "jurisdiction"—to her husband since any legal proceedings would cause "great annoyance to the parties interested." As Lady Shrewsbury's remark indicated, a less appropriate mediator could hardly have been imagined. Wiseman immediately wrote to Lord Shrewsbury asking him, as Pierce's former patron, to intervene in this "madness" to stop Connelly.[17]

In hindsight we see a man in the grip of a serious psychological if not sexual compulsion when he expects to co-habit with the nun his ex-wife has become. More than a few bad jokes circulated in London when a Roman Catholic priest sued a Roman Catholic nun for "restitution of conjugal rights" in the Church of England's Court of Arches.[18]

But this Court of Arches approved Pierce Connelly's suit with indecent haste in 1850, a year of pervasive anti–Catholic prejudice in English culture. The presiding judge, Sir H.J. Fust, accepted Pierce's arguments in toto, even going so far as to say that Mrs. Connelly left her husband in 1847 but "it appeared that they had resided together at the same house for considerable period after her vow" of chastity had been taken.[19] The unspoken subtext was of course that her vow of chastity was bogus or at the very least compromised legally by the cohabitation. Cornelia's attorney met this issue as forthrightly as he could: "It was somewhat startling to contend that bringing the parties together in the same house necessarily involved the breach of the vow of chastity." Judge Fust agreed with Pierce's allegation that even if she were in a convent, Pierce would be responsible for her debts as her legal husband.[20]

Fust was nevertheless sensitive to the implications of the case. He was aware what a decision against Cornelia implied, given "the vows which she had taken." The "Court might," he continued, "hold its hand" since her circumstance "might influence the feelings of the Court, but could not affect its judicial sentence." But Pierce was quite willing to accept his lawyer's judgment that "she may now be compelled by force" to return to him; her supporters "must now therefore know that force can be used, and most surely it shall be used." Cornelia and others heard rumors that Pierce was off the coast of Sussex in a yacht planning to kidnap Cornelia as he had kidnapped the children.[21]

Cornelia appealed Fust's decision to the secular Privy Council. The council was in a moral dilemma: by all common sense and decency it

7. The Ex-Priest and the Nun Who Was His Former Wife   57

could not turn this nun over to her ex-husband, but by English law they seem never to have been divorced. Lord Selborne, Cornelia's attorney, appealed to the council's humanity: "It would be most extraordinary if the Court Christian of England held that after a husband had led his wife to enter into the most solemn vows of chastity before Almighty God he could compel her to break those vows. That would be cruelty of the highest description, and the Court would not lend its aid to enforce it." Furthermore, even if it were granted that they were "together in the same house" it did not "necessarily [involve] the breach of the law of chastity."[22]

Following the temper of the fiercely anti–Catholic times, Pierce Connelly's attorney, Dr. R. Phillimore, argued that the papal approval of the Connellys's vows of chastity was worthless: "There was no principle on which the Court of Rome was to have a power accorded to it which was not given any other prince in the world." In his Protestant zeal to promote Pierce's case, Phillimore made a tactical error: he argued, "In the present case" the "humanity of the court had been repeatedly invoked," but "humanity was the second consideration of the court, justice was the first."[23]

Spectators might have felt the Privy Council was heading in Pierce's favor, especially when Pierce's attorney stated that of the "private vows" of chastity and poverty "no Court would take cognizance." In fact, he argued, those two vows were "expressly set aside by two statutes of Edward VI" in the sixteenth century. Pierce's attorney argued strenuously that the panel of judges should not consider the matter a "religious" question, that is, they should judge that the cohabitation proved that they were in fact still legally married: do not, Dr. R. Phillimore said, "make" the law based on any "new doctrine" but "administer the law" as it is.[24]

Cornelia's attorneys argued, however, from the precedent from the thirty-year-old, notorious case of *Molony v. Molony*, which had been argued in the Court of Arches in 1824. Edmund Molony sued his wife Jane for restitution of conjugal rights and to force her to return from England, where they had resided together as a married couple, to Ireland, despite their four-year separation and her illness.[25] "It would be ten thousand times more atrocious cruelty to compel Mrs. Connelly to return to her husband that it would have been to have sent Mrs. Molony to Ireland," Cornelia's attorney stated.[26]

In a Solomonic gesture, however, the Privy Council ruled that Cornelia Connelly's appeal would be suspended and Pierce's judgment in the Court of Arches would not (yet) be enforced: "Their lordships would pronounce no opinion whatever on the facts of the case" until such time as Pierce re-submitted his case to the Court of Arches with specific motions regarding "the marriage law of Pennsylvania" and the facts regarding their "domicile" while in Rome.[27] Both of these would involve points of law and fact Pierce would have to establish to support his petition that they had never been divorced.

Unlike the legal expenses of the anti–Catholic campaign paid by the Protestant Union for a major libel case against John Henry Newman the same year (chapter 8), Pierce's suit, too outrageous even for the same benefactors, collapsed for lack of funds. The Privy Council dismissed the case in 1856. In order to keep Pierce from a debtor's prison for not paying his court fees, Cornelia characteristically paid his debt.[28]

Cornelia returned to a successful career as mother superior of her order, although her convent was on a high security alert for years, justifiably anticipating a Pierce Connelly raid. Although even Lord Shrewsbury would not encourage Pierce endlessly, Pierce wrote to him in 1848 that he "will now never cease until Mrs. Connelly is placed absolutely & unreservedly under my control. ... Should I fail in the Courts, I will carry it into the House of Commons, & will then make it an affair of the [American Government]."[29]

Pierce, in what must have been a simultaneous and last-ditch effort to sway public opinion, did petition the House of Commons in May 1851 to address his grievances against Cordelia. His intention, presumably, was to develop an even greater opportunity to have the details of his case against her heard in the House of Commons and by attendant public auditors. Some of the members objected strenuously against allowing the petition to be printed and distributed more widely than the "658 copies of the slander" already printed for the members of the House. Other members thought that curtailing circulation of the document would deny parties affected by the bill also presented to the House "the right of contradicting the slanderous allegations." In the end both the bill and petition failed.[30]

Both financial and organizational challenges seemed to strengthen Cornelia's executive abilities. Emily Bowles, an early recruit to the sisterhood on Newman's recommendation, for example, had attained the leadership of one of the order's new satellite houses, but her lack of financial sense soon had Connelly exploring ingenious solutions to pay the debts owed the Bowles family, from whom Emily freely borrowed thousands of pounds to support her ministry. Although losing such an illustrious recruit was difficult for the Society—the imminent dismissal of Bowles was finessed by her voluntary withdrawal—the situation deteriorated when the Bowles family demanded the return of the funds that they had loaned Emily. Although Cornelia maintained it was not a

7. The Ex-Priest and the Nun Who Was His Former Wife

loan made to the Society but to Emily herself, her superiors felt that the Bowles family should be repaid. Cornelia's judgment of Emily Bowles was prophetic because she made very unexpected—one might even say irrational—and unsuccessful applications (twice) for re-admission into the order she had so sharply criticized and demanded the transfer to her of the copyright of the well-received *The History of England for Catholic Children* (1851) she wrote while a nun.[31] By not claiming technical ownership of a copyright achieved while Bowles was a member of the Order, Cornelia avoided still another public legal scandal but still made her liable for backbiting within the Catholic circles Emily led.

Cornelia wisely never let down her guard, however. She annotated carefully her copy of one of Pierce's pamphlets on the case, noting throughout when his comments were "false" or "quite false." His decision to become a Catholic was based on "pride & vanity or by a disappointed ambition or love of power."[32] Nevertheless, from within her order there were even challenges to her original rule or constitution. Because of the notoriety of Connelly's court case, her order kept novices in the dark about her for fifty years. Even Newman, whom one would expect to be sympathetic to Cornelia's dilemma, felt in 1851 that it "not be safe to take up Mrs. C's cause too warmly. She is a Yankee, I suppose this is the reason, but anyhow, though she is a very good woman, it is difficult for an Englishman to follow her." Newman was very concerned about the damage to Catholics from Pierce's eventual petition to Parliament to attack Cornelia by proposing the abolition of convents, once a relatively easy rallying cry among rabid anti–Catholics.[33] Even after the trials were over and one of Connelly's erstwhile patrons, the 17th Earl of Shrewsbury, wrote a preface to the *Report of an Address Delivered by the Rev. P. Connelly, A.M.* (1853) that praised Connelly mildly but exposed the contradictions of Connelly's position, Newman had asked Shrewsbury to use his influence with Connelly to prevent him from "stating the most atrocious things on his own knowledge of persons he once was only too proud to know in Rome." Newman was afraid that "the force and justice" of the earl's preface might keep Protestants from actually reading Pierce's own words. Newman, always the careful tactician, was worried about the pamphlet's effect rather than Mrs. Connelly's terrible dilemma.[34] His timidity in defending Cornelia may have reflected one of Newman's ancient reservations about convent life: "Women (no, nor men, still less)," he wrote to Rosina Maria Giberne in 1840, "would not live together without quarrelling, as things are among us."[35]

The years of Cornelia's neglect ended in the 1930s, as the process of her *beatification*, the first stage towards sainthood in the Catholic Church, was begun, culminating in her being declared *venerable* in 1992, anticipating the final stages of canonization or sainthood.[36] Whether she was (and is) a saint we must leave to her Church to decide. By all standards of the scandalous trials we will consider, she certainly was more sinned against than sinning.

Once Cornelia regained her rightful status in her order, her fame eventually eclipsed the notoriety of her struggles with Pierce. Two sympathetic biographies of her by Julia Wadham and Mother Marie Therese, both with the imprimatur of the Catholic Church and written with the resources of the archives of the Society of the Holy Child Jesus, are good guides to the case, especially regarding the personal tribulations of Cornelia and the grotesque maneuverings of Pierce. Pierce's own *Reasons for Abjuring Allegiance to the See of Rome* (1852) and D.G. Paz's *Priesthoods and Apostasies of Pierce Connelly* (1986) will more than adequately explain Pierce's point of view, while still another biography, *The Life of Cornelia Connelly, 1809–1879* (1922), from a sympathetic Catholic publisher, provides the more or less official counterbalance to Pierce's arguments.

Pierce himself, however, was never able to regain the surprising support his pro-family rhetoric achieved in the early years of his campaign against his wife. Although he himself was never a model for anything but opportunism (and perhaps what we would now call obvious sexual harassment and child abuse), one of his major supporters was a writer, Elizabeth Furlong Shipton Harris, herself a Catholic convert who de-converted, who sought to celebrate the traditional British family over the Roman Catholic celibate priesthood. She had been so taken with Connolly's quixotic crusade that she published a virtually unreadable roman a clef, *From Oxford to Rome* (1847), just three years after the couple's separation, but published in time—and with sufficient notoriety—to support his legal maneuvers financially at first. In the novel an Anglican minister, like Pierce, becomes a Catholic priest by rejecting his children and facilitating his wife's unhappy entrance into a convent. The novel played into some of the anti–Catholic publicity about the Connellys that stressed Cornelia's refusal to be a proper Victorian wife.[37]

Newman's own novel, *Loss and Gain: The Story of a Convert* (1848), published a year later, reversed Harris's acceptance of Connolly's eventual (inevitable, perhaps, given his personality) rejection of celibacy by satirizing the overly sumptuous life of married Anglican clergy in contrast to Catholic celibacy and asceticism.[38] Newman was so adamant about this issue that he wrote in an Oratory memorandum or draft of an essay, *My Illness in Sicily* (1834/1840), that he had "a repugnance to [an Anglican] clergyman's marrying. I do not say it is not lawful—I cannot deny the right—but, whether prejudiced or not, it shocks me." Newman

7. The Ex-Priest and the Nun Who Was His Former Wife

was emphatic: "All my habits for years, my tendencies, are towards celibacy. I could not take that interest in the world which marriage requires." Henry James Coleridge was also critical of the lack of celibacy among Anglican clergymen, despite what he saw as the recognition of the "advantage of the dignity of the virginal life Oxford Movement." In Anglican circles, he argued somewhat slyly, "the celibate movement has been mainly confined to the female sex" in the Anglican "sisterhoods and religious communities."[39]

In fact, Newman always believed in what he called "a marriage with Christ" based on "the virginity of the Christian soul," phrases from his mature Catholicism that have a precedent in at least one of his Anglican sermons in 1843 when he refers to the monastic ideal of celibacy. Since Newman's novel in effect valorized celibacy over marriage, however, he may have inadvertently strengthened the anti–Catholicism rampant in certain strata of Victorian culture.[40]

Pierce proved himself in the end to be remarkably inconsistent: after losing all hopes of regaining his authority over Cornelia, he took over the leadership of an Episcopalian mission for Americans in Florence, Italy, where he lived with two of his children, a third one having left for America.[41] His derangement, however, abated to such a degree that he seemed to acquiesce in Cornelia's contact with their children. In fact, she only ever saw two of them very briefly.[42] Frank, an esteemed sculptor, was his father's close ally and her implacable foe, while Adeline had been an uncanny presence as a teenager when Pierce celebrated his first mass as a Jesuit priest. Adeline died with her mother's crucifix in her hands, having re-converted to Catholicism. Although Frank's contact with his mother was never easy, his daughter eventually attended a Holy Child School in France and married into the Borghese family, close to the Shrewsbury clan, in Italy.[43] The third child passed away thinking, as Pierce taught him, that Cornelia had "been 'possessed by the devil.'"[44]

Always beset by controversy, Cornelia's order moved to St. Leonard's by the Sea, a relatively posh resort near Hastings on the Sussex coast, but their tenancy was only guaranteed when the missing will of the property's owner guaranteeing their claim to occupy the estate was discovered.[45] Cornelia had to return to court in 1877 when one of her nuns, Sister Mary Frances Kenworthy, who had died only four years after joining the order, left the bulk of her 40,000-pound estate—more than 4,000,000 pounds today—to the nuns. Her relatives entered an action against Cornelia's order on the basis of a "plea of undue emphasis," meaning, of course, that the Catholics had planned all along to make off with Sister Kenworthy's money, a recurring motif of a number of trials in this book. Cornelia's attorney, Sir Charles Russell, was ready to defend the order, amidst the array of street posters crying "Great Convent Case. Forty Nuns to Be in Court." As it turned out only sixteen nuns came to court to testify, and one of them was the daughter of the very respectable Sergeant Bellasis, who said that she had witnessed the signing of Sister Kenworthy's will. Her father's repute in the legal world no doubt helped to ensure that the suit was immediately withdrawn. Besides the considerable estate gained, the nuns also scored a psychological victory: their attorney, Sir Russell, announced that four of his daughters would be attending Holy Child schools.[46]

The years at St. Leonard's were tense, as the irrationality of Pierce was always foremost in Cornelia's mind. Only "one or two of the elders" knew the security drill: she was never to be on her own or out of sight of at least one other nun. A "secular outfit" was always ready for immediate escape at any moment. No one knew, however, that she used an intermediary, one of the nuns closest to her, to meet with Pierce a number of times to appeal to his conscience about his virtually illegal sequestration of her children from her. He did eventually allow her to write to them.[47] She died at St. Leonard's in 1879; Pierce, who died in Florence, survived her by just three years.

Details of the Litigation: Connelly v. Connelly, 1849–1851

Court of Arches

Presiding: Sir Herbert Jenner Fust, the Dean of Arches.
Charge: Restitution of conjugal rights.

For the Plaintiff, Pierce Connelly:	*For the Defendant*, Cornelia Connelly:
Dr. Bayford	Mr. Roundell Palmer (Lord Selborne)
Dr. R. Phillimore	Dr. Adams

Verdict: Conjugal rights restored.

Judicial Committee of the Privy Council

Presiding: Lord Chief Baron Pollock, with committee members Dr. Lushington, Mr. Pemberton Leigh, and Sir E. Ryan.
Appeal: From a rejection of a cause of conjugal rights.

For the Plaintiff, Cornelia Connelly:	*For the Defendant*, Pierce Connelly:
Mr. R. Palmer	Dr. Bayford
Dr. Adams	Dr. R. Phillimore

Verdict: Suspension of verdict of the Court of Arches, but Mr. Connelly could

7. The Ex-Priest and the Nun Who Was His Former Wife

"remit the cause to the Arches' Court" with additional evidence if he wished, especially concerning Pennsylvania marriage law and the joint domicile of the Connellys in Rome. He did not, however, do so, because of his lack of personal or publicly raised funds. The verdict remained suspended until 1856 when the Privy Council dismissed the case.

8

The Defrocked Dominican Priest and the Future Cardinal Whose Brothers Were Atheists
Regina v. J.H. Newman, 1851–53

John Henry Newman, one of the stars of the revival of High Church Anglicanism in the early nineteenth century, stunned but did not totally surprise fellow Anglicans when he became a Roman Catholic convert in 1845. His powerful advocacy of his new faith burst forth in dozens of public lectures and books, culminating twenty years later in a spiritual autobiography, the *Apologia Pro Vita Sua* (1864), a bestseller among friends and enemies alike. Although he eventually joined the Congregation of the Oratory of Saint Philip Neri, usually simply called the Oratorians, and lived in Birmingham, he was also closely identified with the Church of the Immaculate Heart of Mary in London, widely known as the Brompton Oratory, founded by his close co-religionist, Wilfrid Faber. He was "Father Newman" to both congregations.

Within six years of Newman's conversion, the Protestant establishment discovered a means, they thought, to humble this upstart: his name was Giacomo Achilli, an ex–Dominican priest who had seduced numerous women in Italy and England, in the end finding London much safer than his native Italian homeland since his exploits had been exposed by the Roman Catholic Inquisition and other religious tribunals. Newman felt safe denouncing Achilli because he had already been exposed in the pages of *The Dublin Review* in 1850 by Nicholas (later Cardinal) Wiseman, perhaps unfortunately, published anonymously. The result was that Newman's Catholic career was almost destroyed before it began.

8. The Defrocked Dominican Priest...   65

Newman's difficulties did not begin with Achilli or even his conversion to Catholicism. Newman had already survived a remarkably large number of crises in the early years of his career. Some of them are well known: his publication in 1841 of *Tract 90*, for example, caused a storm of protest from Anglican authorities, who squelched the series. *Tract 90* argued for the essential compatibility of the Anglican *Articles of the Church of England of England* (1863) and Roman Catholic tradition: "While our Prayer Book is acknowledged on all hands to be of Catholic origin, our *Articles* also, the offspring of an uncatholic age, are, though God's good providence, to say the least, not uncatholic, and may be subscribed by those who aim at being Catholic in heart and doctrine." One of the sections of *Tract 90* that disturbed Anglican critics of Newman—still a member of the Church of England at this time—involved the *lack* of condemnation in the *Articles* of three keystones of Roman Catholic belief and practice: "Purgatory ... Worshipping of Images and Relics.... Of the invocation of saints." Newman wrote back very tactfully, ignoring the content of their critique, but acknowledging it "as expressing the opinion of persons for whom he has much respect and whose names carry great weight."[1] We can only assume that these critics knew an empty sentiment when they heard one.

Newman's subsequent conversion to Roman Catholicism four years later was simply for many the inevitable direction of the Tractarian or Puseyite party. Roman missionaries to England such as Dominic Barberi, however, had expected conversions among the masses and did not really understand the Oxford Movement or its importance to converts among the intellectual aristocracy like Newman.

Newman's personal life suffered when a disturbing competition appeared to arise between Newman and his brother Frank over Maria Rosina Giberne, a relative by marriage of the poet Gerard Manley Hopkins, now Newman's most famous convert. When Maria Rosina met Hopkins, she encouraged him in his early efforts to draw. Her brother George Giberne, Hopkins's uncle, taught him photography, an appreciation of Gothic architecture, and even used him as a model for a number of portraits.[2] Isabel Giberne Sieveking, Hopkins's cousin and Maria's niece, described Maria in her biography of Frank Newman as "a beautiful girl possessing special charm of manner." She became an intimate of Newman's family in the 1820s, especially during the illness and death of Newman's beloved sister Mary in 1828. An accomplished artist, Maria Rosina sketched Mary on her deathbed and admired Newman intensely. In fact, she fell in love with him.[3]

By most accounts Maria was a talented woman—and as we can see from sketches and photos—strikingly attractive and appealing. But since Newman's celibacy was already settled (for about ten years) by the time he met her in 1827, marriage was clearly out of the question. Newman was besieged by another ardent admirer and would-be Catholic in 1844, Mary Holmes, who wished them to have a father/daughter relationship. Newman was clearly aghast at the proposal and when she was received into the Catholic Church before him, she complained that he was "so long in coming over."[4]

Newman's personal problems multiplied when his brother Frank "fell passionately in love" with Maria Rosina during an unplanned mutual visit to her cousin's house near Oxford, in part because she was capable of holding "long talks on scientific and religious subjects." One of Maria's sisters became the wife of one of Frank's mentors, but Maria refused Frank's offer of marriage once, and then a second time when he returned from a missionary trip to Syria. Although he was a brilliant success at Balliol College, he could not hold any academic position because he refused to accept the Anglican *Articles*; "I am anti-everything," he said, with revealing humor. She had another suitor at this time (1828), who, equally rebuffed, went off to India to make his fortune and—when he died—she inherited his estate.[5]

It is difficult to designate a precise moment when Maria's love for Newman turned instead into an affectionate friendship, but for the next fifty years Newman and Maria Rosina Giberne remained friends. The epistolary record (at least mainly from his side) demonstrates their extremely frank and occasionally tempestuous relationship.

Newman's relationship with Frank was more problematical. Frank moved towards agnosticism, even writing a book criticizing his brother's conversion and religious beliefs. Of another volume published by Frank at mid-century, Newman concluded that the independent ideas of "my dear brother ... tend to atheism. God grant that he may be arrested in his course." Frank in the end became a Unitarian and argued that Christ was "a good man" but not divine.[6]

Maria Rosina's niece, Isabel Giberne Sieveking, became Frank's biographer. Maria Rosina's early admiration for Frank was tempered by his "great tendency to free thought," a euphemism for a lack of doctrinal rigor. Frank was admired in these early days for working "amongst the poor" at Littlemore, near Oxford, whose spiritual needs were attended to by his brother John.[7]

But few Victorians then and even fewer people today know that there was a third but even more controversial Newman brother, Charles, and that by the time John Henry became a cardinal all three brothers were irrevocably estranged from one another. Inevitably Galton had concluded that "divines," as he called religious men, "are not founders of influential families," and celibacy ruled out considering Roman Catholics at all in terms of the "inheritability of genius." In fact, Galton's chapter on divines in *Hereditary Genius* virtually gives up the investigation on the first page: "There is commonly so much vagueness of expression on the part of religious writers, that I am unable to determine what they really mean when they speak of topics that directly bear on my present inquiry." He finds that their discourse confuses metaphor and the "plain meaning of language."[8] Later studies of the three brothers could not fathom why their common upbringing should have developed such radically different lifestyles and systems of belief.[9]

Charles was himself an ongoing crisis. Frank had to remind a friend once—or perhaps tell him for the first time—that he had a brother Charles "of whom we do not speak, because he is as unfit for society as if insane." Charles Newman "formally renounced" his family because, Frank added, "we were religious and he was an atheist" as well as a socialist.[10] Throughout Charles's difficult life John Henry Newman nonetheless provided a financial safety net for him. He lived in Wales for thirty years as a recluse until his death in 1884. Although Charles was an atheist and socialist to the end, Newman had inscribed on his tombstone: "Despise not O lord the work of thy hands." Newman had visited Charles just three years before he died, the first time the brothers had met face to face in forty years.[11]

Under Newman's guidance, Maria became as "catholic" as Newman, eventually converting with Newman's direct assistance in 1845. Newman introduced her to Father Brownbill, who first impressed her as "the terrible Jesuit," but he did receive her in the Catholic Church. It is clear, however, that she always regarded him as a spiritual advisor not quite up to her intellectual level.[12]

She moved to Rome for a decade of work there as a professional artist who copied classics of religious art to be used in English churches. There is a coy portrait of Maria in the intelligent and attractive titular heroine who paints pagan images for a living before her conversion in Newman's 1855 novel *Callista*.[13] Maria also did portraits of Newman and his close friend and religious brother, Ambrose St. John, and even drew Pope Pius the Ninth, of whom she was very fond, on a mule. Many of these portraits and other pieces of visionary art made their way back to Newman's Oratory in Birmingham. Before she considered becoming a nun, Newman felt her best course would be to "try to get someone to live with you, and should live in a house, and paint and pray." She could visit a nearby church, "spend all your money on yourself" and "be useful as well as comfortable."[14]

She was clearly a formidable and stunning member of Rome's circle of Catholic intellectuals. The Rev. Thomas Mozley, leader of the Oxford Movement and husband to Newman's sister Harriet, was unstinting in his praise of Maria Rosina, "tall, strong of build, majestic, with aquiline nose, well-formed mouth, dark penetrating eyes, and a radiance of glossy back hair, [who] would command attention anywhere." In Rome "she moved along like a divinity." Her daily life was good preparation for her eventual life as a nun: "Her diet," Mozley wrote, "consisted chiefly of bread and fruit, mostly apples. One apple in the middle of the day she spoke of as a great refreshment." She had trained a local Roman boy as her page, but also taught him how to deliver a sermon at Santa Maria Ara Coeli Church at the top of a magnificent flight of marble steps up the Campidoglio Hill: Caesar had crawled up those steps to the Roman Senate to thank Jupiter for his conquests, and in the church Edward Gibbon had been inspired to write his masterpiece, *The History of the Decline and Fall of the Roman Empire* (1776–88).[15]

Before Maria Rosina became a nun, however, Newman decided she needed some very direct mentoring. In a letter to Newman she had said she would dazzle her mother superior on her first day at the convent, no doubt confident that her friendship with England's most famous Catholic preceded her. That "you should fancy yourself interrogating and flooring your Mother Superior," Newman wrote, "is portentous": "It would be more wicked indeed, but not more inconsistent, for a profligate unbelieving woman, some French novelist, or Italian red-republicaness, to go to the Visitation, than for you, as you showed your feelings the other day."[16] At one point in 1846 Newman suggested she look into Cornelia Connelly's "new congregation" of nuns forming in Rome. Despite her having been married, Cornelia received Newman's support as "an enthusiastic person—of education and great influence in her circle."[17] Newman had met Pierce Connelly at Alton Towers about the same time as when he counseled Maria. Newman was more than a little doubtful about Pierce, "who wishes particularly to give [Newman] some hints about Rome."[18]

It may be terrible to say, but Newman didn't always trust the woman who saved his reputation during the trial. Five years after the trial he suspected that Maria Rosina was thinking of writing his biography. He wrote to Jemima, his sister, telling her that if Maria Rosina called on her not to give her "anything early of mine, handwriting, letters to me, letters from me, pictures." If she outlived him, Newman would not know if she writes "some account of me" but it is a "prospect ... which I cannot endure."[19]

She returned to London during the beginning of the high tide of the Papal Aggression campaign that in part created the context for the

8. The Defrocked Dominican Priest... 69

Achilli scandal and Newman's trial for libel. It had not been easy for her to find her calling. The Benedictine nuns in Staffordshire didn't think the fifty-seven-year-old was robust enough to climb the stairs to the novices' cells at the top of the convent. In part because of Newman's advice she traveled in 1859 to St. Winefride's Well in North Wells, a site of miracles whose efficacy Newman had confidence in, and that Gerard Manley Hopkins had celebrated in one of his poems, in search of a cure for her bad knee.[20] After the Achilli trial she became a nun of the Visitation Order in France until her death in 1885. Newman had written Hopkins that that she had been "very happy" at her convent. Because she took a vow of poverty her estate (as well as her will) was managed by Newman through the Oratory, but Newman was concerned when she used such a large portion of her capital for her (required) novice's dowry, wondering if that would affect her perceived status in her order.[21]

Fortunately for Newman Maria Rosina was in London where not only did she show her deep loyalty to him but also proved to be a spirited and very competent organizer of matters associated with Newman's defense during the Achilli trial. Without her, there is little doubt that the trial would have gone even more badly for Newman. Newman had attacked Achilli in his fifth lecture at the Birmingham Corn Exchange in the series titled "The Present Position of Catholics in England" (1851), confident of the research on Achilli already published by Wiseman in an unsigned review of pamphlets about Achilli that included not only examples of his sexual assaults and his false claims of various offices and titles of the Church in Italy, but excerpts from the "official dispatch" of the Naples police about his rape of a fifteen-year-old girl. The latter was so gross—it included Achill's "sharing" of the girl with one of his friends—that Wiseman could only bring himself to quote the Italian text.[22] Wiseman specifically noted that Achilli's status with the Dominican order "gave him ... access to establishments of female education." He closed with remarks condemning the Evangelical Alliance, who supported Achilli, paraphrasing a quotation from Roman poet Juvenal for their motto, that named Brixton, the oldest prison in England, that should house Achilli: "Would you that saints your glory should proclaim? / Make Norfolk isle, or Brixton-gaol your aim."[23]

Newman's previous or Fourth Lecture was on a significantly higher intellectual level. He did an extended analysis of two radically different species of anti–Catholicism, one kind perhaps best encapsulated by the word intellectual, represented by the peculiar career of an Anglican priest, Blanco White, who was Newman's friend at Oxford—they played Beethoven quartets together.[24] The other kind, "a romance true and terrible," scarcely credible, of Maria Monk and her adventures in depravity in a convent. The public, sighed Newman, chose to follow the second manifestation of untruth. While Blanco White left the Anglican priesthood and ended up "without any fixed belief at all, either in God or in the soul's immortality," he nevertheless would never assume that the Roman Catholic clergy or its nuns were collectively immoral or delinquent. As for Maria Monk, she was nothing more than a farrago of lies and suppositions, most of which were designed to inflame the public's curiosity and pander to their worst instincts.

Because Achilli was guilty of "extraordinary depravity,"[25] Newman's decision to go on the offensive against him was his way of responding to the targeted Catholics of the anti–Catholic mobs at mid-century following the restoration of the Catholic hierarchy in 1850. Demonstrations against Catholic churches and clergy had become widespread, to the point that Newman himself had a bag of flour dumped on him in Birmingham.[26] During the funeral of a young priest who had a lingering case of consumption, a mob besieged the Oratory believing the poor man had been murdered. Rumors spread that Newman had once been married and had "shut his [wife] up in a convent," still another example of Maria Monkism run amuck. Anti-Catholicism was stoked by Achilli's bestseller, *Dealings with the Inquisition: Rome, Her Priests, and Her Jesuits, with Important Disclosures* (1851).[27]

Newman gradually came to understand that Achilli was a diabolical trap, a kind of fire-ship launched by evangelical and other Protestant groups against Newman, a combination of verbal explosives and potential combustibles which Newman could ignore only at his peril. But touch it and he might go down in flames as well. Newman's metaphor was similar: "I had put my foot into a snare; I could do nothing; my enemies had nothing to do but to pull the noose tight at their leisure."[28] "When it first arose," he said in a retrospective sermon, "I said, 'The Devil is here. Look not on prosecutor, lawyers, friends, etc. They are all weapons of the devil.' A net—pulling strings close."[29] The usually sympathetic Earl of Shrewsbury was so frustrated that he commented to Ambrose Phillips: "What a mess poor Newman is in! How could he be so *extremely imprudent?*"[30]

For Achilli had been a Catholic priest, he had debauched young women, and he had used not-so-hidden corners of monasteries and churches to conceal his deeds. He proved what every fanatical Protestant knew in his heart: Catholic priests were licentious. The fact that he had been expelled from his order and eventually excommunicated by his Catholic superiors was not sufficient to belittle him.

Achilli, supported by the anti–Catholic Evangelical Alliance,[31]

8. The Defrocked Dominican Priest... 71

inspired in part by the Irvingites, brought nineteen charges of libel against Newman. The prosecution was at first in a hurry to get the trial going, in November 1850, less than six months after Newman had delivered his denunciation of Achilli in Birmingham. But the prosecution's haste was matched by Newman's side, who sent Maria Rosina Giberne to Italy to gather a number of the women—at least four—whom Achilli had seduced and bring them to London to testify, supplementing significantly four English female victims who were also going to be witnesses.[32] Giberne succeeded at her task remarkably well and returned with a band of wronged *signorine* to testify against Achilli and helped to create much popular support for Newman.

But the prosecution then moved to delay the trial for another five months, no doubt hoping that these foreign women either would not want or could not afford to stay. In fact, Giberne occasionally had to quell mutinies among the women, who—although they knew they would be paid for their troubles—were sometimes ready to give up the ordeal and head back home. On the trip over from Italy matters had grown testy enough that Giberne felt she had to lie to them. She told them that to prevent them from their mission Achilli might arrange to have them all killed. The Neapolitan women had been schooled in such nastiness, so they understood their situation, but their sour moods could only be transformed by the wine and food Giberne supplied them. At one point Newman was so sure he was going to lose and that his witnesses could be imprisoned that he told his friend Ambrose St. John to instruct Giberne to take the women out of the country.[33]

Soon after Achilli filed charges against Newman, Newman wrote in 1851 a remarkable litany or series of prayers that petitioned divine and historical figures to pray for him. It is a startling revelation of Newman's mind, because he clearly believed that the Achilli trial would end with his imprisonment:

> St John Baptist, imprisoned for thy true witness, pray for us
> St John the Evangelist, cast without harm into a cauldron of hot oil, pray for us
> St John, Pope, thrown into a loathsome dungeon, pray for us
> St John Chrysotom, victim of an unjust sentence, pray for us
> St John of Egypt, for forty years shut up in thy cell, pray for us
> St John of God, seized and confined for mad, pray for us
> St John Nepomucene, imprisoned for the law of [Christ], pray for us
> St John of the Cross, imprisoned by the envious, pray for us
> St John Capistran, born anew in prison, pray for us
> St John of Malta, delivered of captives, pray for us.[34]

The litany documents anxiety about his potential public humiliation, but the sure touch of the Church historian and scholar is also obvious, as he calls on the men called John, some known, some not, to intercede. Probably only his fellow Oratorians heard or even knew of this composition, but for us today it highlights the intellectual and moral level only one of the contestants in this trial could possibly attain.

Unfortunately for Newman, Achilles's case of libel against Newman gained a prosecutor—the attorney general, Frederic Thesiger—who was willing to bend the conventions of libel trials considerably. He may have had a special animosity towards Newman because he had been a member of P.M. Robert Peel's government in the mid–1840s and, as unlikely as it seems, Newman had published anonymous letters against Peel and was rumored to have called him a "rat."[35]

The judge, Lord Chief Justice John Campbell, abetted the prosecution's strategy at every turn. Even the "criminal information" against Newman was doubtful, as Wiseman had already published the same "libel" fifteen months earlier without Achilli's reply or any threat of prosecution. Sir Alexander Cockburn, the chief defense lawyer for Newman, had a strong reputation as a defense lawyer, in part based on his successful defense in 1843 of Daniel McNaughten, who was acquitted of a murder because of insanity. This landmark historical victory generated what became known as the McNaughton Rule.[36]

Throughout the trial Newman's attorney endeavored to have Wiseman's *Dublin Review* article with the same attacks on Achilli entered into evidence, but the judge refused. Besides the *London Times*'s usual thorough coverage, we are fortunate in having a virtually verbatim record of the proceedings, although its propagator, W.F. Finlason, a barrister of the Middle Temple, was especially disposed to Newman's side.

Attorney General Thesiger opened his case with an ingenious argument. Once Achilli had left his Catholic faith and arrived in London, he took a position as a preacher at the Italian Protestant Church, catering to immigrants or converts. Because "he appears to possess a strong and determined will, and a spirit of independence which makes him occasionally unwilling to submit to authority" and had "revelations to make respecting the Inquisition" as well as the errors of the faith he had just abandoned, the Catholic establishment knew he would be "a most formidable adversary and one who was by no means to be despised." The Catholic Church decided to "disable his authority, impeach his veracity, and destroy his credit." And there was no person more able to do this than Dr. Newman, who had already in another context denounced "the one-sided intellect of Protestantism!"[37]

Almost immediately, Judge Campbell connived in a legal maneuver by the attorney general that Finlason maintained was contrary to conventional criminal practice: not allowing Achilli to be called as a witness almost immediately so that the jury could check his story against those of the witnesses who will follow him. Instead, Achilli was to be present or could read a stenographic version of all the witnesses Newman's side called to support Achilli's misdeeds, thereby allowing him the opportunity to prepare and formulate his own version of the events. "I should like," Sir Cockburn pleaded in vain, "to have had the opportunity of examining Dr. Achilli himself, before he knew the exact amount of evidence which could be adduced against him."[38]

Newman's attorney was especially incensed by another successful legal posture of Achilli's defense, namely "that every person who swore against him swore falsely, and that any document produced against him was a fabrication." Finlason was stupefied by the possibility that Thesinger did "really believe in the monstrous theory of perjury and forgery he put forward" in Achilli's defense that would come down simply to this: "Whether Achilli or all the witnesses against him swore falsely." The chief justice agreed: "There is no alternative."[39]

Cockburn's opening statement highlighted a titanic battle between the "two converts, each from the faith of the other," two "great champions of these contending churches," ironically comparing a philandering priest, a "nobody" in our parlance, and an esteemed, internationally famous religious scholar. He noted that the jury, who were "composed, perhaps exclusively, of Protestants," had to judge a Catholic, "discharging their duty without being subject to those influences which are so apt to dominate unconsciously over us."[40] Cockburn was perhaps attempting to highlight the absurdity of equating two men of such obviously different abilities and accomplishments. He also was scathing about the very nature of the charges, which implied that Newman was the first to raise them in public when everyone knew that Wiseman had published them openly fifteen months earlier.

Cockburn was able to play to the spectators, many of whom were Newman's supporters. He ridiculed Achilli's pretensions at piety and exposed his interest in the Mary Magdalenes of his circle before they reformed. The gallery erupted in laughter a number of times, not only when Cockburn spoke but also when he questioned some of the women Maria Rosina Giberne had induced to testify. One of the women (Eleni Justini) testified that she was deflowered by Achilli in the sacristy of his Dominican religious house when she was seventeen or eighteen. She explained that Achilli had given her presents: a "silk handkerchief, which was older than he was," and three sausages.[41]

A somewhat different scenario of Achilli's modus operandi was developed in court from testimony of a mother-daughter pair, Signora

Principe and Mary Giovanna Principe, the latter thirteen or fourteen years old. Signorina Principe had joined what must seem to us now to be a bogus religious society—it had no name, the witness said—that Achilli ran to procure women and even make them pay for the privilege. Achilli had sexual relations with her, she estimates, seven or eight times, and she became pregnant. Achilli then told the local Naples police that her father was spreading lies about him. One day Signora Principe and her husband called Achilli out of a church procession to talk to him. Achilli denied their accusations: "I am a priest," he said. He then told the young girl: "Go to the devil if you like, to me it matters nothing." Achilli again reported the family for lying about him, but the police apparently did not believe him, and he fled to Corfu. Later in the trial he said the incident could not have happened because in Italy "it was not allowable to speak to a monk in a procession."[42]

One of the unusual witnesses was an Italian male, Antonio Russo, who testified that he and his friend Garimoni, a tailor, discovered Achilli lurking in the dark near the room of Garimoni's wife. When accosted, "Achilli was trembling, but did nothing." When a police officer was summoned, Achilli escaped and "ran away like a horse."[43]

Although their testimonies had the ring of authenticity to Finlayson, the witnesses were essentially treated by the prosecution as perjurers and objects of mirth. Even the testimony of rape and subsequent pregnancy by another witness (Sophia Maria Balisano) would eventually be considered insignificant despite details—Achilli had sent her out a back door because she was "all red in the face"—that would seem difficult for a young woman to invent. Later, when Achilli testified, the women were brought back into court one by one. He denied ever knowing any of them.[44]

While one might have felt the Italian women were not believable, given the prejudice against foreigners, even the English women who testified that Achilli took liberties with them—and in one case also made one of the servant girls pregnant—fared no better. Judge Campbell joined in the dismissal of one of the witness's testimony at one point by making the spectators laugh at one of his questions about men other than Achilli who came to "court" her.[45]

Although Finlason records the spectators, mostly Newman supporters, laughing at the absurdities of Achilli's exploits—actually less funny than despicable—the jury were clearly not amused. Even when a supporting witness who observed Achilli handling the laundry woman—whom Achilli apparently referred to as a "second Magdalen"—in unsavory ways testified that he clearly was not imparting the lessons of his religion, the audience laughter was even "greater." Cockburn asked rhetorically whether Achilli's marriage just before leaving Italy for England would be "consistent with his vows of perpetual chastity"; he commenced "operations" with English women as soon as he arrived in London.[46]

In the end Newman's case delineated twenty-three impostures, seductions, and rapes by Achilli, both in Italy and England. These "allegations" are "true in substance and in fact, and of fair and reasonable comments therein," Newman asserted, but according to English law, he had to prove each and every one of them.[47]

When Achilli was on the stand, he provided the spectators and even himself with numerous occasions of humor. He did not strike the *London Times* reporter as agreeable because his "black wig, sallow complexion, and somber aspect" were perhaps too "Italian" for English tastes. In any case he denied "criminal intercourse" with his accusers and refused to reply whether he had sexual intercourse with others when he was a monk. He pointed out, accurately enough, that the judge "privileged" him and he did not have to reply to such questions. When he did answer questions, he was cunning and evasive: he said he was never found "guilty" of raping any woman and even when he admitted knowing one of his accusers, he said he "could not commit any sin, because she is shut in a nunnery." As for creating a fake society to seduce women, he said he was merely using a circular to raise money for a church.[48]

His avoidance of direct responses and the use of weasel words drove Newman's solicitor to distraction. "Answer the question!" he shouted over and over, to little effect. Achilli's typical response was that he did "not have intercourse with a woman, according to the tenor of the imputation which has been made against me." When pressed, Achilli said, "I could answer, no." Cockburn exploded: "But I ask you whether you will answer no?" Achilli declined at this point because he "was privileged by the judge not to answer"; in other words, he never denied having raped the women, and thus escaped lying on the stand, i.e., committing perjury. At other times, because his "English was not good," he did not answer a question because he could not understand it, his translator apparently remaining equally mute. At other times Cockburn fairly shouted at the interpreter: "Put the question in Italian!" Once Cockburn confronted Achilli directly: "This is the third time I have asked you, and you understand English as well as I do." Pressure never defeated Achilli's spirits; he obviously had a way about him. When asked if a friend, a chorus singer, was a Catholic, Achilli replied: "Neither a Catholic nor a Protestant, like most of the Italians."[49]

Cockburn's frustrations seemed never to end. Pursuing questions about raping a girl whom Achilli took out hunting with him when he was in his Italian monastery, Achilli defended his un-monkish pursuit of shooting by saying his superiors hunted as well. The judge tried to reassure Cockburn: "Sir Alexander, in Roman Catholic times bishops used to keep hounds." Cockburn's acerbic reply: "Not monks, my lord."[50]

As if Achilli were not enough, Cockburn had the jury to contend with. When he found out that Achilli had been up to his old tricks recently, he sought to introduce his continuing bad moral character into the courtroom mix. "Have you ever had connection," he asked Achilli, "with any other women than" those he had asked about? "The foreman of the jury rose indignantly," Finlason reported, and said "the question was unfair." The judge did not entirely agree with this interruption but said Cockburn could not refer to a specific person not already on the record. Unperturbed, Achilli went on to discuss his similarity to Luther when he finally "was no longer a Christophagus," that is, a Catholic who ate the body and blood of Christ transformed from the host and wine of the mass.[51]

The deployment of Achilli against Newman was a stroke of perverse anti–Catholic success. As Newman's attorney, Cockburn, argued in his opening statement to the court, Achilli was in effect saying, since I have been a monk, I know how bad monks are: "I can tell you of the wicked and sinful things there performed, against the laws of God and man; and for these things I tell you these institutions, and the church to which they belong, should be swept away from the face of the earth, as unworthy any longer to be allowed to exist on it." As Cockburn uttered these words, "one or two of the jury nodded assent."[52] It was as if Maria Monk had spoken through one of the salacious priests she consorted with in her fictional world. Furthermore, like Maria Monk, Achilli argued that he escaped from his monastery, contrary to the fact that he was expelled.

One of the documents Wiseman used in his *Dublin Review* but mislaid was obviously crucial in supporting Newman's assertion that Achilli had been guilty of wanton behavior. Procured at great expense and effort, the trial record before the Court of Inquisition in Rome, a religious court, portrayed Achilli as a priest confessing to the seduction of at least two young women. But other documents, whose particulars corroborating the Inquisition, were records of civil proceedings before a police commissioner in Naples and officials in other cities for similar immoral acts.[53] At the end of the trial Attorney General Thesiger ridiculed the Church document: "It is the first time that a judgment of the Court of Inquisition has been produced in evidence in an English court

8. The Defrocked Dominican Priest... 77

of justice, and I hope it will be the last!" Perhaps the learned gentlemen had forgotten about the contemporary British Court of Arches, specifically empowered to rule on religious matters, not to mention the Reformation acts that Newman compared to the Inquisition in his lecture against Achilli: "What has the Inquisition done at Rome, which the royal name and authority has not done in England?"[54]

But the documents from civil authorities were treated cavalierly as well. Lord Campbell rejected the Naples document as evidence, even though it has "the authenticated seal of the city." Campbell, "with much acerbity," said, "If it were authenticated a hundred times it would not be evidence." This was more a successful rhetorical maneuver than a legal argument because it lumped both civil and Church documents into one category and rejected them all because they supposedly came from the Inquisition. All such documents were automatically suspected as fraudulent by the court.[55]

By the time Cockburn reached the end of the trial, he must have known he was fighting in a losing cause, because one of his final speeches had a desperate air about it. If the women who testified against Achilli were perjurers because they were Italian, then why do we not apply the same standard to Achilli himself: "Is *he* not an Italian? Was *he* not educated by Jesuits? Was *he* not initiated into all the craft and artifice which is ascribed to that well-known fraternity?" In the end he reinforced the absurdity of the case: "I cannot help thinking," Cockburn asserted, "that if, instead of appearing in the garb of a Protestant preacher, he had appeared in a monk's cowl, it would have struck many of us that, having our minds imbued with notions we are apt to entertain respecting the characteristics of that portion of the Catholic clergy, that the man and his habit were by no means ill-suited!"[56]

Not ideal, however, was the section of Cockburn's summation that conceded a little too much to public opinion vis-à-vis British Catholics: "We may differ from Newman," Cockburn began, "we all of us probably do; we may have regretted to see him falling off from the faith in which he had been bred, but it has never occurred to any living soul to impute to him anything which can affect his modesty, his honour, and his integrity!" In the end Cockburn graciously admitted that the jury was confronted by "two great champions of opposing churches—two converts from the faiths they were bred." He could not "shut [his] eyes to the manner in which your feelings on the subject of religion may in this case bias your understandings in determining this case." But, he said, the days of religious intolerance—acted out even in this very courtroom in the past—should be over and they should find Newman innocent.[57]

Despite Chief Justice Campbell's plea that the jurors should not be blinded by religious prejudice against Catholics, he himself was moved to exclaim at one point—in reference to Achilli's supposed imprisonment by the Inquisition in Rome: "Thank God there has never been an Inquisition in England!"[58] Perhaps the remark, especially the word "never," was made in the heat of the moment, but of course Henry VIII was Supreme Head of the Church in England when his parliament passed the *Act in Restraint of Appeals* isolating the monasteries from courts of any kind in 1533, and Thomas Cromwell's aggressive visitation of those same monasteries the following year would probably not be called an "inquisition" in the chief justice's world, as it was supposedly secular. Barrister W.F. Finlason, who wrote the definitive contemporaneous account based on large part on his own presence during the trial, asserted that the rejection of the Inquisition was in fact a key misruling of the chief justice.[59]

The remarks of the chief justice on the Inquisition and his courtroom decorum shocked, positively shocked, the very class-conscious *London Times*. After "some stomping of feet from some of the lowest class in the outer portion of the court; marked indignation and disgust from the educated portions of the audience—including members of the bar—and even clergymen of the Church of England," Lord Campbell "did not check the applause he received!" The *Times* remarked: "We have every respect for the high judicial character and attainments of [Chief Justice] Lord Campbell, and it is therefore with great regret we find him, in a case of so much delicacy and excitement, drawing attention to the Ecclesiastical Titles Act, 'thanking God' that 'we have no inquisition in this country,' and after he had been sufficiently applauded, renewing the remark that it might be applauded again."

In his summation speech, Prosecutor Thesiger applauded Achilli's lack of belief in transubstantiation or "auricular confession," two of the crucial differences between Roman Catholics and Anglicans: if "he is therefore an infidel, I say—without the least levity, but with strong feeling—I hope the number of such infidels will daily increase!" Chief Justice Campbell in his summation of the evidence noted that one criticism directed against Achilli was that "he had made a vow of celibacy, [and] that it was discreditable that he should have entered the holy estate of matrimony. We must remember, however, that Luther married, and married a nun!"[60] Of course Katharina von Bora was a *former* nun, but that perhaps did not matter to his lordship.

Although it seemed routine to the judge, in the middle of Thesiger's closing speech Lord Campbell asked that the Earl of Shaftesbury be recalled for questions. He was one of most celebrated evangelical anti–Catholics in the land, and by what could only be called an incredible coincidence, was on the examining or governing committee responsible for a college in Malta at which Achilli had taken a position after fleeing Italy. Given the judge's lack of support for Newman this recall was curious, because it could only support Newman's perception of Achilli as a person of great suspicion. Shaftesbury would not specify the reasons for Achilli's dismissal from his post at the college. The matter was sufficiently unpleasant, however, that Achilli *was* dismissed, even though Shaftesbury said it was for "general reasons, not of charges officially made before the committee." Shaftesbury added that he wanted to "get rid of the whole transaction, and wash [our] hands of so foul a business." Thesiger was content with this refusal to probe for further specific allegations against Achilli—in any case, the judge make it clear that he would only listen to specific allegations that were not forthcoming—but Finlason could not find any fault in the court's handling of the matter, which clearly was positive in its implications for Newman.[61] In a case full of surprises and unanswered allegations, this Shaftesbury testimony only raised the stakes for all without satisfying anyone completely.

In November 1852, the jury found Newman guilty on eighteen charges of libel but not guilty on one technicality, which Campbell summarized in his queries to the jury: "Then you find it to be true that Dr. Achilli was suspended from the celebration of mass, prohibited from any cure of souls, and from preaching, and from hearing any confession, and from exercising his sacerdotal office in any way, according to the decree of the Inquisition ... but you don't find for the reasons for the decree"?[62] When a juror agreed with this interpretation, Judge Campbell in effect cancelled out the not guilty verdict on this nineteenth charge as well, but said that he would "report to the Court when necessary" their "special finding" on the nineteenth charge. No doubt he was offended that the Inquisition had configured in a verdict in any way.

One of the principal reasons Judge Campbell queried the jury on this nineteenth charge was a startling coincidence: Campbell was applying to this trial for the first time in British judicial history the Libel Act 1843, later known as Lord Campbell's Libel Act, that he himself had drafted and co-sponsored. The act allowed "truth" to be the defense if it was for "the public benefit." Since the jury obviously did not believe Newman's statements about Achilli were true, the guilt would be virtually automatic. Thus the judge in effect erased the jury's "not guilty" verdict on the nineteenth charge.

As he attempted to discharge the jurors, one of them hastened to announce that they "did not consider this case as regards Protestantism and Catholicism" but that they "only looked at it as a matter of fact."

After the judge replied, "Oh, I am sure you have dealt with it conscientiously," the courtroom erupted in a mighty cheer that Finlason, with evident disapproval, noted "the learned judge did not for a moment attempt to check."[63]

Having decided not to appeal, Newman faced the sentencing in court in January 1853, three months later. It was acutely embarrassing for him, because he prepared a statement for the court but never read it. No doubt his attorneys dissuaded him, as Newman intended to announce that he was "going to suffer punishment for a libel, published with an absolute conviction that its matter was true."[64]

John Taylor Coleridge was the sentencing judge. In a statement that to a certain extent even he regretted ("there was something almost out of place in my not merely pronouncing sentence on him, but in a way lecturing him"), Judge Coleridge nevertheless launched into a biting attack on Newman, what Newman called "a most horrible jobation."[65] Coleridge later wrote that he believed Newman was "an over-praised man," one that had been "made an idol of," but in court cited his Anglican phase as "remarkable" for "the tenderness and gentleness of spirit that pervaded the whole," and noted that even in his "writings of controversy there was nothing like personal bitterness." But Coleridge read his attacks against Achilli "with infinite shame and disgust." Newman had lost the gentleness he had demonstrated as an Anglican and should he continue the polemics, he must learn to do so "neither personally nor bitterly."[66]

Newman, however, accepted the verdict and fine of 100 pounds (about $18,000 today) for what it was—a "moral victory"—and despite Coleridge's lecture said he was "grateful to the [sentencing judges] for this act of justice." The fine was paid on the spot, and Newman "walked off in triumph amid the hurrahs of 200 paddies," or Irishmen, who had been some of his greatest supporters.[67] We have already noted that both of Judge Coleridge's sons became strong and lasting friends of Newman. Despite his official victory, Achilli was unable to keep his place in English society, and he went to the United States.[68] Why, as the DNB suggests, the Swedenborgians would facilitate his transit to the United States makes as much—or as little—sense as his translating the New Testament into Italian for the American Bible Union.[69]

Newman's reputation was temporarily blemished by the Achilli scandal, although the *Times* editorial explained that it was British justice that deserved censure. Newman's "witnesses did not break down, were not involved in many material contradictions, and stated nothing in which there was any strong antecedent improbability." And as if to echo the absurdity of the last juror's remark about impartiality among

Protestants and Catholics, the writer noted that Achilli was accused by Roman Catholics "while he was a Roman Catholic and Protestants while he was a Protestant, and always of the same thing." If the jury did not believe these witnesses, "the principle upon which this case was decided would put an end to all proof by human testimony." The conclusion: "We consider a great blow has been given to the administration of justice in this country, and Roman Catholics will have henceforth only too good reason for asserting, that there is no justice for them in cases tending to arouse the Protestant feelings of judges and juries."[70] Finlason overheard a fellow barrister remark after Newman's defense had been presented: "Dr. Newman is morally vindicated." Newman agreed: "I have gained a moral victory," he wrote the following year, "as is testified by the rejoicings of my friends, and the disappointment and mortification of my opponents." As for Coleridge's "jobation" against him, Newman correctly labeled it as "an extra-judicial theory of his own." Newman tactfully omitted that after the sentence of the fine had been pronounced and a warning given that if not paid Newman would be "imprisoned in the first class of misdemeanants in the Queen's Prison," the spectators in the court burst into laughter.[71]

Maria Rosina Giberne had raised, with worldwide support, more than 10,000 pounds for Newman's defense, a substantial sum in 1852 (about a million and a half dollars today), and of course more than enough to pay his fine and costs. Newman used whatever remained from Maria's "defense fund" to help finance the scheme for the Catholic University he wanted so badly to establish in Dublin, "to see," in part, whether "Oxford [could be] imported into Ireland."[72] He would soon spend seven frustrating years trying to make it a going concern. (Later, Gerard Manley Hopkins would follow for *his* five frustrating years there, the years that led to his death.) There were even sufficient funds left from the defense fund to build the Church of Our Lady Seat of Wisdom, the university church for Newman's Catholic University of Ireland in Dublin, designed by John Hungerford Pollen, who had married Maria Margaret Theresa Laprimaudaye, from a family that was close to Maria Rosina; Pollen's son was later schooled at the Oratory and became a Jesuit.[73] Pollen designed a church "in the manner of the earlier Roman basilicas" because these "ancient churches with rude exteriors" represented for Newman "the early history of the Church."[74]

Newman tried to visit Maria Rosina, now Sister Maria Pia, on his return trip from Rome after receiving his cardinal's hat in 1879, but he was too ill to break his journey for a side trip to France. In their correspondence, even more than fifty years after Newman's sister's death, both Newman and Sister Pia exchanged pieties about this moment of shared domestic tragedy. Sister Pia died in 1885: she and Newman had never managed to meet after she left England for her French convent in 1863. Newman offered his condolences to the mother superior of the Visitation Convent at Autun in 1885 for "the death of one in whom I was so much interested, and for whom I had so true and deep an interest."[75] Two days before he himself died in 1890, a visitor recounted to him a moving story of Sister Pia's charity that "touched him deeply."[76] Newman had never been allowed to return to his beloved Oxford, "the only place," he wrote in 1869, where he "could be of service to the Catholic cause; but is it not abundantly for my private comfort, for my tranquility, and for my length of life?"

Since the jury had agreed with the Crown that Newman had libeled Achilli, Newman's exit from the Achilli trial with only a fine and a demeaning lecture from Justice Coleridge on his bad judgment in becoming a Catholic were probably purchased at a price that was actually quite low. After this troubling case, the growth of English Catholicism was steady but slow, but the numbers of Irish Catholic immigrants coming to the cities because of the Industrial Revolution were substantial. Often Protestant evangelicals took out their anger on those in the Anglican church who were aping Catholic ways by introducing fancy papist rituals into Sunday worship. Newman was often the target of these attacks. In a famous pamphlet, *What, Then, Does Dr. Newman Mean?* (1864) Charles Kingsley accused Newman of "cunning sleight of hand logic" in his defense of Catholicism. Kingsley, a virile if not muscular Protestant, had "a score of more than twenty years to settle" with Newman, whose influence had almost turned the aristocratic Frances Grenfell into an Anglican nun before Kingsley rescued her to become his wife. Kingsley's novel *Yeast: A Problem* (1848) had been an earlier polemical cudgel against the Newmanite (and Tractarian) ideal of celibacy, to be countered by Kingsley's fulsome celebration of married love and conjugal embraces. His rhetoric—and later his published letters to his wife—often embarrassed his friends and followers.

The Oratorians, as well as the Oratory itself, proved to represent additional crises in Newman's career because his Birmingham Oratory was having some "family" problems of its own. A member of the Oratory had to be expelled because he advocated a concept of "spiritual love" between Catholic celibates (especially himself) and laywomen who helped at the Oratory. Newman was even afraid that his friend Maria Rosina may have talked to this troubled Oratorian "in the most idiotic way of her spiritual love" for *him* so that the expelled Oratorian may have thought that Newman's "impatience" with Giberne came from his "fear that I [Newman] felt too much spiritual love for her."[77]

The concept of the Oratory as a *building*, as opposed to a religious movement, inspired by the Italian Renaissance and even Baroque architecture, brought him into sharp conflict with A.W. Pugin, despite Newman's intellectual adherence in the 1840s to some forms of the Gothic architecture Pugin championed as the protégée of the Earl of Shrewsbury. The latter's estate at Cotton Hall in North Staffordshire was the first home of Frederick Faber's early community of proto–Oratorians in a Pugin-designed church that became known as St. Wilfrid's. Faber had a memorable confrontation outside St. Wilfrid's with Pugin and another Gothicizer who was Pugin's patron, Ambrose Phillipps de Lisle, when they asked Faber what had happened to the sixteenth-century-style rood screens they expected to see. Faber said Newman didn't want them; the Oratorians believed they came between the celebration of the mass and the participation of the poor and working classes who were their chosen people.[78] When Pugin asked what Faber would do with the screens, Faber replied: "Burn 'em all." Phillipps shouted that God "will curse and destroy" the Oratorians if they "go on thus." Pugin, uncharacteristically, urged Phillipps to hold his tongue.

These quarrels went deep. Ambrose Phillipps at one point wrote to Newman that he didn't "expect" Newman or his "disciples to preach a crusade against us." If he did, Newman would be responsible for "dividing the Catholic Body, already too much divided, by throwing [his] talents ... zeal, and ... piety in the scale against the noble efforts of that admirable man Pugin."[79]

There is paradox in positing Newman and Pugin as rivals in architectural taste. Newman was actually a co-founder of the Oxford Society for promoting the study of Gothic architecture in 1839 with, among others, his close friend Tom Mozley (soon to be his brother-in-law) and John Ruskin. Newman had already sponsored a chapel at Littlemore before his conversion in the parish of St. Mary the Virgin at Littlemore. This chapel of Saint Mary the Virgin and Saint Nicholas was Gothic. Newman's mother laid the cornerstone in 1835. The curate, John Rouse Bloxam, was a wealthy architectural amateur, and his stained-glass windows were complemented by an altar cloth created with church needlework contributed by Newman's sisters. Pugin approved of this chapel, and the building served as a model for the Margaret Street Chapel in London, high praise indeed. Newman's Gothic allegiance and respect of Pugin were at their high point in his three years at Littlemore from 1834 through 1836. Newman had in fact been confirmed as a Catholic in St. Mary's Collage Chapel, built with the assistance of Pugin's patron the Earl of Shrewsbury. The church at Oscott, built in 1837, a Pugin gem, was his first major commission for which he contributed the interior decors—a nave roof of blue strewn with gold stars and other sacred emblems—and a polygonal apse to the chapel.[80] He used a very similar design for the chapel roof at Alton Towers.

While Pugin's Gothic worldview was shaped by the thirteenth century in Catholic Britain, the original Oratorians were founded by Philip Neri in Rome in the sixteenth century as a kind of secular or public order of priests. This tension between Gothic and classical mirrored the division between the Old and New Catholics. The former were wealthier, as a rule; in some cases descendants of the most powerful Catholic families of the pre–Reformation period, most notably the earls of Shrewsbury in the Midlands and the dukes of Norfolk in the south. Not all of the Old Catholics supported the Gothic tendencies of Pugin's quixotic quest for a feudal relationship to a church that dominated both aristocratic manse and countryside. The New Catholics were either middle- and upper-middle-class converts, like Newman and his followers from the Oxford Movement, or working-class and poor immigrants, mainly from Ireland.[81] For these latter Catholics, heavily Rome-leaning by inclination or tradition, the norm was a Roman basilica, in the Renaissance style, naturally. Newman, of course, was in the end resolute: "How is not a dome beautiful? Poetical and solemn? Is not a row of columns beautiful? By my taste they are as beautiful, nay more so, than anything Gothic."[82]

In the end Pugin transformed Alton Towers, the Old Catholic family seat of the Earl of Shrewsbury, a complex of stately house, church, and convent, into a medieval showpiece[83] (see chapter 10), while the rising order of Oratorians and Newman preferred the Italianate approach popularized by the Duke of Norfolk's favorite architect, Herbert Gribble, for the Brompton Oratory, home for the order which was spiritually Roman in papal obedience and architecturally Roman in classical design. Roderick O'Donnell, scholar of Victorian church architecture, summarizes this tension: "The Oratorians were mostly converts who had followed either Newman or Faber into the Church. Paradoxically, they already had their fill of Pugin's teachings through his Anglican admirers in the senior and junior Common Rooms of Oxford and Cambridge. As converts they wished to forget Gothic Oxford, and the obvious reaction was to turn to Classical Rome." Pugin, pugnacious as ever, was not impressed: "I give the whole Order up forever."[84] The war with the Oratorians really only ended because Pugin died prematurely, more or less in dementia, in 1852 at age 40.

In his letters in 1848 Newman was rarely diplomatic. He believed that Pugin had both the "merit" and "the great fault of a man of genius." But, Newman, concluded, he was "intolerant" and a "bigot." Pugin never accepted that the whole of the Church should not be Gothic: "The

Canons of Gothic architecture are to him points of faith, and everyone is a heretic who would venture to question them." Newman, on the other hand, was emphatic in *his* preferences: "We do not want a cloister or a chapter room but an Oratory." Pugin would "as soon build a mechanic's institute as an Oratory." The latter cannot be Gothicized. As for what we now see as the third or Butterfieldian High Church approach, Newman found that the "present practice" at St. Margaret's were "extravagances," the most common fear of Butterfield's inventiveness[85] (see chapter 6).

The major exceptions to the Old Catholic support of Pugin's approach were the 14th and 15th dukes of Norfolk, consistently pro–Jesuit, who contributed significant sums towards the building of the Oratory; the 15th duke energetically put forward Gribble as the choice for the commission. Gribble was already his favorite architect for many reasons, especially for researching the architectural proof of the duke's ownership of the Fitzalan Chapel in the Arundel chapel challenge in 1879 (see chapter 13).[86] Despite enthusiasm for other candidates in the non-binding competition for the Oratory, Gribble was eventually selected for the job.

The Oratory was the largest Catholic church in England until Westminster Cathedral was completed in 1903. That cathedral itself was also a fairly radical departure from the norm, with its neo–Byzantine—one might even say Butterfieldesque—alternating orange brick and white stone courses.

But Gribble's Oratory has the heft of a Roman building. Like Italian basilicas, its essential form is a massive cube with a dome. It does not have the strictly cruciform structure of typical Anglican or Catholic churches, divided or no, nor the soaring Gothic towers of Pugin's fevered dreams. It does have a pseudo-transept with a Lady Chapel to the east and the Altar of St. Philip Neri to the west, as well as the Chapel of St. Wilfrid (the seventh-century founder of a Northumbrian monastery and later canonized) that is situated parallel to—and to the south of—the sanctuary with its high altar.

Within Roman Catholicism, there was a third way (discounting Butterfield as a "third way" because he was Anglo-Catholic). An influential Catholic such as Lord Arundel and Surrey wrote to Phillipps that he should accept that "the Oratorians themselves are compelled by the rule of their order to an exact copy of the Mother House in Rome, even to the most minute details." Their discipline does not "appear essential anywhere that the return of Christianity [i.e., Catholicism] should be accompanied by a return to the architectural tastes of our ancestors." He found Phillipps's attacks on the Oratory wearying. It is "strange," he wrote, "in a Catholic to forget that, under the much-abused churches of Roman and Greek form, so many Saints have received their inspirations." God does not "bestow His graces and favors" because of the architecture of church buildings. In fact, Phillipps positively revels "while traveling" to "find in one place a Gothick, in another a Grecian, and in a third a Byzantine Church." There are many of us "heartily tired of unnecessary disputes." To "feel a repugnance to any one form in which it appeared due attention in the ornament of the temple dedicated to God would appear to me actually wrong."[87]

The architectural form of the Oratory became synonymous with the Oratorians and of course with Newman itself, although Newman's Oratory was in Birmingham and the two houses, while under the same rule, were occasionally at odds. There was a major disagreement between the houses in 1855 over the hearing of nuns' confessions, an issue eventually resolved. Nonetheless Newman chose not to attend a celebration at Birmingham because of scruples that "his presence might create a false impression of interdependence between the two houses," according to the historians of the London Oratory, who add that his decision may have been "due to [Newman's] excessive delicacy."[88]

The identification of Newman with the rebirth of English Catholicism is secure, certainly in terms of his leadership and the rise of a Catholic architecture on a different course than Pugin's. Pugin was a convert as well, but his premature death deprived the Gothic movement of its most formidable force. If Pugin had done nothing else but publish *Contrasts: Or, a Parallel Between the Noble Edifices of the Fourteenth and Fifteenth Centuries and Similar Buildings of the Present Day Shewing the Present Decay of Taste Accompanied by Appropriate Text* in 1837, his name too would be secure. The book was a brilliant illustrated argument for the (partly) mythic past of an organic Catholic society so superior to a contemporary world of poorhouses and factories that little text was needed. In his struggle to establish himself as the leading Gothic trailblazer of a restored Catholic England, Pugin was tempted to shorten Roman Catholic to just Catholic and even began using the expression "natural architecture" for his work, denoting his experiments with using rough local stones rather than professionally cut blocks.

Perhaps the judgment of Rosemary Hill, Pugin's latest and perhaps most architecturally astute biographer, would not satisfy this man who was frantically in pursuit of a united *Catholic* kingdom: "The architectural texture of [British] towns and countryside is still largely nineteenth-century and none of it would look quite as it does had A.W.M. Pugin never lived."[89] Pugin's end is too terrible to re-count: psychosis, Bedlam, leeches, death. But his churches really represent the living Pugin.

Details of the Litigation: Regina v. J.H. Newman, 1851–52

The Queen's Bench

Presiding: Lord Chief Justice Campbell, with a special jury.

Charges: Nineteen charges of libel.

For the Prosecution:	For the Defendant, J.H. Newman
Frederic Thesiger, Attorney General	Sir Alexander Cockburn
Sir Fitzroy Kelly	Mr. Serjeant Wilkins
Mr. T.F. Ellis	Mr. Joseph Badeley
	Mr. Bramwell
	Mr. Joseph Addison

Verdict: Dr. Newman guilty on eighteen charges of libel; not guilty on the nineteenth ("that Dr. Achilli was suspended from the celebration of mass, prohibited from any cure of souls, and from preaching, and from hearing any confession, and from exercising his sacerdotal office in any way, according to the decree of the Inquisition"), but since the jury did not "find for the reasons for the decree," Judge Campbell decided that their "special finding" on the nineteenth charge would be reported "to the Court when necessary," in effect establishing a guilty verdict on the 19th charge as well.

Sentence: Fine of 100 pounds, imposed by Sir John Taylor Coleridge in court, January, 1853, with Justice Campbell present.

9

The Royal By-Blow, the Wandering Statue, and the Religiously Divided Church

FitzClarence v. Blount, 1851–1852

> On Queen Caroline
> Most gracious Queen, we thee implore
> To go away and sin no more,
> But if that effort be too great,
> To go away at any rate.
> —Anonymous (c. 1820)

In 1625 when Protestant Charles I married the Catholic princess Henrietta Maria (daughter of Henry IV, king of France, and Marie de Medici), their first wedding was executed by proxy, with George Villiers, the Duke of Buckingham, standing in for Charles for the first wedding on French, i.e., Catholic, soil. For the second wedding in St. Augustine's Church, Canterbury, Charles and his bride participated in an "Anglican" ceremony. Religiously, those were fluid times.

Queen Henrietta remained a staunch Catholic but was assuredly a British royalist, actively raising funds and troops to defend her husband during the Civil War. Her tenacity became legendary and was the source of what has become a virtual folk saying in British culture when she reportedly told her ladies-in-waiting aboard a ship during a North Sea storm after a fund-raising mission to the Netherlands: "Comfort yourselves, my dears, Queens of England are never drowned."

This accommodating royal couple had the perhaps unexpected consequence of encouraging Catholic or Recusant activity in the Thames Valley, straddling both Oxfordshire and Berkshire. At least four of the churches in the valley experimented with a novel approach to religious divisions by permitting a Catholic aisle or section or chapel in an otherwise Anglican church. At least three other well-known parish (primarily Anglican) churches in Arundel, Mapledurham, and Tichborne already had Catholic services, usually only burial services, in a section of the church privately owned by the lord of the manse (see chs. 12 and 13).

The architectural separation of the two contending religious persuasions within one physical building was also successful at first in the villages of Mapledurham, Noke, Stonor, and Brimpton. It may have been because of the stressful issue of partisan burials in parish churchyards, but the compromises, with the exception of Mapledurham, did not hold. Mapledurham is the only divided church in the Thames Valley still in existence, although the three other parish churches maintained their medieval cohabitation of Catholic and Anglican sections of the church for some time.

Brimpton, for example, had a separate aisle with a chapel on the parish church, built by William Wollascott III, a Roman Catholic, who died in 1637. It was similar to the Catholic-owned private aisles, as at Mapledurham, Noke and Pishill (the latter serving the Catholics of Stonor village). William Wollascott III was buried in a vault attached to his chapel. He was succeeded by his son, William Wollascott IV, whose wife Susan Fryer was also a Catholic. But the Wollascotts's aisle no longer exists as a separate entity.[1]

A divided church, on the other hand, persisted in Mapledurham. The architectural configuration of St. Margaret's in Mapledurham would bear little obvious parallel to the Duke of Norfolk's Collegiate Church at Arundel, as the south aisle or the Bardolf or Blount Aisle, as it has been known in various eras depending on the manse's owner's family name, is clearly a chapel that was "added on" and is visibly thus when one stands on the south side of the church.

The church proper may date as early as the thirteenth century, but the south aisle was described in a will as "new built," intended for the tomb of Sir Robert Bardolf, who died and was interred in the aisle in 1395. The lord's estate was sold a century later to Richard Blount, whose descendants retain the aisle as the property of the Roman Catholic lord of the manor, despite the vicissitudes of the Reformation in the sixteenth century and the Civil War in the seventeenth century.[2]

The estate was sequestered by Parliament during the Commonwealth years because the Blounts were Royalists and their property was sacked by the Roundheads in 1649. By the end of the seventeenth century another Blount cousin, Lyster Blunt, regained the property.[3]

St. Margaret's Church, Mapledurham, with Roman Catholic Bardolf Aisle. Restored by William Butterfield; led by noteworthy vicars Augustus Fitz-Clarence and Edward Coleridge (photograph by the author).

The most famous members of the family were the Blount sisters, Theresa and Martha, with whom the (Catholic) poet Alexander Pope was inordinately smitten.[4] Pope really was a horny little devil, visiting Mapledurham often and writing poems about these beautiful, accomplished young women, one (Martha) pleasant-tempered, the other (Theresa) rebellious, sharp, and flirtatious, despite—or perhaps inevitably because—having been educated by nuns in an English convent in Paris. Pope seemed to have a preference for Theresa, for she is immortalized in one of his greatest and best-known poems, the mock-heroic satire *The Rape of the Lock* (1712), in which a maiden's curl of hair is the symbolic quest of a gentleman.[5]

The royal presence came more directly to Mapledurham, however, in the nineteenth century in a number of unexpected ways. The Duke of Clarence, sixty-four years old, the third son of King George III and Queen Charlotte, ascended the throne in 1830 as King William IV. He succeeded his elder brother George IV, much to the astonishment of the royal entourage. The Georges—as well as Queen Caroline—were part of one of the most unpopular royal lines in a cycle of monarchs. Neoclassical poet Walter Savage Landor was appropriately unmerciful to them in his oft-reprinted, circulated, and recited poem "The Georges":

9. The Royal By-Blow...

> George the First was always reckoned
> Vile, but viler George the Second;
> And what mortal ever heard
> Any good of George the Third?
> When from Earth the Fourth descended
> God be praised! The Georges ended!

King William IV did not fare much better with other critics: "Neither George I, nor George II, nor William IV were patterns of family merit; George IV was a model of family demerit," according to Walter Bagehot in *The English Constitution* (1867).

King William IV's quixotic hunt for a fecund queen resulted in his marriage to Adelaide, a German princess. The new royal couple had two children who did not survive infancy, but the King already had ten (others)! One of these children, FitzClarence, was destined to be the vicar of Mapledurham church.

FitzClarence was perhaps the best known of the king's cohort of offspring, the consequences of an earlier twenty-year affair, if that's the right word, of the Duke of Clarence (before he became King William IV) with the Irish actress Dorothea Bland (known by her stage name, "Mrs. Jordan"), who, for all those years, was the most popular actress in the kingdom, reigning at Drury Lane's Theatre Royal. Her roles were the standards of her age—Shakespeare's Juliet, for example. She performed in the theater owned and managed by Richard Brinsley Sheridan, who also wrote two of the most highly regarded plays of the previous era, *The Rivals* (1775) and *The School for Scandal* (1777).

Both the Duke of Clarence and Mrs. Jordan, as the actress styled herself (there never was a Mr. Jordan), had been to their own school for scandal, but it did very little harm to her reputation and drawing power in the world of Covent Garden. Since William had not been expected to be king, he was somewhat free to throw himself around, and on the receiving end was usually Dora Jordan. They lived together in London for all those twenty years, most of the time on her earnings as an actress in great demand. The broadsheets that hit the streets were, however, unmerciful:

> As Jordan's high and mighty squire
> Her playhouse profits deigns to skim,
> Some folk audaciously enquire
> If he keeps her or she keeps him.[6]

Not that he was forever ungrateful, even with a very mixed bag of offspring.

Soon after he ascended the throne and became King William IV, he commissioned Francis Chantrey, the leading sculptor of the royal family, to memorialize his Convent Garden "queen." Surely this was a cheeky if not downright odd decision, given that he had a legitimate queen who had had terrible problems trying to give him an heir.

Although Mrs. Jordan had been dead for fifteen years, William was in tears as he explained the commission to Chantrey. These may have been crocodile tears, however, as his behavior to her after their separation was another scandal: he did not help her when she was forced into bankruptcy by an evil son-in-law who stole her money, driving her into exile to Paris, where she died alone.[7] Her fans were outraged, as the street ballad recounted:

> What, leave a woman to her tears?
> Your faithful friend for twenty years,
> One who gave up her youthful charms,
> The fond companion of your arms?[8]

But he wanted a life-size sculpture of her, based on her numerous portraits, with two of their children. Her biographer, Claire Tomalin, found the figure not as impressive as most of us now do, quite "bare and rudimentary."[9] The statue may not literally resemble Mrs. Jordan, except for her curls and bosom, the latter an impossible compromise between Victorian breast-feeding sentimentality—her hand is pulling back her shift so the baby can suck—and neo-classical nudity. It is nonetheless a strangely powerful "family" group.

Chantrey proudly noted in his studio ledger, "Mrs. Jordan's Monument" would be "erected in Westminster

Sacred to the Memory of an Affectionate Mother, Dora Bland (1834), statue of Mrs. Jordan, celebrated Convent Garden actress and Augustus FitzClarence's mistress, by Sir Francis Chantry (by permission of Royal Collection Trust/© Her Majesty Queen Elizabeth II).

Abbey."[10] Not likely! The dean of Westminster, an insider among insiders, having proffered the crown to both William and his father at their respective coronations, ruled that a sculpture of Mrs. Jordan—even if some people thought its facial features indistinct—was not an acceptable companion to portraits and busts of other former queens of England. All of the most influential literati of the realm who admired Mrs. Jordan to excess—the poets Coleridge and Byron, as well as many others—tried in vain to change the dean's decision.

When the dean of St. Paul's came to the same conclusion about *his* building receiving the statue, it then languished in Chantrey's studio, becoming an endless item of speculation for Victoria, the new queen, who was, after all, technically the royal "cousin" to all of Mrs. Jordan's children: her father, Edward, and William IV were two of the four sons of George III. She became queen because Edward and all his brothers were deceased.[11]

When Queen Victoria heard that an end-run was being proposed—that the statue, labeled "Sacred to the Memory of an Affectionate Mother, Dora Bland," would be placed in still another venue, Henry VII's Chapel, that was Crown property but not under the authority of the dean—Victoria flinched: "Why shouldn't it be Dora *Jordan*?" The queen was reminded—or informed for the first time—that there was no record of a *Mr.* Jordan.[12]

But even Queen Victoria couldn't resist this scandal. Dear diary, she wrote, Mrs. Jordan "was beautifully formed, as this statue is," according to Lord Melbourne, her very close (too close?) insider source, plus "she had a beautiful enunciation."[13] But Victoria could not bring herself to welcome her theatrical "aunt" into the royal precincts. It remained in Chantrey's studio until one of King William's by-blows was surprisingly appointed to the vicarage of Mapledurham, the beautiful little church near Reading with the religiously divided floor plan. The new vicar's name was FitzClarence, using the archaic but accurate Scottish "Fitz," denoting "son of Clarence." In fact, he was the first child of the royal liaison with Dora Jordan.[14]

Mapledurham parishioners were easier marks than Westminster's or St. Paul's stiff-necks or even Victoria: the statue was placed in their church by FitzClarence, the new vicar, without a plaque or notice of any kind. Biographer Claire Tomalin speculates that the parishioners thought it was a statue of Mary with St. John and the infant Jesus![15] Not likely, as a semi-clad Virgin Mary breast-feeding became increasingly rare after the Council of Trent's more restrictive codes in the mid–sixteenth century, but the statue's mostly Anglican admirers no doubt assumed that their Catholic brethren were always a little bit more daring than they were.

The statue, completed in 1834, remained at the church long after FitzClarence passed away, in fact for at least sixty years before it was "re-discovered" by Mrs. Jordan's great-grandson, Aubrey, when he became the fourth Earl of Munster.[16] He moved it to his London house until *his* son in turn moved it to his Surrey country house. When the fifth Earl of Munster died, he bequeathed the statue to Queen Elizabeth, who installed it in Buckingham Palace in 1980,[17] where it still stands, finally in royal company, in the Queen's Gallery.

FitzClarence on the surface was an attentive and even generous vicar from his appointment in 1829 until his death in 1854, but a few questionable details about his life and career have come to light, suggesting that his flights of religious fervor may have been will-of-the-wisps. Claire Tomalin reports that he used to absent himself from Mapledurham to stand in the wings of the Covent Garden and Drury Lane theaters, "sometimes waving his gloves about in sympathetic dumb show when, for instance, Fanny Kemble played [Shakespeare's] Juliet; later he danced with her at a ball."[18] Juliet of course was one of his mum's grandest roles, but FitzClarence would have seen Kemble in many roles, as she herself reported that he "attended every one of her performances" in the winter of 1829.[19]

My readers must stifle such remarks as "like father, like fitz," but surely very few rural Church of England clergymen visited the playhouses as joyously as he (and his father before him) did.

Given FitzClarence's convivial public presence, it is hard to imagine him having any desire to contest the Blounts, the lords of the manor, about their Catholic aisle of the church. But contest them he did, before Dr. Phillimore, the chancellor of the Diocese of Oxford, with the goal of the parish church's "annexing" the Bardolf Aisle, the Blounts's private property.

FitzClarence had been enthusiastic about decorating *his* new church, not only with his mum's statue but with other, more traditional, church furnishings donated by his father, William IV, including a clock for the tower with a royal crown and the king's initials and an organ for the gallery (since removed). FitzClarence himself provided a "splendid Service of Plate" to be used at Holy Communion.[20]

And one cannot help wonder if perhaps he initiated this ill-fated suit not simply to dispossess the Catholic lord of *his* aisle, but perhaps to make more room for the statue? It *is* a small church, after all.

The Blount family was not amused, for after all they possessed copies of the wills of both Sir Robert Bardolf, who was lord of Mapledurham from 1375 to 1395, and his widow. The latter's will describes the south aisle as a "new chapel ... lately built," an addition to the church as

Roman Catholic Bardorf Aisle, 15th century, added on the south side of the 13th century St. Margaret's Church, Mapledurham (photograph by the author).

it stands, replacing the original south wall with the three arches that still remain.[21]

Long after his suit failed and future vicars learned to live with the medieval arrangement, Roman Catholic funerals and burial services were held, at least as late as 1879, when, as a result of publicity from the *Arbuthnot v. Norfolk* case (see chapter 13), a correspondent to the *London Times* noted, "When an interment occurs" in the portion of the church that "belongs to the Blount family," the "Burial Service of the Romish Church is performed therein."[22]

Another correspondent was shocked, positively shocked, at this news because the decision of Judge Phillimore delivered to Mr. Bount more than twenty-five years earlier was crystal clear: "Remember, in declaring you the owner of the aisle, I also expressly declare that no service, rite, or ceremony of or belonging to the Church of Rome can at any time be used in it." This correspondent declared, "Romanists in Mapledurham are buried by the vicar of the parish" with "no other service either before or after the public service of the Church of England." Phillimore also granted FitzClarence the right to collect fees for any burials there.[23] FitzClarence himself is buried in the church graveyard.[24]

Had Phillimore gone too far? Phillimore's brother judges in the courts across the land presumably thought so, since they made short work of his pronouncement, especially at Arundel, where the court acknowledged that both Anglican and Roman ceremonies followed one another from Anglican church to Catholic chapel whenever a Duke of Norfolk was buried. After all, on private property one worships as one wishes.

While FitzClarence chose the court as a vehicle for his ambitious seizure of the Catholic aisle of his church, his successor as Anglican vicar, Edward Coleridge, was more circumspect, in fact conducting an Anglican burial service for one of the Catholic Blounts in 1874. And rather than the courts, he used his Coleridge family connections, preferring pounds instead of writs to gain his ends during his tenure as vicar from 1862 to 1883.

Coleridge hired William Butterfield, the favored architect of the Coleridge clan, to restore the church. Butterfield's architectural strategy was coy, and only a cynic could find it suspect. Clearly the roof would benefit from a pyramidal uplift, and the west tower would also look better if were higher. In a telling maneuver, however, he created a "false north aisle divided from the nave by two timber piers," according to architectural critic Nikolaus Pevsner.[25] Butterfield therefore created the appearance of a trendy unified Anglican church, with a nave bounded on each side by traditional aisles.

When the question of the Mapledurham church arose in the *London Times* during the Norfolk trial, Butterfield was dismissive: he deliberately ignored his own reconstruction and suggested that the cases were not related since "at Arundel the great chancel of a church is in question, while at Mapledurham the part of the church referred to … is only an aisle and minor chancel."[26]

The Blounts, however, certainly understood the precedent of the Norfolk decision and the power of a dividing wall to reinforce ownership, because afterwards they replaced the wooden fence formerly separating the nave from their aisle with a stone wall, thereby offsetting the "parallel" wooden piers erected by Butterfield, canceling out (visually) the impression of a single traditional church plan. They also fenced in the openings between nave and north aisle so that simple entry was forbidden to the general body of the church.

Although Edward Coleridge funded all of Butterfield's renovations at Mapledurham Church, in the end Butterfield would not prevail over the Catholic aisle, as he would not prevail years later when he supported the vicar of at Norfolk against the Duke of Norfolk and *his* Roman Catholic "wing" of the Anglican church. Like FitzClarence, Coleridge was buried in the Mapledurham Church graveyard, when he died in 1883.

The two campaigners against a divided church rest in peace together a short distance from their nemesis, the Blount family.

In the British courts, private property almost always trumps architectural verity, if not religious motive. The Blount Aisle is still in place, still Roman Catholic, still in the possession of the Blount family. Fitz-Clarence is all but forgotten, except perhaps for his mother's statue on exhibit in the Royal Collection. His father's memory lives on in the form of still another notorious statue, this one really a kind of ghost statue: a statue of King William on horseback was supposed to grace the now-famous fourth (northwest) plinth in Trafalgar Square, constructed in 1841, but owing to a shortage of funds the statue never appeared. Instead the Fourth Plinth (as it is now known), was empty for 158 years. King William's accomplishments, which included supporting the great Reform Act of 1832 and the idea of building a canal at Suez, were not enough to earn him the coveted spot.

Really Good, **sculpture by David Shrigley on top of Fourth Plinth, Trafalger Square, London, 2017 (photograph by the author).**

Rumor has it that the Fourth Plinth will be used for a statue of Queen Elizabeth II, the longest reigning monarch in British history, if she ever passes away. Whether she wants to occupy the top of the plinth where for twenty years cheeky biennial contributions by sculptors with outsized and often postmodern ambitions are awarded commissions is unknown; since 2001, for example, we have had Katharina Fritsch's giant (fourteen and a half feet high) blue rooster, *Hahn/Cock*, now crowing on the roof of the National Gallery of Art in Washington, D.C.; Rachel Whiteread's self-reflexive (meta) *Monument*, an upside-down resin cast of the plinth itself; and Michael Rakowitz's *The Invisible Enemy Should Not Exist*, a replica of the Taliban-destroyed Lamassu, the winged bull-god of Nineveh, made of 10,500 empty tin cans of Iraqi date syrup. More appropriate to King William, perhaps, was David Shrigley's *Really Good*, a giant hand with a thumb's-up gesture, with an especially elongated thumb, that appeared in 2017; we may assume that it means: King William, good luck, sorry about your space on the plinth, but rest in peace.

Details of the Litigation: FitzClarence v. Blount, 1851–52

Diocese of Oxford Court

Presiding: Dr. Phillimore, Chancellor

Plaintiff: Lord Augustus FitzClarence   *Defendant*: William Blount

Verdict: The Roman Catholic Blount Aisle remains the private property of the Blount family. Burials in the aisle may only be facilitated by the Anglican Church. The latter part of the verdict has been ignored ever since it was made.

10

The Medieval Architectural Folly, the Tenth Cousin, and the Earl Who Was a Jesuit

Talbot v. Earl of Shrewsbury, 1857–1867

Most of the visitors today to the Alton Towers Resort owned by Merlin Entertainments in Staffordshire might be surprised to know that the medieval buildings they see tucked amidst the monorail and the rollercoaster were in fact reconstructed in the nineteenth century to strike awe and wonder in their beholders not for entertainment but for religious value. Alton Towers, one of the monumental achievements built—perhaps more precisely, rebuilt—for the 16th Earl of Shrewsbury by the great neo–Gothic architect A.W.N. Pugin, may have at first appeared to many Victorians as a kind of *folly*, an architectural term for a structure built more on an owner's whim for spectacle rather than practical use—in a sense, the expression of an owner or builder that often reflects vanity rather than common sense. Followers of Pugin's idiosyncratic remarks and dismissive analyses about contemporary architecture would expect him to engage in a folly even if one of the kindest and richest men in England was willing to bankroll it in the name of his faith. Pugin as a rule did not build follies, but he defended his work as if his critics always suspected him of pursuing the unlikely for effect.

But *folly* is perhaps better reserved for the superficially similar Fonthill Abbey in Wiltshire, the outrageous country house and tower built at the turn of the eighteenth century for William Thomas Beckham by the architect James Wyatt, but whose tower collapsed just twenty-five years after it was built, primarily because in the rush to satisfy the owner's whims the construction crews who were working by bonfire through the night neglected to build a solid foundation under the tower.[1]

Rushton Triangular Lodge in Northamptonshire, the two-story building in the form of an equilateral wedge of cheese, has also been called a folly, although its history is more complicated. It posed as a rabbit warrener's lodge at the turn of the sixteenth century to protect its Roman Catholic owner and designer, Sir Thomas Tresham, from further abuse and incarceration by his Protestant overlords. Unlike Fonthill Abbey, however, this wedge of cheese is still quite solid, as the illustration indicates. Another one of Tresham's idiosyncratic creations, a residence hall called New Bield at Lyveden, also in Northamptonshire, was a hunting lodge with gardens that included a labyrinth. The project was never finished, and only the shell in the shape of a cross remains. (See chapter 17 for further discussion of Tresham's buildings.)

Both the owner of Alton Towers, John Talbot, the sixteenth Earl of Shrewsbury, and Pugin, its fanatical rebuilder and defender, died in 1852, ending a remarkable British experiment in Roman Catholic architecture. Its finale, drawn out through a series of four judicial hearings and trials, created a virtual shell of an estate. And though its inspiration was medieval, Alton Towers' Roman Catholic foundation was ultimately not as solid as the religiously divided medieval churches of Mapledurham (chapter 3), Tichborne (chapter 6), and Arundel (chapter 7), all of which are still standing virtually unchanged after centuries, despite significant legal challenges to the ownership of the Catholic aisle or chapel of the churches.

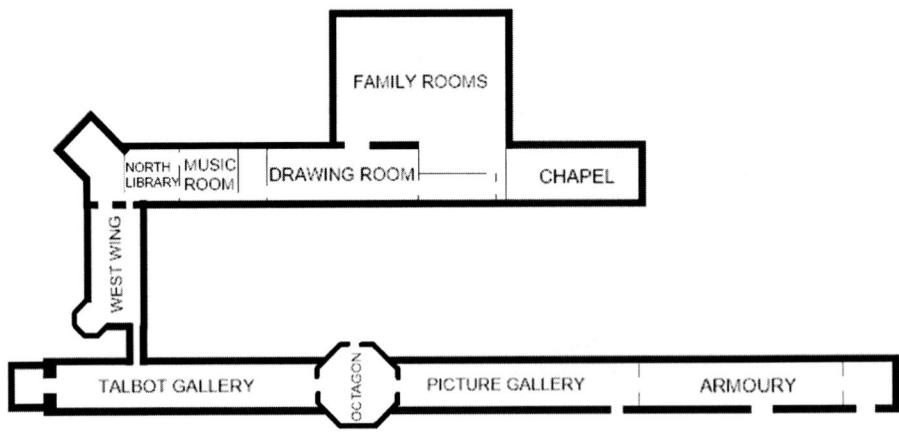

Alton Towers, c. 1860 (designed by Emily Taylor).

Alton Towers in northeast Staffordshire was the primary estate of the Talbot family, whose male heirs were the fabulously wealthy earls of Shrewsbury. Alton Towers as an experiment in a new form of religious architecture revived the semi-mythical thirteenth-century erasure of difference between the religious and the secular, popularized by Pugin's obsessive medievalism. Novelist Wilkie Collins found Pugin easy to satirize in *The Dead Secret* (1856): a rich Londoner buys Porthgenna Tower, an estate like Alton Towers, and decides "to beautify the old house from top to bottom with brand-new mediaeval decoration" by hiring "a gentleman who was said to be an architect, but who looked ... the very image of a Popish priest in disguise," in brief, Pugin personified and satirized.[2]

Rushton Triangular Lodge, an unusual three-sided structure, was designed and built by Thomas Tresham near Rushton in Northamptonshire. It functioned as a rabbit warren keeper's lodge and esoteric symbolic structure (photograph by the author).

Especially important for Pugin's fevered imagination were the quasi-medieval parades, fests, and other events he brought to the grounds of Alton Towers. When there was a wedding, such as the marriage of the earl's daughter to an Italian prince, or a visit of Queen Adelaide, the widow of William IV (the royal father of Mapledurham's notorious pastor, Augustus FitzClarence—see chapter 9), with a procession of 300 men, or the inevitable sad day when the 16th earl died and he lay in state in the chapel at Alton Towers and was taken in a very large funeral procession from the chapel to his burial in the family vault in St. John's Church ... all of these events unfolded with a pageantry that had been typical for royalty and aristocrats alike for centuries and that Pugin now celebrated as essential for an organic Catholic community.[3]

The 16th earl had been immensely popular among Catholics. Educated at Stonyhurst, he had the reputation for living a simple lifestyle despite his incredible wealth. His nickname, the "Good Earl," recognized his acts of charity and support for Catholics and Catholic institutions across the land. Despite his aristocratic bloodline, he had a touch of the spirit of peasant Catholicism about him, probably because he visited Italy so often. For example, he even had the highest regard for the *stigmatics*, the women who bore the wounds of Christ from the cross, usually regarded by British Protestants as one of the most vulgar obsessions of foreign Catholic, fanatics by definition.

Both the earl and his travelling companion, T.W. Allies, an early Roman Catholic recruit from the Oxford Movement, published detailed reports in London on two stigmatics, Maria Domenica Lazzari, known as L'Addolorata ("the woman of pain"), and Maria Morl (or von Moehrl), known as L'Estatica ("the woman of ecstasy"). The former had the "five wounds" of Christ from the Crucifixion, while the latter in addition to those wounds exhibited "ecstatic" and extended trances and contorted postures. London's Wellcome Library owns a remarkable contemporary watercolor of Maria, showing the mask-like facial covering of blood Allies described as the result of the blood flowing from the punctures on her forehead from a "crown of thorns."[4]

Most of this fervent defense of extreme examples of Roman Catholic behavior in Italy would probably make even a number of British converts uncomfortable. As for Pugin, he chose instead ideological purity in his Catholicism and flashy costumes and architectural flourishes rather than bloody manifestations. In his own religious crusade, more British to the core, Pugin was able to institute the medieval concept of a *hospital* at Alton Towers, where poor or retired priests would have a dignified sanctuary rather than the horrors of the workhouse so graphically dramatized by Charles Dickens in *Oliver Twist* (1839).

This mixture of building and function appealed to Pugin, the leading Gothicizer of his era. Simon Jenkins, author of *England's Thousand Best Churches* (1999), called Pugin's St. Giles, Cheadle (1841–45), a "complete thirteenth-century re-creation ... the outstanding English church of the nineteenth century." It shines with Pugin's fanatical sense of detail: "Not an inch of Cheadle," Jenkins concludes, "is without paint, carving or gilding."[5] As the architect of choice for the Good Earl, he began ambitious plans to renovate the Alton Towers complex.

Pugin was never, therefore, a casual medievalist, because his guiding principle was resolutely anti-classical: "Revivals of ancient architecture, although erected in, are not buildings of, the nineteenth century." As a result he was the sworn opponent of every religious and architectural principle represented by the neo-classic and French-style buildings of the Oratorians, Newman's order. Newman's ideal was sixteenth century, Pugin's the thirteenth: "We do not want," Newman wrote, "a cloister or chapter room, but an Oratory." In fact, Newman reported that Pugin said that he "would as soon build a Mechanics' Institute as an Oratory."[6]

Pugin believed that the blend of the secular and religious at Alton Towers would triumphantly fulfill the central thesis of his classic study, *Contrasts: Or a Parallel between the Noble Edifices of the Middle Ages, and Corresponding Buildings of the Present Day; Shewing the Present Decay of Taste* (1836), in which medieval Catholic England was celebrated precisely because there were not a strict demarcation between the religious and the secular: monastery and manor had their appointed functions and they were complementary. But we must not forget that in particular instances, medievalism even won over parochialism: he rebuilt or redecorated at least five medieval Anglican churches, we presume, *because* they were medieval: even after working on Alton Towers, his West Tofts project in Norfolk, restoring a medieval church, was especially noteworthy.[7]

Curiously, Pugin was not the one who first transformed Alton Lodge, the Shrewsbury country estate originating in the eighteenth century, into Alton Abbey. No actual "abbey" ever stood on this site,[8] it should be stressed, although the ruins of a nearby Cistercian abbey often fell into the hands of literary Gothicizes and scribblers whose fanciful notions were satirized in Jane Austin's *Northanger Abbey* (1817), in which her heroine, Catherine Morland, imagines grotesque horrors of forced imprisonment or murder behind every locked door.

Before Pugin took charge, a few other features of the Gothic revival, especially an octagon room, were already in place on Shrewsbury's estate, an architectural gesture attempting to rival Ely Cathedral's octagonal tower or the Wells Cathedral's octagonal Chapter House.⁹ Other Gothic touches included the Gallery Range and an armory, the latter a symbol of the "Talbots' recreation of their medieval past," according to Michael J. Fisher, author of the best contemporary guide to the complex.¹⁰

John Talbot became the sixteenth earl in 1827. Pugin, practically foaming at the mouth in high combative mode, arrived in 1837. It is an understatement that both Protestants and even fellow Roman Catholics were handled with an edge if and when Pugin perceived them as enemies to his concept of the Gothic revival. "Impressed with the strength of Catholicism" in the Staffordshire area, Pugin was ecstatic about the ruins of the White Ladies Augustinian priory in Shropshire, for example, because "no Protestant has ever polluted the consecrated ground, and this in England. Delightful."¹¹ When Pugin's projects began to devour too much of the earl's patrimony, the latter suggested that instead of building a wing of the medieval *hospital* for retired priests, they should be lodged instead in the castle. Pugin was aghast: "I would sooner jump off the rocks that build a castellated residence for priests. ... I can bear things as well as anyone but would as soon cut my throat as to cut that hospital to pieces."¹²

Pugin had fifteen years to transform Alton Towers. He added the Talbot Gallery and reconstructed the Octagon, among other ambitious projects. So costly was the upkeep of the new complex that the earl estimated that he saved 2,000 pounds a year by not living there in the summer.¹³ Instead he spent his time in Rome with his daughters, who had married into families of the Roman nobility, and used the money he saved to bankroll other churches that Pugin would build in Staffordshire, of which St. Giles in Cheadle was the most spectacular.

The Alton Towers complex as Pugin imagined it—and for the most part completed—is described by Michael Fisher as "an apsidal-ended chapel, a high-gabled entrance hall, and an embattled Long Gallery, all set transversely and separated by irregular blocks of domestic apartments with diverse windows."¹⁴

The complex forms an inverted U with a northwest-southeast axis. One enters the most southern or "left" arm of the U, to a range of rooms, set up in a continuous line-of-sight Pugin insisted on, by first entering the armory, then a long picture gallery that ended at the octagon at the base of the tower. The picture gallery featured the works of art of English and European masters, while the Talbot Gallery, heading out of the octagon, was lined floor to ceiling with numerous portraits from the family dynasty.

Down the northern or "right" arm of the inverted U were the

10. The Medieval Architectural Folly... 105

Lyveden New Bield residential lodge, East Northamptonshire, designed in the shape of a cross by Thomas Tresham (Sharpshotaero/Alamy stock photo).

specialty rooms—the north library, music room, and drawing room. North and east of these rooms was an extended wing or complex of bedrooms, dining rooms, kitchen, and other family rooms. The eastern end of this arm was the chapel. Each of the major rooms had either a Shrewsbury or a Pugin signature. The armory, 120 feet long, evoked the Shrewsburys' medieval heritage through a collection of arms and armor, many of which were brought in from other Shrewsbury residences to enhance this collection. Were they actually used by a Shrewsbury knight? Doubtful. Michael J. Fisher notes that during and after the Napoleonic Wars, for instance, London brokers brought in batches of armor for sale. When the "movables" themselves of Alton Towers went up for sale in 1857, 300 lots of arms and armor were on offer.[15]

Not only did a great Gothic house had to have an octagon, it had to have a magnificent library. The north library was noteworthy for its collection of books on Catholic history and theology, but other scholarly works were on hand. Novels, except for the great Sir Walter Scott's evocations of the medieval past, were rare.

The enthusiasms of neither Pugin nor the Good Earl survived these remarkable men. Unfortunately Pugin had rarely been without distressing periods of instability, mania, psychotic breakdowns, and, in the end, as Rosemary Hill points out in her biographical study of him, insanity.

His manic fits grew so violent that for a time he was confined to Bedlam, although in the end he died at home with his family in 1852.[16]

Those who knew that even his fevered imagination had often broken loose in the past were not prepared for his apocalyptic rhetoric at the end. Witness his description of the state of the nation in this rhetorical rush at the close of one of his last essays, in this case, in the Catholic *Dublin Review* (on, among other topics, his work at Alton Towers), an amazing passage reminiscent of the Irvingites, one of the radical sects of his youth. Pugin imagined, "A dark speck soon appeared on the horizon, and a whirlwind destruction arose, and the foundations of this vast fabric were undermined, and the choirs ceased to echo with the sound of praise, and soon they were roofless ... and the altars of God were overthrown, and the image of Christ was defaced, and strange ministers stood in the temple of God and mocked the olden solemnity."[17] Even if skeptics had not known of his (likely) manic fits, they might have been amazed at this evocation—so suggestive of William Blake's illustrated poems or John Martin's apocalyptic landscape paintings—of Pugin's failure to rescue England from the grip of an enemy he could feel but not see.

In a different but related arena, the sixteenth earl, without a son as heir, could not have imagined what would happen to his estate, which passed in 1856 to a first cousin, Bertram Arthur Talbot, thereafter designated the seventeenth earl. Bertram's confidential advisors were Edward (Serjeant) Belassis and James Robert Hope-Scott, two of the most influential lay Catholics in the country. Both men had been friends of Newman and active supporters of the Oxford Tractarians. Both had been received into the Roman Catholic Church by the Jesuit priest Father James Brownbill, Hope-Scott having been accompanied by his friend, Henry (later Cardinal) Manning.[18] One of Hope-Scott's tutors had been the Rev. Edward Coleridge, John Taylor Coleridge's brother, who later became master of Eton College.

Hope-Scott had managed Newman's defense when he was sued for libel by the ex–Dominican priest Achilli in 1851, and eventually married (as his second wife) the eldest daughter of the fourteenth duke of Norfolk, Lady Victoria Fitzalan Howard. She was buried with two of her children in the Duke of Norfolk's Fitzalan Chapel (see chapter 13).[19] The Church of the Immaculate Conception in Kelso, built at Hope-Scott's expense to serve a small but growing population of Irish Catholics, had been attacked by a Protestant mob and burned to the ground in 1856.[20]

Bellassis had been an ardent "devisor"—in his own words—of "some Popery" at the Margaret Street Chapel in London,[21] the forerunner of All Saints, Margaret Street, the great Anglo-Catholic masterpiece

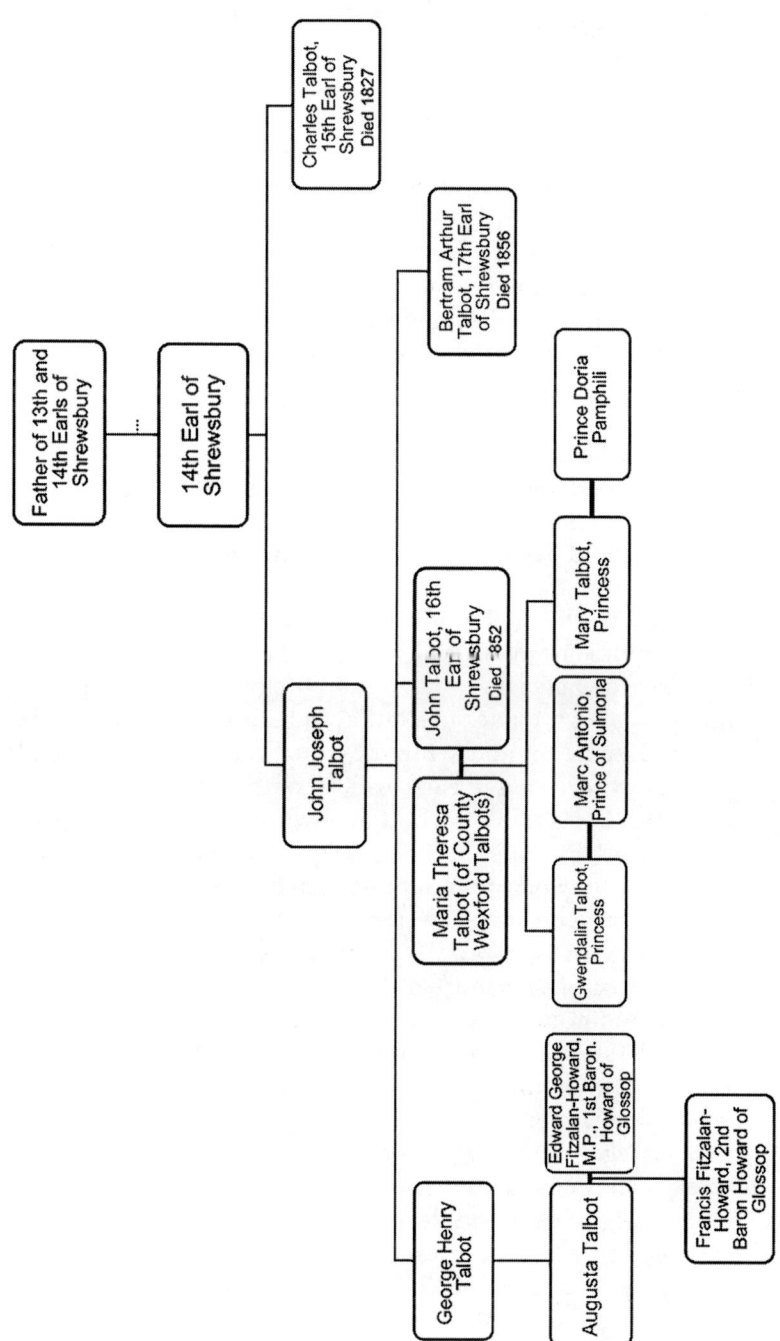

Family tree of the Talbots (template courtesy Family Echo, http://familyecho.com).

of William Butterfield, as well as a benefactor of the oldest "Catholic" property in London, the thirteenth century St. Etheldreda's Church of Ely Place, which was purchased at auction by the Italian Rosminian order in 1874 and became their British mother-church (see chapter 17).

Although nothing improper was ever alleged publicly, the two advisors also became the executors of the seventeenth earl's estate when he died only four years later, in 1856, leaving in his will an immense fortune—including Alton Towers itself—not to a blood relative but to Lord Edmund Howard, the younger son of the fourteenth Duke of Norfolk. The seventeenth earl had believed he was the last male descendant of the Shrewsbury line.[22] The two advisors had also become legatees of part of the seventeenth earl's estate, but their request to remove their status as legatees, a potentially compromising role, given their status as advisors to the expected eighteenth duke, was granted before his death.

Henry Chetwynd Talbot, a Protestant and no closer than a tenth cousin once removed from the late seventeenth earl, challenged the will on every financial and personal level—the ownership of buildings and land, as well as the aristocratic title. He was descended from the second Earl of Shrewsbury, who died in 1460, a 400-year separation from this Catholic earl, a more distant relative being hard to imagine.

Henry Talbot's challenge resulted in four closely related trials and appeals that persisted for a decade, but even before the legal proceedings occurred, an auction house hired by the executors proceeded to sell, permitted by the deceased earl's will, all of the "movables"—furniture, antique objects, six thousand bottles of wine and spirits, and paintings, including work by Raphael and Van Dyck. Even a consignment of new panels and woodwork, no doubt designed by Pugin, delivered to Alton Towers but never installed, were sold.[23]

Henry Talbot's first successful legal maneuver was before the Committee on Privileges of the House of Lords in 1857, who awarded him the title of Earl of Shrewsbury. He became known as the 18th Earl of Shrewsbury and Talbot, the latter from his previous (family) title—the third Earl Talbot. The committee's action ended irrevocably the Catholic line of the Shrewsbury dynasty.

His second legal victory in 1858 came in the Common Pleas Division, in an extremely convoluted and challenging decision. Clearly the court had done significant and deep research into the dynasty's history of primogeniture and inheritance. Since the Shrewsbury line was remarkably balky in creating male heirs, Judge Cockburn in the end based his decision almost exclusively on the legal status of Gilbert Talbot, the 13th Earl of Shrewsbury, who became known on the street as the "tenth cousin" and who held the title from 1713 until his death in

1743. Gilbert renewed the Catholic line of the titled earls, but he had no heirs, and at his death the earldom passed to his brother's son (the 15th earl), who was childless.[24]

Judge Cockburn discovered that by an act of settlement in 1700, the Shrewsbury estate had been "annexed" to the earldom. Because "the settled estates were rendered inalienable by any future tenant-in-tail," they could not be separated from the male Shrewsbury heir. But there was a catch, one that transcended birthright: since as a Jesuit, Earl Gilbert Talbot lived away from England in a Catholic seminary most of his life, he was not eligible for the estate unless he declared himself a Protestant! His attendance abroad was a serious breach of the English anti–Jesuit laws that forbade sending any "child or person beyond the seas ... to enter any college, seminary, or house of any Jesuits, seminary priests, and recusants."[25]

A paradox: although his Catholicism, in itself, the justices ruled, did not allow him to have "labored under a special incapacity to inherit, take, or enjoy" the Shrewsbury estate, to keep it he would have to renounce his Catholicism. He chose not to. In any case, Gilbert himself had no son who could become the fourteenth earl.[26]

The judge turned philosophical at this point, because this remote Jesuit earl, the key historical avatar of the Shrewsbury estate in the matter, "had nothing, he could give nothing to the plaintiff [Henry Chetwynd Talbot], and the plaintiff could take nothing from him." It did not matter that it was 1858, since the 1718 act "cannot be impeached after the estates had been dealt with for a century and a half." The plaintiff, who was "issue male of the body of John the first Earl of Shrewsbury," therefore prevailed: the judge ruled against any act of ejectment of Henry Talbot in favor of Lord Edmund Howard (through his trustees) and awarded the grounds and the empty buildings to Talbot. Lord Edmund Howard, not descended from a Shrewsbury male, would seem to have lost everything—title and estates.[27]

All through 1859 the race to control public opinion raged outside the courts. The *London Times* reported that the new eighteenth Earl of Shrewsbury and Talbot was celebrating his title (awarded by the Committee on Privileges of the House of Lords) at a public ceremony establishing a waterworks in his new home area. He was nonetheless clearly nervous about the decision, since as recently as two months earlier Hope Scott and Serjeant Bellasis, the trustees of Lord Edmond Talbot, still held "possession of the mansion and demesne of Alton Towers" and the "new" earl was only "in possession of those parts of the estates the tenants of which have, in spite of advice to the contrary, voluntarily came forward and acknowledged him as their landlord."[28] Henry Chetwynd

Talbot spoke to the crowd "as if I were the actual and positive landlord of the place. The judgment may be reversed; I do not think it will, and I am sure that if it is, it will not be of long duration." His argument was unimpeachable: "I do not like to count my chickens before they are hatched."[29]

But subsequent appeals resulted in split decisions for Lord Edmund Talbot's trustees, Bellassis and Hope-Scott. In the first decision in 1860, the Lords Justice of the Exchequer Chamber unanimously rejected the *appeal* of the act of ejectment without even needing to hear from Henry Chetwynd Talbot's attorneys, thereby formally establishing the 18th earl as the sole owner of the buildings and all the *entailed* land, that is, property that is entailed to the heir and cannot be sold, which, at Alton Towers, was the majority of the property. But not all: based on a separate decision from the Chancery Court in 1867 the income from the *unentailed* portions of the estate would still be in the control of the recently deceased earl's trustees. Five years later, still another suit in Chancery, this time favoring the new 18th earl, disqualified specific holdings in Broadstone, Dorset, from that trustees' unentailed award. And still a further five years passed when the 18th earl died and his younger son sued his older brother, the 19th earl, to prevent the "the wills and trusts of their father brought into execution." When the 19th earl died the administers of the estate even sued his widow, Anna Theresa, Countess Shrewsbury.[30] As for the endless curse of inheritance litigation, the Shrewsbury dynasty could even compete with the Tichbornes (see chapter 12).

What came to pass is that regardless of the favorable rulings for the new earl's family, the Chetwynd-Talbots, they were still without the funds that the earlier Shrewsbury dynasty controlled. They could not will the return of the glory that was Alton Towers: it took cash, and a lot of it. Outwardly still spectacular, inwardly in decline, Pugin's Alton Towers suffered irrevocably because of the loss of its last great benevolent patron, the 16th Earl of Shrewsbury.

But Alton Towers did not go quietly. Benjamin Disraeli, the former prime minister and novelist, kept it in the public consciousness as a folly-like fantasy in 1870 by placing it—re-named Muriel Towers—as the country estate at the heart of his novel *Lothair*. The titular hero Lothair was the orphaned heir to a mighty estate, with two guardians, one a Presbyterian and the other a Roman Catholic convert from the Anglican Church. These guardians wage a spiritual war for his religious allegiance. His Catholic guardian eventually becomes a cardinal who schemes with the English Jesuits to secure the young aristocrat's wealth for the Catholic Church.

Disraeli peoples his novel with characters named after famous British Catholics: we have a Monsignore Chidioch (a Tichborne name) and a

Miss Arundel (from the dukes of Norfolk), who becomes a nun. Disraeli even borrows the armory, the octagon, and the chapel from Alton Towers, although in the novel the latter is used for Anglican worship even as the young Lothair at first plans to build a Roman Catholic cathedral with his abundant inheritance. In the end, after a hard-to-fathom stint as an officer in the army of the Italian revolutionary Garibaldi as the latter launched his ill-fated attack on the Vatican, Lothair becomes a Protestant convert and secures Muriel Towers as the Protestant seat of his new family, as did the new 18th Earl of Shrewsbury in real life.

Regardless of century, entrepreneurs reimagined Alton Towers as a mock-medieval masterpiece but were always challenged to pay the footman's bills. In the early twentieth century, the 20th Earl of Shrewsbury and Talbot, in desperate need for funds for Alton Towers, flogged a polo club, a hansom cab service, Greyhound bus routes, and even an imported French auto dealership. He finally sold Alton Towers to local businessmen who had no choice but to turn it over to the army during World War II for use as a barracks and training center.[31] No record indicates how the army used the armory.

Tussaud's Group became the first modern entertainment conglomerate to take over Alton Towers in 1990. Partly in ruins, it eventually passed to the Merlin Entertainment Group, the current owner, who now succeeds in catapulting children past Alton Lodge on a roller coaster, eventually coaxing them into the armory on another ride called "Hex: Legend of the Towers." Before their ride, park employees narrate the "Chained Oak Tree Curse" that is responsible for the deaths of the wishy-washy men in the Shrewsbury line: every time a tree branch falls an heir perishes. It would not be difficult for us to guess that the Good Earl and his pugnacious ally Pugin are two of the ghosts the children encounter on this ride.

Details of the Litigation:
[Earl] Talbot v. Earl of Shrewsbury, 1857–67

Common Pleas Division, 1858

Presiding: With jury

Suit: Act of ejectment for the recovery of Alton Towers.

Plaintiff: Henry Chetwynd, 3rd Earl Talbot

Defendant: Lord Edmund Howard [through his trustees]

Verdict: Alton Towers (the buildings and grounds) awarded to Earl Talbot.

Committee on Privileges of the House of Lords, 1856–58

Decision: 3rd Earl Talbot of Ingestre awarded title of the 18th Earl of Shrewsbury.

Exchequer Chamber, 1860

Appeal: The act of ejectment (#1 above)
Verdict: Lord Edmond Howard's appeal rejected; the act of ejectment sustained for 3rd Earl Talbot.

Equity, Chancery, 1867

Presiding: Lord Chancellor (Frederick Thesiger, Lord Chelmsford), Lord's Justices Hugh McCalmont Cairns and George James Turner
Charge: Appeal of Common Pleas Decision of 1868
Verdict: Part of property in #1 appealed successfully: therefore the unentailed portions of the Shrewsbury estate (income from the property) will remain under control of the trustees. Most of the property was entailed and therefore under control of 3rd Earl Talbot.

11

The Convent Scandal, Fatty Mutton, and the Goosebury Fool

Saurin v. Star and Kennedy, 1869

The specter haunting the streets of London seemed to come alive in the case of the convent scandal, because a number of the alleged abuses Maria Monk suffered seemed to have really happened to a nun in Hull in the 1860s. The *Saurin v. Star and Kennedy* convent scandal in 1869 must have reassured many Protestants who had for a generation been titillated by the outrageous stories of the best-selling *Awful Disclosures of Maria Monk*. Even those who believed there was a real Maria Monk who could not have been of sound mind and had certainly been duped by ghostwriters or booksellers or both into detailing sexual liaisons between priests and nuns and the murders of the babies born from such unions, all outrageous tales church officials could seemingly not debunk, might have given Maria Monk another look.

Although one would expect Harriet Martineau, Charles Dickens's competitor for middle-class readership, would be above the sensationalism represented by Maria Monk's tales, she could not resist the historical intrigues she imagined for a convent during the days of Henry VIII's movement to suppress religious houses in the 1540s. Her novella *Sister Anna's Probation* (1861) is—in fact—about a failed *probation*, as Anna attempts to pursue her vows of chastity, poverty, and obedience at a nearby abbey whose abbess believes that this novice's father—who, like the novice's former ardent suitor, lives in the neighborhood—has cheated her convent of a rightful share of the family's dowry. The abbess also enforces what seems like her order's over-righteous suppression of the Bible.[1] The story was illustrated by John Everett Millais, the Pre-Raphaelite painter whose interest in religious subjects in his early paintings, especially nuns, seemed to support Protestant prejudice about Catholics. Anna's rescue imitates *The Escape of a Heretic, 1559* (1857), one of Millais's much-admired, sensationalist anti–Catholic paintings, in which a priest is tied up with his own crucifix and cincture (a rope-like belt) while a suitor prepares a young nun for escape. In Martineau's tale, Anna's escape is foreshadowed by the footstool she will steal from her cell that had concealed a copy of the Bible she secretly studied to discover the truths suppressed by the Catholic Church. Millais had also painted a notorious convent scene in the *Vale of Rest*, exhibited at the Royal Academy in 1859. One nun is laboriously digging a grave while a second nun sits by with her gaze directed at us, encouraging the viewer of the painting to imagine that this scene smacks of a suspicious burial.[2] After all, aren't most burials done by professional gravediggers?

Although Cardinal Newman should have had no illusions about rampant anti–Catholicism, he was nonetheless scandalized that Monk's fictitious memoir had sold at least a quarter of a million copies. Although Newman could not have ignored the *London Times*, whose news stories in 1869 of *Saurin v. Star and Kennedy* rivaled those of Maria Monk, some of his friends and associates expected him to come out in public on the side of the accused nuns, as did the Catholic newspaper the *Tablet*. Given the specter of Maria Monk, no Catholic could rest easy with the testimonies in this trial. Although there were no murders or secret burials revealed in the Queen's Court, this "very remarkable case ... promises to excite an unusual degree of public interest," according to the *London Times*, when it began on February 4, 1869.[3]

Newman chose not to go public with his opinion of the case, but he was certainly mistaken that, as he wrote to his friend Emily Bowles, "there has been no great scandal." Newman did admit, "There is a good deal of petty tyranny and injustices in the small places and out of the way corners of the Church, and authorities may be roused to put them on a better status." In another scandalous case (chapter 7), *Connelly v. Connelly*, he unfortunately seemed to be taking the side of Emily Bowles in *her* grievances with Mother Cornelia Connelly; he was also surely mistaken by supporting Bowles in that contretemps[4] (see chapter 11). Like other Anglican converts Newman was always conscious of the public image of Catholic sisterhoods: when the nuns in a Norwood convent were acquitted of expelling one of their number, they remained liable for court costs, which Newman paid from the surplus from the Achilli trial funds.[5]

Saurin v. Star and Kennedy was a remarkable case because both plaintiff, Susanna Mary Saurin (formerly Sister Scholastica), and defendants, Mary Ann Star (Sister Mary Joseph) and Julia Kennedy (Sister Mary Magdalene), all seemed to be on good terms when Saurin joined the Order of the Sisters of Mercy in Clifford, Ireland, and then moved to their convent in Hull.[6] As Sister Scholastica, Saurin had, however, to struggle to remain in her order at the very convent house she was invited to transfer to by her superior, Star. Co-defendants Star and Kennedy were equally determined to kick her out for what must seem to us today to be an unfathomable case of jealousy or competition over clothes and ecclesiastical jewelry or perhaps even friendship gone awry.

At one point Saurin testified, naively, that she was a "favorite with the girls" in the convent school.[7] Perhaps for a nun in this convent, that was presumptuous behavior. She was later accused of stealing food from these children: in fact, one of the times she was stripped of many of her clothes in a closed room was when Star and Kennedy wanted to see if she was secretly bringing to the convent the dinners of the children at the school she was teaching.[8] Clearly Saurin's superiors were obsessed with food: Star testified that she surprised Saurin in the pantry one day stuffing ham in her face. She could not explain her behavior to her superior because "her mouth was so full and the lower part of her face was besmeared with grease." It is hard to say whether anyone in the courtroom believed this testimony since everyone apparently was convulsed with laughter.[9]

By the time her case reached the Queen's Court, Saurin was no longer Sister Scholastica, but she appeared as if she were still a nun, dressed in a black robe, her face masked in a thick veil. Spectators partial to her were noisy and supportive, drawing Judge Mellor's disciplinary remarks quite often. His court would not become a theater, he often repeated, with spectators making remarks aloud. But a live re-staging of Maria Monk was hard for the spectators to resist. Saurin's own brother, Matthew Saurin, a Jesuit priest, had written in letters to his family that what his sister endured could have appeared in a book, *The Lives of the Saints*. Furthermore what she had endured would "far surpass the minds of the most fanatical enemies of the convent."[10] In 1865, at the time of the trial, it had been seven years since he had seen her last.

In her civil action, Saurin charged her former mother superior and deputy with conspiracy (depriving Saurin of her right to remain a member of her religious order), false imprisonment (confining her to various rooms and punishing her to make her want to leave of her own free will), libel (accusing her of theft), and assault (forcibly stripping her of most of her religious garments).

The court heard, therefore, a scenario out of many Protestants' nightmares of life in a convent, especially those who had read Maria Monk. Saurin was accused by her superiors, according to court testimony, of stealing a religious medal from a dead sister's corpse, of stealing the very habit of this same deceased nun (a friend, as it turned out), and of "a great forwardness in her as regarded a certain priest. She put herself continually in his way, and sought to attract his notice by various little arts; talked to him frequently, though as frequently forbidden to do so; was in a state of excitement quite remarkable whenever he was about the convent."[11] The court heard from another nun, a lay sister, formerly a pupil when Saurin taught in Hull, that Saurin was "very forward" compared to the other nuns, and often interrupted a priest who was repairing desks, urging him to go somewhere with her. (Later Coleridge would point out that Saurin was instructed to inform the priest that lunch was ready.)[12] Saurin's superiors summarized her years with them as a time of "the grossest falsehood, deceit, and treachery."[13]

Although it would be clearly forbidden by all that these nuns held holy, Sister Mary Joseph, Mary Ann Star, according to Saurin, wished to hear the details of Saurin's auricular confession to the convent's ministering priest. This may have been the flashpoint of Saurin's—perhaps any nun's—difficult status as a nun: she owes total obedience to her mother superior, who must be informed of all infractions of convent discipline; but her confessions to a priest must be absolutely confidential.[14] Her confessor would later testify that he concluded "that both intellectually and morally she was warped" and that he agreed with the bishop examining the case that she was a kleptomaniac.[15] Needless to say, this confessor was skirting the rules himself, since confessions were supposed to be secret.

When a Catholic bishop's commission and then the bishop himself determined that Saurin should leave the convent, she refused, whereupon she was stripped of her habit, searched, and made to stand for hours in a cold, dark attic room. This was a violation considerably beyond the earlier occasions in the past when she had some of her clothes removed so that they might be searched for food she was supposedly stealing from the children in the convent school. Saurin had accused Star of stripping her five times.[16] Her clothes, especially those of any quality (such as a "knitted petticoat"), were taken from her, sometimes violently, and later she saw that Star and other nuns were wearing some of them. She was told to wear the equivalent of rags "for her sins."[17] Her ring, symbolizing her status as a bride of Christ, was taken from her. Furthermore, her meals were always the same disgusting mutton—"lukewarm, then lukewarm and fatty, next lukewarm, fatty, and the leavings of others' plates," as she testified. She had mutton every day *for two years.*¹⁸ The other sisters, however, used to have the occasional stewed rabbit or ham for variety.¹⁹

Saurin had written to her brother, "I think I will get my request to leave the convent in my coffin." As a result Star told her that she, Star, was privy to all communications between Saurin and her brother. Star knew Saurin had told him "she had stripped" her. Star told her that if "she were to take [her] by the hair of the head and drag me downstairs from the top of the house to the bottom [Saurin] ought not to mention it."²⁰

She was often deprived of any nutritious food, could only drink water from a recently used coffee pot, and was forced to stand for seven or eight days in a bathroom.²¹ As she was also forbidden any normal intercourse of any kind with any member of the convent, that she survived at all may indeed have been a saint's miracle. A doctor testified that three years earlier he had examined her and found her scantily dressed in a secular outfit, extremely thin, her "circulation feeble," and "her hands were almost blue." She testified that it was often made difficult for her to use the common toilet and sometimes entirely forbidden to do so.²²

The courtroom *did* become a theater, despite the efforts of Sir Alexander Cockburn, the lord chief justice, to rein in the numerous outbursts of laughter and occasional hissing from the spectators. What could he do when testimony from the defendants dwelt obsessively on Saurin in the larder stuffing her mouth with ham—"she could not answer me her mouth was so full, said her accuser," or eating gooseberries and cream on the sly. Coleridge then asked "if they make such things as gooseberry-fool in a convent?" The solicitor-general already knew the answer because laughter broke out when Star admitted that not only did she herself make gooseberry-fool but that she sometimes ate some in the morning.²³

Although some of Saurin's testimony was intrinsically disturbing—she had to kiss the floor if she were late, for example—she was a natural if not a naïve comic. Although she frequently kissed the floor, Mrs. Star and Mrs. Kennedy "never kissed the floor, whether late or not." No, "there was no particular spot we had to kiss—we kissed where we liked." Gales of laughter continued all through this testimony.²⁴ Even when Star complained of Saurin's presence as "an enemy living in our midst" and hoped for a technicality in her convent admission process to make it possible to free themselves from "so dangerous a person," the spectators also erupted in laughter. Clearly Star's testimony showed a personality lacking in human warmth or discernment. The solicitor-general was intent on showing that she had a real character flaw and was not suitable for leadership. He asked her how she could take away Saurin's ring, "a sign of her union with her Lord." Was it within her rights to do so? No, Saurin replied. "Well," he pushed, "where did you get the right to take away the symbol?" Star replied that she "did not consider" that she "exceeded" her right to do so. "It was an indignity," was it not? Solicitor General John Coleridge asked and pressed again: "Will you have the goodness, without my again asking the question," to repeat your "answer to the jury?" She said: "I do not know that it was an indignity." Since she did "not obtain the right" to take the ring from "rule, custom, and tradition," her moral inadequacy was clearly exposed.[25]

To be fair, the social class of the Lord Chief Justice and Solicitor General Coleridge may have interfered with courtroom decorum. When Coleridge heard that Saurin was late for "community exercise," he asked what that was. Laughter greeted the answer: supper. He was not amused: "It would be convenient if you called supper supper."[26] Likewise Cockburn had to be told what a "retreat" is, not to mention his exasperation at the nuns' names: "Sister Mary what? They are all Sister Marys."[27]

It may have been that class was playing more of a role in the matter than even the jurists realized. Kennedy, who admitted that she had a "bad memory," nonetheless remembered that Saurin was disciplined for using an unladylike but common Irish expression—"as sure as my hand is on my body"—as a colloquial affirmation of telling the truth.[28]

The question of the hostile removal of all of Saurin's papers and possessions came up often. Star took a relic that Saurin believed was a "piece of the True Cross." Apparently, the defendants took away all the papers without reading them, since one of the papers turned out to be a remedy for toothaches. How could Coleridge *not* know the audience would break into laughter when he asked: "I suppose they have toothache even in convents?"[29]

At a relatively early stage in the drive to expel Saurin, the convent resorted to a kangaroo court hosted by the local bishop, the Reverend Cornthwaite, who now testified that he believed it possible that she had the "disease" of kleptomania because she stole things like "a medal from a dead body."[30] It was to this paragon of objectivity that Star wrote of Saurin in 1865, "We now fear she steals from the school-children."[31] Star added that she would even be willing to give up her leadership position because she could not control Saurin's behavior.

But even before the bishop testified, Coleridge had set him up by asking Star why Saurin's hoarding of "ribbons and bobbins, and hooks and eyes" had been subsumed into the category of an "unaccountable accumulation of materials of every description" in the accusation: "Would 'accumulation of materials' have conveyed the notion of bobbins to the Episcopal mind?" Of course the spectators roared.[32] Some of the bishop's testimony included reading a heartbreaking letter written by Saurin to him asking why she was being treated so strictly, considering that she had spent sixteen years as a nun and never wanted to leave or reside in the outside world. Later, Saurin testified that she would rather die than leave the convent. Her superiors' response was to lock her in the attic.

Why, then, are we not surprised that spectators carried "flasks of sherry and packets of sandwiches" rather than give up their seats during the break for mid-day "refreshment"? They gave up the opportunity, if that's the word, to join an "outside mob" who in effect "hooted Mrs. Star in the persons of at least half a dozen Sisters of Mercy" who were attempting to enter a cab.[33]

It seemed that even the attendees in court did not always grasp the finer points of exchanges between Cockburn and Coleridge, when the question of Saurin's confiscated papers came up. In addition to the remedy for toothaches a poem titled "St. Cecilia" appeared, of which, Coleridge noted, "the subject is much better than the poetry." When Cockburn wondered, "It is not [John] Dryden's, I suppose?" Coleridge gently replied; "No, my lord, that [poem] is better known as *Alexander's Feast*."[34]

Coleridge's summation was a rhetorical masterpiece, as he had to avoid any grave insult to the women in the dock while asserting his client's version of the truth. Coleridge noted that Saurin was the victim of a concerted effort to keep her uninformed of various charges that had been forwarded to their bishop, who, in an attempt to forestall further scandal, convened a commission that was so transparently biased against Saurin that Coleridge could scarce contain his contempt.

Coleridge, too, could not resist playing to the crowd. He ironically suggested it was believed that she entered the convent "to gratify her love of dress, and her love of eating, and her excessive affection for externs," i.e., those individuals, men and women, outside the convent walls. To rolling laughter from the spectators Coleridge suggested such ideas were ludicrous: "The dress of a nun was not very attractive, nor was the diet of a nun exceedingly luxurious." Furthermore, if she wanted to consort with externs, "all she had to do was keep outside the walls of a convent."[35]

He turned to an analysis of the rules of obedience required of convent life to demonstrate that it was no surprise that so many sisters would corroborate their mother superior's views of Saurin. "The evidence, therefore, was, so to say, poisoned at its very source." Saurin's peers would have "an eternal, a sacred, a conscience-binding duty" to defeat her. It would also be imperative, "whether Miss Saurin was right or wrong," to avoid "a great scandal to the order."[36]

Coleridge said that Mrs. Star should have had "that spirit of charity which would have befitted her religious professions." In a daring maneuver he quoted a line of poetry from "a great man, one of the most distinguished ornaments of the Roman Catholic communion, Dr. Newman." Quoting from "My Lady Nature and Her Daughters," one of Newman's allegorical *Verses on Various Occasions* (1829), Coleridge intoned: "Nature amid the spheres hath sway / Ladies rule where hearts obey," leaving no doubt that this noble sentiment did not apply to the convent of the Sisters of Mercy.[37] In fact, "petty malignity" ruled the convent's life. Don't forget, he told the jury, that awful truth that appears in John Bunyan's *Pilgrim's Progress*, that "there was a bye-way to hell from the very gates of Paradise itself."[38]

Coleridge could spar with the court's witnesses and even the lord chief justice, but he would not play to the crowd as often as the latter did. Throughout the trial the sorry state of Saurin's stockings were a sticking point: at one point she stated that she blacked her feet so that the holes would not show her bare skin. When Star's attorney Mellish was examining a witness about Saurin's clothes, the lord chief justice interrupted him: "There is an error in the report of Dr. O'Hanlon's evidence which he may wish to have corrected. What he said was not that he had never seen such stockings on a nun before or since—[laughter]—but that he had never seen a nun's stockings before or since."[39]

In a recognition of how high popular feeling might be influencing a Protestant jury, Coleridge reminded them of the central irony of this case, that Miss Saurin was in fact a Catholic and wanted to remain a nun. In response to the defense attorney's suggestion that her future would be safe regardless of their verdict, he became passionate: "Do not believe it! It is not so! His opinion is nothing; mine is nothing; the opinion even of my Lord Chief Justice is nothing. But your verdict is everything. Clear away, therefore, from her—for you can—the dark cloud with which the defendants have overshadowed her! Bring back to her—for you can—the bright light from which they have shut her out!" Coleridge was keenly aware of anti–Catholic sentiment in both polite and working-class society, for he asked the jury, "twelve honourable and high-minded men," to believe his client. As Coleridge concluded, the *Times* reported, "a burst of applause broke out, which was promptly suppressed." It was paradoxically a Protestant anti–Catholic outburst in favor of a Catholic nun.[40]

The charge to the jury of twelve "merchants"[41] by the lord chief justice was long and clearly favored Saurin, although his contempt for convent life was palpable because this "monster case" of twenty days about the "miserable squabbles of a convent" should have been "disposed of" by their bishop.[42] The jury, he said, could—as Protestants—easily favor the plaintiff, since they "may think that convent life is an object of dislike and suspicion." Furthermore, in a remarkable defense of Victorian Protestant family values, he warned them against the following belief which he then so very carefully outlined for them: "You may think that withdrawing women from the sphere for which by nature they were destined, that of being wives and mothers, and thus forming and cementing ties on which, in the main, human happiness must rest—that this is an attempt to obliterate human instincts, to chill human affections, or at all events to repress them within the narrow bounds and limits of an artificial and unnatural life, contrary to the laws of nature and the ordinances of God."[43]

Despite the fact that they are all Protestants, the lord chief justice issued an unusual injunction: they "must try" the case as if they "were twelve right-minded Catholics, members of the Roman Catholic Church," accepting convent life and its own rules, especially the "unlimited powers of the superior and unqualified subjection in the subordinates." The defendants offered what lawyers call a "plea of leave and license," that is, Saurin "gave her consent to these acts of which she complains." However, there was nothing in the "rules and customs of this association, the convent, that permits personal violence, restraint of an individual against her will, and conspiracies against her."[44] For him the turning point of the matter was that the convent authorities tried to force her to reveal her confession. Even her brother, a Jesuit priest, was moved to say in a letter that her superiors were "torturers and tyrants."[45]

The sundering of her own "natural" family ties had been the leitmotif of the trial: Miss Saurin had not been told of the death of a brother, and she was forbidden to see her mother and another brother—the Jesuit priest—even when they came from a great distance (Ireland) to visit her. (This Jesuit brother, the court was frustrated to learn, favored his sister's case, but had strangely disappeared, no doubt raising suspicions that his superiors had ordered him away.)[46] When her mother finally insisted on a face to face meeting, she grasped her and said: "My child, are they going to make a prisoner of you?" The jury had heard this plea, strange enough because it came from the mother of three nuns and two priests, whose daughter wished to remain in a convent and could not. It is unlikely, at this point, that an earlier injunction for nuns to regard "the voice of the mother superior as the voice of angel" would be very convincing.[47]

The chief justice asserted that this was not a case everyone would have expected, in which "Protestant parents complain that a daughter has been inveigled and subject to restraint" when she wished to leave the convent or "has been ill-treated because her better judgment has revolted at the practices she has been called upon to perform." No, the irony of this case persists in the fact that the plaintiff "does not complain of being kept in a convent, but of being turned out of a convent"![48] As absurd as it may seem, Cockburn argued that—inverting Hermia's banishment to a convent by Theseus, Duke of Athens, in Shakespeare's *Midsummer Night's Dream* for refusing to marry her father's choice—Saurin "desired" to:

> Endure the livery of a nun;
> For aye to be in shady cloister mew'd.
> To live a barren sister all her life.[49]

Cockburn's instructions to the jury seemed not to support much merit in any of the charges except the one of conspiracy and, in fact, suggested that giving voluntary (and absolute) obedience to a superior in a "common association" like a religious order may preclude any complaint about discipline being imposed for infractions of the association's discipline, because of the (now quite dubious) legal maxim *volenti non fit injuria*—"no wrong is done to a person who consents to a wrong." But her case would succeed, he added, if she has capably demonstrated—as an example of the development of a conspiracy against her—that Mrs. Star insisted on her revealing the contents of her confession and maltreated her when she would not do so. After a lengthy review of the relevant evidence, Cockburn's final example of the likelihood of the conspiracy came down to Star's allegation that Saurin had "stripped off the grave clothes from the body of her deceased sister, that she might afterwards wear them."[50]

And while Cockburn did not dismiss the possibility of guilty verdicts for all charges, he seemed preoccupied by the long delays church authorities manifested in solving this dispute among themselves, implying that there was not good faith on their side. Furthermore, the notion of Star's forcing information about Saurin's confession was especially "odious and detestable." And finally, "the cruel act of oppression" in openly exposing her in a "state of semi-nudity and humiliation," not to mention the insinuations of Saurin accosting a priest—if true—would assure her of a verdict in her favor.[51]

Also alluding to the public disorders of the last ten years, Cockburn asked the jury to "allow no prejudice to influence" their judgment: "The current of popular feeling, the echoes of which have been heard within these walls, ought to find no entrance here. The cries of an unthinking populace ought to find no response in the breasts of twelve honest and intelligent men."[52]

The jury deliberated for three hours and returned guilty verdicts for the counts of conspiracy and libel. The defendants were to pay Saurin 500 pounds if her dowry of 300 pounds was not returned, but only 200 pounds if it were. Although this was in the end only a modest settlement (in effect) of 200 pounds, the verdict "was communicated like lightning to the multitude outside, and a loud cheer was heard reverberating through Westminster Hall"[53]; an observer reported that in the streets outside the Court, "the dense crowd there congregated gave expression to their gratification in a loud and long-continued and right hearty English cheer."[54] Star and Kennedy were acquitted of the charges of false imprisonment and assault.

While that acclaim was surely Protestant in essence, within four years Coleridge would be back in court for the first trial of the Tichborne Imposter, a judicial struggle of even greater duration, excitement, and potential anti–Catholic animus, to which we will turn in the next chapter. We do not know what the Roman Catholic bishops, canons, nuns, and families of the plaintiff and defendants in the spectator boxes did while the crowd roared its approval of the verdict, an acute embarrassment for the Roman Catholic establishment, one of whose aristocratic members, the 14th Duke of Norfolk, attended a number of sessions of the trial including the day of the verdict and would find in ten years his own family's chapel at Arundel subject to public scandal and a court case as well (see chapter 13). In matters of religious controversy, it seemed to many, class and rank would not matter.

Star and Kennedy did not, in the end, go quietly: they hired new attorneys who tried to get the successful prosecution of the two guilty verdicts invalidated by the Vice-Chancellor's Courts, without success. In the end all parties in the case agreed to seek a settlement in Chancery, the details of which were not announced, but was achieved in April 1870, more than fifteen months after the original verdict.[55] Ex-nun Sister Mary Scholastica then disappeared from the public world.

Details of the Litigation:
Saurin v. Star and Kennedy, 1869

Queen's Bench

Presiding: Lord Chief Justice, with a special jury.

Charges: Conspiracy, false imprisonment, libel, and assault.

For the Plaintiff: Mrs. Saurin (Sister Mary Scholastica)

Sir John Coleridge, QC, Solicitor General

Mr. Digby Seymour, QC

Mr. A. Willes

For the Defendants: Mrs. Star (Sister Mary Joseph) and Mrs. Kennedy (Sister Mary Magdalene).

Mr. Henry Hawkins, QC

Mr. George Melish, QC

Mr. Charles Russell

Verdict: Guilty of conspiracy and libel, not guilty of false imprisonment and assault.

12

The Twenty-Six-Stone Claimant and the Invisible Stonyhurst College Quadrangle

Tichborne v. Lushington, 1872–1873, and *Regina v. Tom Castro*, 1873–1874

> My tale was heard and yet it was not told,
> My fruit is fallen and yet my leaves are green,
> My youth is spent and yet I am not old,
> I saw the world and yet I was not seen.
> —Chidioch Tichborne, from
> "Elegy Written with His Own Hand
> in the Tower Before His Execution" (1586)

The Roman Catholic line of the clan Tichborne in Hampshire possessed a family tree with far more than its share of legends and curses. Perhaps the curse of all curses came in the form of Arthur Orton, a Cockney, but lately of Wagga Wagga, New South Wales, who returned to his native London in 1866, obviously a working-class bloke from stem to considerable stern. Londoners always commented on his weight, twenty-six stone, about 364 pounds. He claimed to be the long-lost Roger Tichborne, drowned in a shipwreck. The young Tichborne weighed about ten stone, or 140 pounds, when he was last seen in England in 1851. In Queen Victoria's courts Orton would come to be known as the Tichborne Claimant, as he sought to be named heir to the immense Tichborne family fortune, then up for grabs. For the Tichbornes, he was almost the final curse that destroyed them.

The family itself traced its origins at least from the twelfth century, but St. Andrew's, the parish church of the village of Tichborne in

Hampshire, has a chancel dating from the mid-eleventh century. The village and church are situated on the "Itchen bourne" or bank of the Itchen River east of Winchester: hence the Saxon name "Tichborne."

One of the family's legends was the thirteenth century Tichborne Dole, a charitable distribution to the deserving poor, carried out to this day on March 25, the Feast of the Annunciation, a holiday celebrated by Christians of all denominations. More than seven hundred years ago, Lady Mabella Tichborne, suffering from a crippling disease, asked her husband to donate food to the poor. Apparently both miserly and perverse, he said he would only give away the corn from any plot of ground that his pathetic wife could crawl around. The formidable lady was able to circumnavigate a twenty-three-acre plot, later to acquire the name of The Crawls. She then cursed her own family: if seven generations of sons were born, seven generations of daughters would follow, the family name would collapse, as would the manor house itself.[1]

Sir Henry Joseph Tichborne, grandfather of the Roger Tichborne whose disappearance and possible reappearance kept mid–Victorian London on the virtual edge of a record-breaking trial, fulfilled much of this curse early in 1845 by having only daughters, seven of them—a remarkable genealogical feat, perhaps, but he made it seem easy. The estate remained Tichborne in name, but later passed to near relatives, the Doughtys, who decided to be known as the Doughty-Tichbornes.

The Tichbornes of the sixteenth and seventeenth centuries felt the curse inflicted by both the divided Elizabethan church and the Cromwellian Commonwealth or Protectorate, respectively, resulting in three of Tichborne ancestors being imprisoned in the Tower: two of the three died in the Tower, but only one, Chidiock Tichborne, was executed there. Chidioch was a melancholy but accomplished poet. He was a minor conspirator in the Roman Catholic Babington Plot to assassinate Queen Elizabeth and was executed in 1586. The Babington Plot was only one of a number of Catholic-inspired attempts on Queen Elizabeth's life. Sir Francis Walsingham was Elizabeth's principal secretary but became known as her "spymaster." Because of Walsingham's craft, some say imposture, all of the conspirators were easily rounded up and sent to the Tower for execution. Chidiock's elegy, "Written With His Own Hand in the Tower Before His Execution," is now a textbook gem of the plain style epigram: "My prime of youth is but a frost of cares," reads the first line, for Chidiock was only twenty-eight when he died, and concludes: "And now I live, and now my life is done."

The seventeenth century Henry Tichborne was King James I's governor of Drogheda and later lord justice in Ireland who—when the parliamentary rebellion broke out in 1641—fought against the confederate

Irish rebels as a royalist. He was captured by the parliamentary army, who suspected him of collusion with the Catholics—no doubt because of his family's ties—and sent him to the Tower. Soon after, he switched allegiance to the Commonwealth and regained a tentative hold on his old post in Drogheda. His kinsman, Robert Tichborne, who also fought in the parliamentary cause, was not as fortunate, because he was imprisoned in the Tower for twenty-two years for his role in the trial and execution of Charles I in 1649. He had apparently saved the lives of some Royalists, and this gesture saved him from execution but not imprisonment.

The descendants, the local lords of the manor, of these historic Tichbornes did not escape the difficulties of sectarian struggle either. St. Andrew's Church in Tichborne has itself been a divided church since the Reformation: the Tichborne Chapel remained Roman Catholic and the property of the Tichborne family, despite widespread Protestant confiscation of church properties and buildings. This chapel takes up the whole of the north aisle to this day. Viewing the church from outside, the external features of both north and south aisles seem structurally similar, but inside the church the dense array of monuments, wall-plaques, and even sculptures make it clear that the south aisle is a very special place if not an especially sacred one, with an intensity not quite as evident in the rest of the very minimally appointed church interior. An article in the *Gentleman's Magazine* in 1810 reported, "The original Altar-table of oak, with I.H.S. and crosses carved on it,"[2] i.e., a Roman Catholic altar, was in front of the window at the east end of the aisle, but it is no longer there.

The chapel, because it was a relatively narrow aisle, was used primarily as a burial chamber, with more than a dozen memorials and tombs. In keeping with the family curse, perhaps, the most striking monuments feature children who died very young. The monuments capture the premature deaths of numerous Tichbornes; perhaps the youngest, who lived only a year and a half and died in 1619, is represented by a small recumbent sculpture, arrayed now in a bright red smock or gown.

The aisle is divided from the rest of the nave architecturally by two bay arcades; an iron railing prohibiting access from the main body of the church, architectural historian Nickolas Pevsner speculates, is Elizabethan in origin and may simply reflect the right of ownership rather than of religion, a distinction that studies of other divided churches would *not*, however, support. Although there was a door leading from the chapel to the outside at one time (obvious traces of which are still visible from outside), access to the chapel, as at the divided church at

Roman Catholic Tichborne Aisle, interior of St. Andrews Church, Tichborne (photograph by the author).

Mapledurham, is possible only when the gate in the interior railing is unlocked by the Catholics of the manor house.

Tichborne House was built in 1803, although the family seat has been on this site since the thirteenth century. The Tichbornes were unusually successful Recusants, with a Catholic chapel in the house and "priest's holes"—hiding places in case of a raid on a religious service. It is from the porch of the house that the Tichborne Dole was distributed. And it was the house and of course its land and family fortune that became the potential prize of one of the longest running pair of trials in British history, the trials of the Tichborne imposter or claimant (or three trials, if you include the Chancery hearing which began the business). The trials were still another curse, many locals believed, in the long line of curses inflicted on the family, because they came about as a result of the untimely death at sea of the family's heir, Sir Roger Charles Doughty Tichborne, in 1854.

The name Doughty had been added to Tichborne by Roger's uncle, the ninth Baronet, when a fourth Tichborne cousin, Elizabeth Doughty, left him a considerable fortune, including parts of Bloomsbury in London that has its own Doughty Street, as well as agricultural estates across the land.[3] The ninth baronet's only son died, of course (the ancient curse!), and the title passed to his younger brother, Roger Tichborne's father.[4]

Roger Tichborne was raised in France, his mother's home, then schooled at the Jesuits' Stonyhurst College, the Catholic prep school that features prominently in a majority of the cases in this book. It appears that Roger's father, Sir James Tichborne, had an extended lapse of judgment that resulted in *his* illusion that Roger could be Anglicized at Stonyhurst and therefore be fit to become head of the Tichborne clan. Roger and his mother fought strenuously to avoid his matriculation at Stonyhurst, but the family more or less forced him to return from France, where he was living with his mother. Novelist Bram Stoker, in his book *Famous Imposters* (1910), suggested that Roger was virtually kidnapped from the funeral of the seventh baron of Tichborne, his uncle Henry, and dragooned to Stonyhurst. Somewhat inevitably, he was a poor student and decided quixotically to begin a sailor's career, although he seemed to have neither an interest in or propensity for military discipline. Before leaving for his military service he naturally became much more interested in matters of his Tichborne heritage, because he fell in love with his cousin, Miss Catherine (Kate) Doughty, later Lady Radcliffe. Now his family were even more enthusiastic about his military career, hoping that the separation from his cousin would make what seemed an unhealthy—especially for Catholics—relationship with his cousin recede.

The *London Times* concluded that after an unsuccessful military career three years in length, he "escaped, for the present, Paris, Stonyhurst, Tichborne, and too full a compliance with the ordinances of his Church," by embarking on a South American voyage that provided him with almost a year of hunting and other expeditions.[5] He then boarded an English ship, the *Bella*, bound for Jamaica. The *Bella* never arrived, and search parties found elements of its wreckage with no survivors. In the meantime the family of Roger's cousin, Kate Doughty, had more than loss interest in this wayward aristocratic youth and prepared her for marriage with Mr. Percival Radcliffe, an heir to a Yorkshire baronetcy.

All of this aristocratic folderol might have passed notice except for two related moments. Before leaving for the military the impetuous and probably ardent Roger left a letter, dated June 22, 1852, for Kate:

> I make on this day a promise that if I marry my cousin Catherine Doughty, this year, before three years are over, at the latest, to build a church or chapel at Tichborne to the Holy Virgin, in thanksgiving for the protection which she has thrown over us, and in praying to God that our wishes may be fulfilled.[6]

Such a letter might have become any family's talisman to a lost child, but that was not to be. It became the focus of the Tichborne imposter's campaign to support the slander that, as Roger Tichborne, he impregnated his cousin before leaving England. And to add to the general scandal, his mother went not-so-quietly mad with grief for her lost son and the simultaneous belief that in fact he had never died.

Neither his wrecked ship nor his body were ever found. He would not be missed except (perhaps) by his French mother, for "he was not a good Catholic, or an affectionate son, or a soldier at heart, or a true lover, or a warm friend, or a scholar, or a kind master, or a genial companion," concluded the *London Times*, perhaps too snidely, if not accurately.[7]

His younger brother, Arthur Joseph, was named the eleventh Baronet of Tichborne, but he died in 1866, leaving his baby, the posthumous heir, Henry Alfred Joseph. Because of his age, the infant heir did not occupy Tichborne House; it was let to a local gentleman, a distant relative, Colonel Lushington.

Arthur Orton, originally from Wapping in London's East End, is now known as the Tichborne Imposter, but his supporters, almost universally working-class Protestants, called him the Tichborne Claimant, obviously the more sympathetic term. He was the twelfth and youngest child of a butcher who emigrated first to Valparaiso in South America, where he was befriended by a family named Castro from whom he eventually took his new (second) name, Tom Castro. He returned to England to learn his father's trade but changed his mind again and emigrated to Wagga Wagga, New South Wales, breaking off relations with his London family and taking up odd jobs both legitimate and elsewise. Even by the standards Down Under, he mixed with a rum lot.

When and why he hit upon the scheme of claiming to be the long-lost heir of the Tichbornes is open to debate, but he perhaps at first he simply did not accept how different in size, manners, and deportment he was from the legitimate heir, for whom Lady (Tichborne) Doughty had sought through widespread South Seas announcements and advertisements. But once the game was on, he was relentless and cunning, beginning in 1866 by writing semi-literate letters to her from Wagga Wagga that said he was her son, had lived a poor life, but had not "disgraced" her or his family. (Only the second part of that self-description was even close to being accurate.) But most importantly, he begged, please send me money so I can come home.[8]

Soon after he encountered, perhaps coincidentally, Andrew Bogle, the former Jamaican servant and valet of the Tichbornes now living on a small pension from Lady Doughty, with whom he was in contact on occasion and who knew of her quest. When he finally met Orton, the latter told him he noticed that Bogle could see that he had quite stout and that might explain why Bogle did not recognize him immediately.

Nonetheless, Orton suggested that Bogle recognized him as the long-lost Roger Tichborne.

Next to Lady Doughty, the imposter's second-best ally would turn out to be Andrew Bogle. He had been pensioned off and ended up in Australia, where his path accidentally—or by intention—crossed the path of Arthur Orton. Most likely irritated by the Tichborne's family's lack of generosity, he decided to identify the imposter as Roger Tichborne; as a means of revenge, possibly, but more likely as a way to return in comfortable triumph as a newly paid retainer of a long-lost aristocratic heir. Bogle knew every detail of the family intimately, of course, and could coach the imposter with little-known facts and stories of the old days that Orton could never have discovered on his own. When Orton arrived in Hampshire, he went down to Tichborne village as unobtrusively as a 364-pound man could and gleaned additional information from locals that would also prove invaluable in establishing how much he "knew" about the family and the community. With Bogle's tutoring, of course, he could mingle with the locals familiarly and often "knew" their names. But his progress through the village was not always successful. He asked the village blacksmith for directions and announced to him "they say Roger Tichborne has come back." "O! no, he has not," the blacksmith said, "he was drowned." Orton tried a more direct approach: "Do you believe," he asked the blacksmith, "I am Roger Tichborne?" The reply: "No. I'll be damned if you are. If you are, you've turned from a race-horse into a cart horse."[9]

Eventually Lady Doughty released the funds that would enable Orton to come to Paris to meet her. Orton was "recognized" by the distraught—some say insane or at the very least senile—mother of the real Tichborne heir, who was of a very slight figure: remember, he weighed only about a third as much as Arthur Orton when last seen in England. Raised in France, his death at sea had been presumed since his body was never recovered. So fierce was Lady Doughty's desire to regain a son lost virtually without a trace that she identified the Cockney Orton as her French-schooled and French-speaking son who had gone to Stonyhurst. It did not seem to bother her that at first he thought her name was Hannah Frances, although it was really Henriette Felicite. Later she realized that she had omitted the word "thin" in the descriptions she circulated when she was searching for him. She provided him, the *London Times* argued, "every letter, journal, and token of every kind, and all the information—that is, the fabrication—of an identity."[10] They took meals together and he no doubt learned a lot about the childhood he never had at Tichborne from her.[11] When she interviewed Serjeant Ballantine as a potential barrister for the case, she said to him: "How can a mother be mistaken in her son?" That heartfelt remark and her assertion that there were "marks upon his [Orton's] person which she had remembered noticing in his infancy" convinced Ballantine to take the leadership of the imposter's team.[12]

John Moore, Roger's servant on an earlier voyage he took to America, had initially been sympathetic to Lady Tichborne's identification of the imposter as her son, but he eventually testified, "If they had sent over to her an Egyptian mummy, and ticketed it Roger Tichborne, she would have acknowledged it as her son." It was an open secret, he said, that she had a "touch of insanity."[13]

Significantly aided by Lady Doughty's identification of her son and her thousand-pound-a-year allowance that supported his prodigious appetite for cigars and whiskey, Orton and Bogle returned to England. Orton attracted a core of cronies who guided his claim into the Court of Chancery to gain control of the Tichborne and Doughty estates, currently administered by the trustees for the underage second son since the real Roger Tichborne's estate had been executed in 1854, the year he drowned. Separate bills or actions of ejectment, as they were called, were filed for both estates in 1867. The same legal remedy was sought in both: in the words of J.B. Atley, a barrister and one of the many chroniclers of the hearing, Orton's strategy was to press for "permission to bring certain actions at law without hindrance from the outstanding terms of years vested in the trustees." In the meantime Orton's advisors entered a motion in Chancery that all "rents and profits of the estate" be placed in receivership, that is, removed from the control of the current trustees.[14]

Orton had the remarkable good fortune of serving as the escort of his own "mother," Lady Doughty, who came over from Paris and accompanied him from her hotel back and forth to Chancery hearings as he testified.[15] His claque went so far as to print up a book of statements and affidavits they gathered as to Orton's authenticity for distribution and, ideally, to refresh the memories of other potential witnesses.[16]

Things could not have been going better, until the imposter made a grievous error: he asserted that his cousin Kate Doughty Tichborne, now Lady Radcliffe, with whom Roger had agreed to suspend their romantic attachment in 1854 when he left for his travels, had been pregnant with his child.

Had Orton in all his confidence not understood that cousin Kate was in fact the extremely respectable Lady Radcliffe, who would soon testify that this imputation of pregnancy was a slander? Why did Orton make up such an outrageous story? To prove his Tichborne manhood? (More, however, about his manhood will eventually be forthcoming!) It was an unnecessary fabrication. Orton could be called determined and perhaps even confident, but he was never clever. Did he believe that this would be a revelation only the *real* Roger Tichborne would know? Ironically, Orton was simply unknowingly anticipating the strategy of Edward Vaughan Kenealy, his absurdly capricious attorney for his second trial, who characterized his seduction of his cousin as "the result of Stonyhurst teaching" that was corrupt and morally polluting, not to mention leading to lust. Kenealy, an ex–Catholic (among many other things), had served a month in jail twenty-five years earlier for beating his illegitimate son but went on to father twelve legitimate children with a woman he married when she was sixteen.[17] He was brilliant but bent, the ideal lawyer Orton would need to survive a difficult second trial, when his schemes were running out.

Kenealy had also a messianic complex, a personality curiously like Orton's. Kenealy believed that not only was he "the chosen one" but that his delusions and conspiracy theories would justify volumes of self-published prose.[18] His opening statement for the defense was typical: "If I had the gold of the Treasury at my back I might bring witnesses here who might immediately annihilate the sort of evidence brought before you. I might bring people here to prove there is no such place as Nowhere-Else." If only the jury knew that there was no Nowhere-Else, he could succeed: instead he was "like a person bound with fetters."[19]

In the four years—characteristically and absurdly drawn out—in which the Chancery suit was investigated, both sides hardened. Lady Doughty's death in 1868, however, deprived Orton of his biggest supporter, who, he maintained, had been poisoned, presumably by her own family to keep him, the claimant, from his rightful inheritance. When Orton heard the news of her death, he rushed to her living quarters in London. He was confronted by her brother, Henry Seymour, who was very much anti–Orton: a confrontation ensured, whereupon Orton called Seymour a "bloody blackguard" and demanded an inquest, which ruled she died of heart failure.[20]

A variation of the charge was made later by Kenealy in the second trial, when he accused the Tichborne family of driving "her into the grave by their persistent opposition" to her decision to accept Orton as her son. When the lord chief justice tried to correct Kenealy—"Why, she died of heart disease"—Kenealy shot back: "Probably aggravated by emotion." The lord chief justice had had enough: "You are charging the family with a sort of homicide. Really it is exaggeration."[21]

A requiem mass was said for her in the chapel at Tichborne House, and she was buried in a vault in the Tichborne or Roman Catholic family aisle of the divided St. Andrews parish church. Orton attempted to attend the funeral service, but he was blocked by the Tichborne family members from entering the church. Orton always maintained that if his "mother" had remained alive he would have been unstoppable until he gained control of one of England's largest fortunes. Given the inexplicably widespread support he received in the streets even without her, he was probably right.

Nonetheless, Orton argued that his supporters, not to mention those in the jury box later, would not have resisted a mother's heartfelt plea if she had appeared in court for him. He may have had a point, for certainly the moment she died, his official progress stalled and the remaining Tichbornes gathered their forces against him, ironically aided by his childhood sweetheart, Mary Ann Loder, his own brother, Charles Orton, and two of his sisters from Wapping, all of whom identified him as Arthur Orton.[22] He still had his mob, however, and he knew how to gain their favor: attack the perverted Roman Catholics, especially the Jesuits, and like Maria Monk always allude to secret forces—and sordid acts—behind the scenes.

His refusal to accept the original Roger's Catholicism, coupled with his attorney's attempt to defame the Catholic education the imposter claimed to have received at Stonyhurst College—suggestions of priests sexually abusing their pupils and plays performed in drag, for example—made the Tichborne case another public ordeal for English Catholics. The Stonyhurst boys who performed plays, by the way, were not allowed to take female roles and certainly could not wear female clothes, as male actors did in Shakespeare's days: when the boys performed *Macbeth*, for example, Lady Macbeth became Uncle Donald.

Orton's knowledge of his Stonyhurst days was irregular, to be kind. He knew that Roger's Arundel cousins—John (the current Lord Arundel) and Everard (later a Jesuit priest for a time)—were in residence when he was there, but he could not recall a single building, courtyard, or walkway with a scintilla of accuracy.[23] He did not know exactly what a "quadrangle" was but assumed it "was a staircase or some other part of a building."[24] He also wildly misrepresented the different classes or forms of the student body, suggesting at one point that the more elite "philosophers," like Roger Tichborne, lived eighteen or twenty to a room. They actually had a room each.[25] He did not know that the detached building where he and the other philosophers lived was the "seminary," which Orton thought was called the "cemetery."[26] Perhaps his "memory" of the Arundels was colored by his oft-stated belief that the entire campaign against his rightful inheritance as a Tichborne was orchestrated by the Arundel family in particular and the Jesuits in general.

Both of his trials after the referral of the Chancery hearing were extremely complicated: it is perhaps best to begin by emphasizing Orton's overall strategy, which, not to put too fine a point on it, involved his blatant and prejudicial attack on Roman Catholicism in general and Stonyhurst College, its leading prep school, in particular. Since he had adopted the posture of being a legitimate heir, raised as a Catholic, to a Catholic fortune, his rhetorical pitch that required him to demonize the Jesuits, the order in charge of Stonyhurst, was odd at best.

Orton's instinct was to build on contemporary waves of Victorian anti–Catholic prejudice. He responded to questions with what he believed to be cutting comic remarks about Catholicism. His solicitor usually followed his lead. The young Tichborne heir had been educated both at Stonyhurst, originally a school derived from a similar Jesuit foundation in France, and privately in Paris. Orton's ingenious argument went roughly like this: the education he received at both Stonyhurst and Paris were similarly depraved and thus he—as Tichborne—was driven to a number of unsavory deeds, not the least of which was seducing the cousin he said he had been secretly engaged to. When he realized the depth of his depravity, he sent himself into a long exile where his French accent, all of the Greek and Latin studies he had acquired at Stonyhurst, and the memory of many other family routines had been lost. If he were an impostor, he would have tried to re-learn those things to fool the court. But he honestly did not remember them. Q.E.D., he was Roger Tichborne.

Most of the public knew the Tichborne case through the two public trials that followed Orton's bid for the estate that had begun with the Chancery hearing. The first trial (1871–72), a logical outcome of the Chancery hearing, was a civil action of ejectment, designated Tichborne v. Lushington; that is, Tichborne, i.e., Orton, the "real" heir to the Tichborne estates, was attempting to eject Lushington from *his*, the claimant's, home. Lushington was the name of the Tichborne relative who was the current sitting tenant of the Tichborne property. Still another irony of the proceedings was that Lushington, based on—at most—a single "courteous" meeting with the imposter at Tichborne Park, actually believed that Orton was Roger Tichborne.[27] Lushington always believed in the imposter, even after the evidence in the first trial—in part named after him—went against Orton. Soon after, the Crown decided to arrest Orton and prosecute him for perjury. He was able to get himself released on bail by appealing to the Court of the Queen's Bench, however, and then used the fact of his bail as "proof" of his innocence. All of these developments made Lushington persona non grata in his very own family. His defense of the imposter could only have meant he expected somehow to stay in residence at Tichborne House if the imposter prevailed.

In a remarkable letter to the *Times* on April 27, 1872, Orton asserted that his identity as Roger Tichborne was virtually self-evident, given his successful release on bail after the first trial, as well as the increase in funds donated to his defense fund. His ace in the hole, however, was the fact that despite an appeal in the *Daily Telegraph* to Roger Tichborne's fellow officers for any testimony attesting to Roger's tattoos—tattoos that Orton did not have—no one had come forward in eight days to vouch for such tattoos. Therefore—as always—he was Roger Tichborne. The fact that the *Times* published this letter as "signed" by "R.C.D. Tichborne" was probably the best news and support he could wish for, although not surprisingly he neglected to mention that in fact eleven brother officers of Roger Tichborne from the Carabineers had already written to the *Times* on April 1 attesting that Roger Tichborne had never returned to England since his departure in 1853.[28]

Despite this seemingly authoritative report from the genuine heir's peers, the only way to understand the confidence of Orton and *his* supporters is when we realize that just three months later, Orton attended a rally of 12,000 people in Loughborough in the East Midlands, where the local MP told the assembly that he had just read in a Welsh newspaper that a man had arrived in Swansea who had lived in Melbourne, Australia, and had met Roger Tichborne, then living under the name of Tom Castro, one of Orton's admitted aliases: the man before you *was* the genuine heir to the Tichborne estate, he told the rally.

One recurring theme of his testimony was the guilty knowledge possessed by Catholics, especially priests. In the first trial, Orton snapped at the prosecutor, John Duke Coleridge, about a detail of French Catholic practice: "You appear to be very innocent just now. Considering that your brother [Henry James Coleridge] is a Jesuit, you must know." Coleridge was outraged: "I don't know that I am to submit to that from anybody. I have the highest love, regard, and veneration for my brother."[29] Coleridge was so keenly disturbed by Orton's remark that he discussed it again in his closing address: "Do you suppose," he said, "that a Roman Catholic gentleman would have attempted to insult a man, in cross-examination, by calling his brother a Jesuit?" He called Orton's question the work of a "blackguard."[30]

John Duke Coleridge confided to his diary early on that the trial was "impeding over him like a black cloud of fate." Two months later, so exhausted was he from interrogating the slippery Orton that he wrote that the claimant "will kill me before I do him." Nonetheless, his attack on the claimant and his supporters was relentless, and his defense of the Tichbornes against this "cunning and odious scheme of a conspirator, a perjurer, a forger, an imposter—a villain" was convincing. He intended, in J.B. Atlay's summation, to demonstrate that "the claimant differed in physiognomy, style, habits, taste, language, and education from Roger Tichborne" and that all that he claimed to know about the original Tichborne "came from careful coaching, from gossip, or from documents to which he had access."[31] Coleridge would learn, to his dismay, that it was not going to be that simple. In the end, Coleridge's rhetorical tic, directed at Orton numerous times—"Would you be surprised to hear?"—was so effective in exposing Orton's ignorance about the actual Tichborne family and experience that it remained a memorable catchphrase of Coleridge's courtroom style for decades to come.[32]

Coleridge's frustrations were so great that the Crown decided to stop the relentless attacks on him and others on the prosecution team during the imposter's public rallies. Especially active in the leadership of these rallies was a true believer in the imposter, the MP George Whalley, who, according to one chronicler of the trials "was one of the most notorious ultra–Protestants in the House of Commons."[33] The Crown resorted to the little-known *sub-judice* proceedings that charged Whalley and others with contempt of court. This "fringe court" soon proved quite controversial throughout the nineteenth century because it was held without a jury and because the likelihood of the individuals accused actually influencing the trial was not always manifest.[34] But whenever a Victorian judge read a speech like the following from Whalley, appearing with Orton at a rally in Piccadilly, there was no doubt he would regard it as an act of contempt:

> It has been said there was a conspiracy. He had no doubt there was.... The Attorney-General and the Government were attempting to prosecute under a penal Act a man whom they knew was innocent of the charges made against him. The object was to keep the large Tichborne estates in the hands of the ARUNDELL family—a family which they all knew was influential in certain sections of English society.[35]

Whalley really did not have to say the *Catholic* "Arundell family" since the Arundells' religious standing was public knowledge.

Coleridge's summation was the longest address ever given to an English jury, lasting thirty-seven days. It was an incredibly thorough review of the damning evidence that the Tichborne family's legal team had assembled. It was not enough for Coleridge that the prima facie evidence and testimony should be overwhelmingly successful in exposing the Orton's imposture. Coleridge was not a flashy speaker, but he was an authoritative one. Fellow barrister Sergeant Ballantyne once remarked that the future lord chief justice "never could deliver a charge without also preaching a sermon."[36]

We can see this kind of fervor in one his daring arguments at this point in the trial, however, as he in effect accused Tichborne's attorneys of bad faith: "They ought not," he asserted, to "defend persons of whom they have a suspicion of being or whom they know to be, guilty of a crime of which they are accused." These attorneys "make themselves accomplices of the guilt of the person whom they so represent." So much for the decorum and gentlemanly regard the profession had labored to maintain. Two of the attorneys he attacked were especially indignant that he had not told them in advance what he was going to say so that they would have been sure to be present to hear it directly from him. Coleridge would not apologize for his remarks.[37] Such was the chaos the claimant continued to foster.

Coleridge, however, was not above surprising the court with a piece of material evidence that he had just received from Australia that had not been available earlier during his cross-examination of Orton. It was Orton's notebook, clearly in his handwriting, with revealing entries of varying degrees of literacy and revelation. One page appeared to be Orton's practicing his various names, aliases, and—"some day I hope"— his future title. Thus we read "Thomas Castro, Wagga Wagga," one of his earlier aliases, as well as "Roger Charles Tichborne, Tichborne Hall, Surrey" (although the Tichbornes lived in Hampshire), "Roger Charles Tichborne, Bart." It included the exact date of Roger Tichborne's arrival in Hobart Town before he boarded the ill-fated ship as well as the address in London of Mary Ann Loder, Orton's early sweetheart who identified him in court as *her* Orton.

The journal also contained what became a virtual meme of the imposter's style, a paragraph he oft repeated, not realizing his Cockney pidgin was self-incriminating: "Some men has plenty money and no brains, and some men has plenty brains and no money. Surely men with plenty money and no brains were made for men with plenty brains and no money."[38]

Like so much of what Orton with his "plenty brains" did, this remarkable passage was plagiarized from a villain's speech in *Aurora Floyd* (1863), one of a number of bestselling sensation novels written by Mary Elizabeth Braddon, and a sequel to her bestselling novel about bigamy and murder, *Mrs. Audley's Secret* (1862). Lord Maugham's analysis of the Tichborne case concluded that Orton's version was "perhaps an improvement" of the standard English of the novelist's original speech: "I should think fellows with plenty of money and no brains must have been invented for the good of fellows who have plenty of brains and no money, and that is how we contrive to keep our equilibrium in the universal see-saw."[39] One thing Orton did do well was not ape the language of the aristocrats whose treasury he wished to loot: his followers were

12. The Twenty-Six-Stone Claimant... 139

not so big on keeping their "equilibrium in the universal see-saw," as witnessed by their heckling and "rushing" at the opposing attorneys as they left court after a particularly embarrassing session for Orton.

Coleridge concluded his summation after twenty-five sittings at court of the first trial by quoting Chidioch's "Elegy," in which the young Tichborne, about to be executed in the sixteenth century, asserts in the last stanza of his only famous poem the inevitable bathos of the situation:

> I sought my death and found it in my womb,
> I looked for life and saw it was a shade,
> I trod the earth and knew it was my tomb,
> And now I die, and now I was but made;
> My glass is full, and now my glass is run,
> And now I live, and now my life is done.

Coleridge said the poem was so good that it was attributed for many years to Sir Walter Raleigh. This Tichborne had an "melancholy" and "ill-starred life" but it was the "life of an affectionate, perhaps ill-educated, but still honorable, kindly, warm-hearted, interesting person."[40] Even allowing for the lawyer's natural hyperbole for his clients, Coleridge wanted to show that misfortune came to both Tichbornes, but that the jury had in its decision to come "the hopes of a great and ancient house ... centered in the little child," the real Tichborne heir.[41]

The jury really determined the end of the first trial, ironically without issuing a final verdict. After Coleridge's devastating oration, the foreman on March 20, 1872, the 102nd day (a British record) of the trial, announced that the jury required no "further evidence." They remarked pointedly about the tattoo evidence—Tichborne had one, Orton did not—and were ready to retire to reach a verdict.

Orton's attorneys scrambled for a way out from a sure "guilty" verdict if the jury retired to reach their verdict. Orton's lead attorneys considered two different strategies. Sergeant Ballantine suggested they should be "not-suited," that is, basically withdrawing their charge against the Tichborne family, hoping that without an official guilty verdict a subsequent prosecution would be avoided. Giffard preferred a "hostile verdict" that would lead to a new trial or appeal on the grounds of "errors of ruling" by the lord chief justice on "disputed points of evidence."[42] Lord Maugham stated in 1936 that he could find no record of how the two attorneys reached their final decision, but that Ballantine's views prevailed. Giffard agreed, but years later said he believed his would have been the better course.

Giffard's hindsight was clearly influenced by what in fact *did* happen. Ballantine asked the jury if their decision was based solely on the tattoo marks or on the "whole case." After retiring for only a half hour, the jury said their decision was based on all the evidence, not just the tattoo issue. Whereupon Ballantine announced that his client and his legal team elected to be "non-suited," what Lord Maugham called "a peculiar feature" of British law by which neither jury nor judge reach a verdict. It also meant Orton was responsible for all the Tichborne family's costs of defence.[43]

The lord chief justice, however, had other ideas. Since Orton had been guilty of "willful and corrupt perjury," he referred the case to the grand jury of the Central Criminal Court because of the preponderance of the evidence against the imposter. His bail was set at ten thousand pounds. Accordingly the grand jury dutifully charged him with perjury and forgery and instead of continuing to live at his posh digs at the Waterloo Hotel on Jermyn Street, he was taken to old Newgate Prison in his own brougham, complaining all the while that this business was very inconvenient for him. The crowd at Newgate apparently agreed, as his entrance there was accompanied by their cheers.[44]

Orton's case was soon transferred to the Court of Queen's Bench, with Kenealy heading a new defense team. Because forgery is a felony and perjury a misdemeanor, the Crown dropped the forgery charge because the same jury was not allowed to sit on the two different classes of charges at the same time. The current law prevented Orton from testifying at all, but all his statements from the first trial could—and were—used as evidence against him. He did not have to remain at Newgate, however, until the trial began sixth months later, because four gentlemen, including his stalwart defenders, the MPs Onslow and Whalley, gave their security for five thousand pounds that matched the imposter's own "recognizance" of five thousand pounds, even though he did not have sum of money like that on hand.[45]

Being free on bail seemed to increase the imposter's populist standing. Rallies from Manchester to Bradford drew thousands of Orton fanatics, most of them paying into his purse two to three shillings to see him. In some cities he gave multiple lectures—ten at Leeds, six in Birmingham, and so on across the land. He was greeted at the railway station as a hero and mobbed if he just popped out of his hotel.[46]

Because this was a "trial at Bar," three justices presided: Sir Alexander Cockburn, the lord chief justice of the Queen's Bench, and two other estimable judges, Mr. Justice Mellor and Mr. Justice Lush. Because the only weapon left in his arsenal was public opinion, the imposter spent all of his time agitating at rallies. He was often joined in reckless speech by his attorneys Onslow and Mellor, who were fined in court for contempt. Another one of his barristers was fined *and* imprisoned for three months. It is clear that the Crown would no longer be a relatively easy mark for this grafter, as it also ruled that unless Orton paid forty thousand pound in costs from his first trial, he could never sue for the ejectment of the Tichbornes again.⁴⁷ Of course this fanned the claimant's position that the trial was really about the "classes and the masses," that he was fighting "the power of wealth and position and political influence," possibly related to "a vast Jesuit conspiracy."⁴⁸

The list of Orton's perjuries numbered twenty-three: it included most of the obvious lies—that he was not Arthur Orton, that he had been an officer in the army, that he had seduced Lady Radcliffe (Miss Doughty), that he had not seen any of his own sisters before his first trial, and that he had never been in Wapping, his London home.⁴⁹ Both sides called even more witnesses in this second trial, the prosecution because they had witnesses "left over" from the early stoppage of the first trial, and the defense because, well, Kenealy was unhinged and thought that three hundred witnesses would sway the jury.

Kenealy pushed the misbegotten strategy of impugning the integrity of all of the Tichborne family as well as accusing the Crown's advisors of bribery and conspiracy.⁵⁰ Part of Kenealy's cunning was also to take advantage of what lay close to hand, so to speak, and that meant riding one of the waves of public discussion of the imposture of Roger Tichborne that often featured the medieval case of a relatively prosperous, sixteenth century French peasant, Martin Guerre, who deserted his well-off family. He returned after seven or eight years to reclaim his place in the family leadership now vacated by his dead father. This newly arrived Martin Guerre was in fact an imposter, burrowing his way into his wife's bed and his community's good graces, even if he could not speak the Basque dialect he was once fluent in.⁵¹ Kenealy commented on the Guerre imposter: "The imposter was perfectly acquainted with the facts of the real man's life, while the real man himself had forgotten them."⁵² This conclusion was actually ludicrous and untrue, as evident by the return of the real Martin Guerre. His wife eventually confessed that she had been mistaken, despite having had two children fathered by the imposter. The lord chief justice could not resist commenting that the French imposter actually had three trials, winning the first, almost winning the second when the real Martin Guerre appeared, and then being convicted in the third and sentenced to hang.

Michael Gilbert, author of one of the six major books about the Tichborne case, believes that the government and the Tichborne family did not pay enough attention to the pattern of "previous impostures" like Martin Guerre's, because almost all of them share the same characteristics of the claimant's campaign. Joseph Brown, queen's counselor, soon after the trial published "The Tichborne Case Compared with Previous Impostures of the Same Kind" (1874), which analyzed the pattern. The jury, Gilbert argues, might have had an even easier time if they had had copies of Brown's pamphlet.[53]

Kenealy wanted to demonstrate how Orton could in fact not be an imposter but was simply a Martin Guerre figure who has forgotten his earlier life. In his zeal to use the Martin Guerre story Kenealy missed—or believed he could finesse—the real upshot of the matter: the Martin Guerre "claimant" was in fact the imposter and was soon executed.

Orton pursued a somewhat different strategy. He—or his literate secretary—wrote an extended plea for funds from the general public to get him out of jail on bail before the second trial began. The British public has always supported him, he wrote, and now was more important than ever, as the government intended "to punish me first and try me afterwards," all part of the "grossest conspiracy ever concocted." And "one word more," he wrote: no one has been able to prove that "Roger Tichborne" had been tattooed. He, the rightful claimant, certainly isn't.[54]

Kenealy was clearly frustrated that Orton could not take the stand. One can see desperation in any number of the speeches Kenealy made to the court. One instance is especially revealing. The lord chief justice did not wish for Kenealy to devote court time to establishing exactly *who* had interviewed various witnesses and taken their statements. Kenealy said it was important because obviously the questioners had manipulated the witnesses' statements. His lordship objected to this possibility, only to be told by Kenealy to stop insulting him. "What did you say?" asked the amazed lord chief justice. "I said," Kenealy replied, "I was perpetually receiving insults from your Lordship." "Do not use that language to me, because I will not bear it," replied the judge, who was then seconded by Mr. Justice Lush: "It is quite time that you should end this cross-examination which has wasted a good deal of time." And no doubt flooring everyone, a juryman then said: "And which has no effect on the mind of the jury whatever."[55]

The lord chief justice then stated, "During the seventeen years I have sat on this Bench, I have never had an unpleasant word from Counsel before I had the misfortune to be presiding on this trial." Kenealy refused to apologize. "Very well then," the judge said, "let us go on."[56] Since the chief justice and Kenealy had been reasonably friendly colleagues before the trial (Cockburn had sponsored his "silk," or status designation, and even was godfather to one of his children),[57] this exchange reveals a barrister beyond all reclamation.

Although Orton could not recall any of the classical authors he supposedly had studied at Stonyhurst—not to mention even the language they were written in—Kenealy was keen to have him testify instead about a comic opera, Samuel Arnold's *The Castle of Andalusia* (1782), that the real Roger Tichborne had acted in at Stonyhurst, as it provided more evidence of the decadent material the Jesuits really preferred the students to perform. The comic opera had been staged about fifty years earlier in Convent Garden and performed afterwards by numerous amateur theatrical troops, and concerned a bevy of dandies, damsels, and brigands consorting about the countryside singing such lines as these, clearly anticipating what happened to Roger Tichborne:

> The hardy sailor braves the ocean
> Fearless of the roaring wind,
> Throbs to leave his love behind.

One of the robbers notes, "A rich old fellow ... has lately come to reside in the castle on the skirts of the forest—what say you to plunder there?" But his comrade has a different idea: "I love to rob a fat priest." We don't know which if any of these lines were quoted in the courtroom, but their relevance to the Tichborne disappearance was no doubt suggestive. Kenealy wanted it on the record that the songs, "descriptive of the life of robbers, and containing language rather loose" were exactly what the "Jesuit fathers" wanted their students to hear.[58]

Exasperated to hear such lines read aloud in his court, the lord chief justice "asked what was the relevancy of all this?" Kenealy's reply was, "Such literature was a good preparation for a bush life,"[59] no doubt hoping that the jury would see that Orton was obviously no longer an upper-class Tichborne but was able to handle the Australian outback (like the Andalusian "skirts of the forest") with such specialized literary preparation.

An episode in the second trial was also of a piece with this strategy. Part of the depravity of Stonyhurst boys in particular and French men in general was their addiction to the novels of Paul de Kock (1793–1871), the Parisian chronicler of working- and middle-class life. Such novels, the imposter's solicitor reminded the court, were inevitably found in the knapsacks of French soldiers in the late Franco-Prussian War, not to mention Roger Tichborne's own bag before he left for France. They were manuals of "seduction made easy." When Orton's solicitor began to read extracts from de Kockian horrors, the lord chief justice interrupted him and said that he could continue tomorrow but that the courtroom would be closed to the ladies because the extracts were "indelicate and immoral."[60]

The next morning Kenealy read the damning excerpts from de Kock to an all-male audience. These excerpts, alas, were not printed in the *Times*, but later commentators retrieved this one salacious passage that Kenealy selected, no doubt because it featured a licentious nun:

> Frederick dared everything and Sister Anne soon surrendered herself to her lover without regret—without remorse.... She delivered herself up to his advances, she abandoned herself to love; she shared the burning ardor with which he was inflamed.[61]

The judge pointed out that these excerpts should have been from novels that Roger Tichborne had actually read, not just random passages chosen, no doubt, for their immorality. Of course, Kenealy could not prove Tichborne had actually read these passages. The judge confessed that he himself had Daniel Defoe's novels in his library, but that did not mean he read some of the coarser passages from his *Moll Flanders* (1722) about that titular amorous and profligate lady.

In the meantime, like all good con men, Orton knew how to raise money from the masses: Orton's supporters and free-lance speculators were asked to invest in "Tichborne Bonds" or the "Tichborne Estate Mortgage Debenture." Debentures are bonds backed by the good name or creditworthiness of the issuing party but not necessarily by any tangible collateral. Since Orton had no money, these bonds would be redeemable only when their hero came into his fortune. These were speculative instruments indeed. Besides those who were naturally gullible, many investors would have to believe that there was a Protestant ruling-class alliance with the Jesuits to deprive one man of an income of 10,000 pounds a year. (A person in the artisan class was considered lucky to receive a pension of ten pounds a year.)

Orton apparently appealed to those Protestants who wanted their claimant to have persevered despite Catholic knavery. Kenealy, for his part, expected the long tradition of English suspicion of the "sly, artful, Jesuitical school" of deception to win over the jury. What Roger Tichborne learned from the Jesuits of Stonyhurst was a character "of guile and deceit and cunning."[62] But his strategy failed for many reasons, including a change in the ruling-class acceptance of Catholicism.

The Tichborne trials represented a generational change at the highest levels of the British judiciary. Judge (Lord) Campbell just twenty years earlier had been at ease openly abetting witnesses against Newman in the Achilli trial. But the Tichborne family's first solicitor, John Duke Coleridge, who eventually also became lord chief justice, included both Newman and John Keble (who in the end did not defect to Rome) as his friends at Oxford. Coleridge in many ways was as close to Catholicism as a High Church Anglican could get. His brother, Henry James

12. The Twenty-Six-Stone Claimant... 145

Coleridge, whose name the imposter took in vain, had been received into the Catholic Church by Newman and was a Jesuit priest who edited the most prestigious Catholic journal in England, *The Month*.

And although Orton could rally thousands of supporters, trial chronicler J.B. Atlay finds his conclusion, in part, among the classics:

> The possibility of the Claimant having been Roger Tichborne has long been abandoned by all sane persons, but there are some who still maintain he was an illegitimate member of the Tichborne family. Of this theory, no proof has ever been adduced and the facts elicited at the two trials render the identity of the Claimant with Arthur Orton as clear as a proposition in Euclid.[63]

After the second criminal trial of 188 days, Kenealy's comment on the Lord Chief Justice Cockburn's summation of the case proved prophetic and for him unusually accurate: "Like the venom of the cobra, it means death." The deliberation by the jury to reach a verdict of guilty was astonishingly brief—just thirty minutes after Cockburn told them that their verdict would be welcomed favorably by everyone except "fanatics and fools." The jury had left the court to deliberate only after convincing their foreman that his plan to vote immediately while still in the jury box would look bad.[64] Perhaps they still had bad memories of the court's robing room, where they were forced to view the imposter's regressive or retractable penis (look it up!) because Roger Tichborne's nickname in the military among his unsympathetic mates was "Little Cock."[65] Whatever similarities in appearance there might have been, did not, however, impress the jury.

As the junior or *puisne* judge, Justice Mellor repeated the jury's verdict of "guilty on all counts," but only after he blasted the motives and behavior of the accused. Mellor's ire was greatest when he discussed Orton's lies about Lady Radcliffe's pregnancy, designating it as almost worse than his deception of Lady Doughty. Orton received two terms of seven years each to run consecutively, the maximum, Mellor said with frustration, allowed by the law. When the first sentence of seven years ran out, the House of Lords ruled in 1881 that while perjury was perjury, Orton had committed it in two distinct contexts (in his first Chancery hearing and in his first libel trial) and therefore deserved separate sentences of seven years each.[66]

Orton never spoke a word aloud during this record-breaking criminal trial of 188 days. When he specifically requested to be allowed to say a few words after the verdict was announced, the lord chief justice refused.[67]

With the collapse of the Tichborne imposter's case, Stonyhurst College returned to safer ground. Catholic families would have no fear in sending their sons to be educated there. But perhaps more to the point, at least some non–Catholics (either in court or out) could no longer assume that Catholic values meant "perverted" values.

Orton was taken to Newgate, while the streets were lined with thousands of supporters, and was eventually transferred to Dartmoor Prison, where later the public learned that he did not pick oakum, a typical prisoner's task involving untwisting old strands of rope, because his fingers were "too delicate," according to one account. The imposter would reply only when addressed as "Tichborne." The crowds that gathered to see him transported to jail no doubt knew what to call him, but the police presence was more than sufficient to deter any untoward demonstrations of support or censure.

Kenealy was disbarred as a result of his verbal shenanigans, not the least of which was calling 300 witnesses during the second trial, many of whom provided dubious, ludicrous, and offered unsubstantiated testimonies of support for Orton's claim. Kenealy's hysterical denunciation of the proceedings encouraged minor rioting among the spectators in the streets near the court as well, with both Crown counselors and jurors being rushed by Orton's fanatical supporters. Kenealy kept up his crusade for the claimant for years, even during a brief stint as a member of Parliament, although he was soon expelled from that body as well. As for Dartmoor Prison, he said: "To this fearful place, the Jesuits who are now our masters have sent Roger Tichborne."[68]

Orton served a somewhat reduced sentence of ten and half years for good behavior. Towards the end of his years in jail, he sold a confession of his imposture to a London newspaper, then characteristically recanted it. He died on April Fool's Day (All Fool's Day in the UK) in 1898: his coffin, with a plaque inscribed with the name "Sir Roger Charles Doughty Tichborne," was placed in an unmarked pauper's grave (#1470/2A) in Willesden Land Cemetery, now called Paddington Old Cemetery. The location of his grave is still unmarked, except for a small generic sectional sign, "A2." Five thousand people attended the funeral. The man of whom Coleridge said there was never "a cleverer and more slippery scoundrel I have had to do with in my life" was finally gone.[69]

What sets this extraordinary imposture apart even from the other scandals in this book is its staying power. A hundred and twenty-five years of corroboration and denial have now gone by. Perhaps because of the sheer enormity of the claimant or even as a result of his widespread working-class support, the Tichborne case has generated more attention than any of the other trials in this book, with at least six full-length studies about it. (See books by Douglas Woodruff, Michael Gilbert, Geddes MacGregor, Robyn Annear, Lord Maugham, and Rohan McWilliam.) All

Potter's Field, Section 2A, in the former Willesden Land Cemetery, now called Paddington Old Cemetery, the unmarked burial zone of Arthur Orton, the "Tichborne Imposter" (photograph by the author).

these books reveal even more unseemly details about this imposter, who seems to have led at least three unlikely, shifty and probably criminal lives even before claiming to be Roger Tichborne.

Did anyone ever believe the claimant? A simple guide to any book's point-of-view is whether the author calls Orton a claimant or an imposter. Woodruff has probably done the most exhaustive research, but his insistence that Orton's identity is still "doubtful" flies in the face of so much of the evidence against Orton, especially Orton's ignorance of all things Stonyhurst and his pathetic mishandling of coaching from Lady Doughty and Bogle, not to mention hiring local people to tell him about the Tichborne family, that I weep at the second clause of Woodruff's conclusion: the first jury accurately said that the claimant was not Roger Tichborne, but the second jury that said he was Orton "was much more doubtful." Really? Not at all. In the end, students of this trial should also read the daily reports on the trials in the *London Times* and "The Tichborne Trial," in *Famous Trials of the Century* (1899), the trial narrative recorded with comments written by the indefatigable barrister-at-law, J.B. Atley.

Even an insatiable pursuit of more information will come up against the wall that is the nine volumes of Kenealy's *The Trial at Bar of Sir Roger Tichborne* (1875–1880): although much of it is transcript from the trials, his often deranged commentary puts one in mind of Mary McCarthy's comment on her rival Lillian Hellman during the Dick Cavett television show in 1979: "Every word [she] writes is a lie, including 'and' and 'the.'" In the end, Kenealy would try anything to win because, he believed, he had already lost a sure victory when Lady Tichborne had died: "Had Lady Tichborne lived and gone into witness-box and swore that this was her son, which of the family would have dared to confront her, and what jury would have dared to convict him? What could deceive a mother's instinct?" He concluded this opening statement in the perjury trial with this appeal to the jury. There was "some applause, which was checked by the Court."[70]

The fascinating, somewhat parallel, story of the rich, sixteenth century French peasant and his—for a time—successful imposter, is the subject of an excellent novella, *The Wife of Martin Guerre* (1941), by the Palo Alto, California, poet and novelist Janet Lewis, who included the story in her series of "novels of circumstantial evidence." Even during the Tichborne trial, the name of Martin Guerre was often a topic of comparison. Kenealy bizarrely thought that the eventual exposure and execution of Martin Guerre's imposter somehow supported his client's veracity.

But perhaps we need to realize that even the great comic writers Gilbert and Sullivan wrote their first opera while the court was still sitting. Their very first public co-production, *Trial by Jury* (1875), was inspired by the trial, although their subject matter concerns a breach of promise suit by a spurned lady, related very vaguely to the real Roger Tichborne's pathetic promise to Lady Radcliffe. Sullivan himself often sat with Chief Justice Alexander Cockburn at the judge's bench during the trial. Sullivan's brother then played a "Learned Judge" made up to resemble Cockburn. Cockburn returned the favor by attending a performance, but thought the operetta was in danger of encouraging disrespect for British justice. He had a point: at one point in dress rehearsal all the members of the jury/chorus made themselves up to resemble Orton's barrister, Kenealy. In the operetta the Learned Judge decides to marry the plaintiff himself, having long jettisoned the "elderly, ugly daughter" of a rich attorney.

The unlikely figure of Bogle, the Black servant once faithful to the family who casts his lot with the imposter, has also attracted spirited attention. Jorge Luis Borges, the great Argentine fantasist, wrote a short story, *The Improbable Imposter Tom Castro*, in which Bogle is *not simply* a former servant who *knew* Roger Tichborne but a conniver who engineers Orton's transformation into him. And when Borges's story finally reached the screen in 1998 as *The Tichborne Claimant*, directed by David Yates, its Bogle initially does think Orton *is* Tichborne, but no matter, because he soon conspires with him to win the case and split the inheritance.

Mark Twain, a writer who surely knew a humbug when he met one, visited Wagga-Wagga many years after the trials, where he was reminded that he had in years past actually attended a reception for the claimant, as Twain called him in his travel book, *Following the Equator* (1897). During the second trial, Twain attended a reception in Orton's honor, in "sumptuous quarters provided him from the purses of his adherents and well-wishers" with "twenty-five gentlemen, ... educated men, men moving in good society, none of them commonplace, some of them were men of distinction, none of them were obscurities." These "cordial friends and admirers" all addressed him as "Sir Roger." Twain believed it was only because Orton's tale was so preposterous that people believed it, as these fine gentlemen demonstrated: "No one withheld the title, all turned it from the tongue with unction, and as if it tasted good."[71]

Although it has proven impossible to trace a copy of the libretto, I am sure that the Neapolitan opera *Roger di Ticciborni*, appearing soon after the trial and boasting a love triangle among Roger di Ticciborni, Arturo Orton, and Katarina Doughty, would make time travel to the 1870s very desirable.

As for poor Roger Tichborne, who would really never return, the *London Times* was in the end reasonably convinced that he was in fact buried on Sydney Island in the South Pacific, now known as Manra Island, by an itinerant English sailor who worked in the *beche de mer* or sea cucumber industry and had met the seriously ill survivor of a shipwreck who said he was Roger Tichborne.[72] Today the island, part of the Phoenix Island Protected Area of the Republic of Kiribati, has no inhabitants.

Details of the Litigation: Tichborne v. Tichborne

Court of Chancery

Presiding: Mr. Charles Roupell

Hearing: Roger Tichborne [Arthur Orton] filed two bills against the trustees of the Tichborne and Doughty estates for recovery of all rents and profits of the estates as well as the estates themselves.

For Tichborne [Arthur Orton]:	For the Tichborne and Doughty
Sergeant Ballantine	*Estates*: Mr. Chapman Barber, Equity Bar

Decision: Vice-Chancellor could not settle the case and referred it to Court of Common Pleas.

Tichborne v. Lushington, *1871–72*

Common Pleas Division

Presiding: Lord Chief Justice William Bovill

Suit: Action of ejectment against Col. Lushington of Tichborne House

For Tichborne [Arthur Orton]:	For Lushington:
Serjeant William Ballantine, QC	John Duke Coleridge, Attorney General
Hardinge Giffard, QC	Henry Hawkins, QC [Baron Brampton]
Mr. Pollard	Sir George Honeyman
Francis Jeune	Mr. Chapman Barber, Equity Bar
Mr. W.B. Rose	Charles Bowen

Verdict: Plaintiff chose to be "non-suited" and withdrew complaint.

Regina v. Tom Castro, *1873–74*

Queen's Bench

Presiding: Lord Chief Justice (Alexander) Cockburn, Mr. Justice Mellor, and Mr. Justice Lush

Charge: Perjury

For the Queen: *For Defendant Tom Castro*
                                         [Arthur Orton]:

Henry Hawkins, QC   E.V. Kenealy, QC
Serjeant Parry   Mr. Patrick McMahon, MP
Mr. Chapman Barber   Mr. Cooper Wyld
J. C. Mathew
Charles Bowen

Verdict: Arthur Orton, guilty of perjury.

Sentence: Two terms of seven years, to run consecutively.

Regina v. Tom Castro, *1879–81*

Court of Appeal

Presiding: The Lord Chancellor (Lord Selborne), 1879–80; with Lord Blackburn and Lord Weldon, 1881.

Appeal: "Writ of error challenging the validity of consecutive sentences."

For Plaintiff Arthur Orton: *For the Crown*:
Judah Benjamin, Q. C.   Solicitor General Hardinge Giffard

Verdict: Writ denied because perjury had occurred twice, first in Chancery and then in the first trial; verdict affirmed by the House of Lords.

13

The Catholic Lord and the Protestant Vicar in the Valley of Martyrs and Queens
The Duke of Norfolk v. Arbuthnot, 1879

> Side by side, their faces blurred,
> The earl and countess lie in stone,
> Their proper habits vaguely shown
> As jointed armour, stiffened pleat,
> And that faint hint of the absurd—
> The little dogs under their feet.
> —from Philip Larkin,
> "An Arundel Tomb" (1956)

Visitors to the lovely village of Arundel, about sixty miles slightly southwest of London, encounter a phenomenon very atypical of British villages. If they wish to visit the Anglican parish church of St. Nicholas, they enter the church through the main doors at the eastern end of the building on the main thoroughfare of the village; if they wish to visit the Catholic Fitzalan Chapel at the western end of the church, they must enter from the grounds of the Duke of Norfolk's Arundel Castle.

The Fitzalan Chapel, originally called the Collegiate Church of the Blessed Trinity, with its south-facing, fourteenth century window with Early English stone tracery, is clearly of the same style as the church itself. Standing before the chapel on the castle grounds, you would readily assume that you are facing a single church with a small roof cross. In fact, the chapel before you occupies about forty percent of the entire (combined) structure's square footage: it is physically but not legally a part of the church.

13. The Catholic Lord and the Protestant Vicar... 153

Arundel Castle, Arundel, residence of the dukes of Norfolk, from publicity photograph, c. 1980 (author's collection).

If you were ever skeptical of the idea of a religiously divided church, you would say that this Fitzalan Chapel you enter from the castle grounds was actually the chancel of the church, with its own traditional Lady Chapel, usually a private chapel erected or subsidized as a chantry or private space of worship for the local lord or benefactor, and a sacristy. But these three chambers have always remained Roman Catholic and independent, both the symbol and the reality of the Norfolks' lasting grasp on their ancestral religion, and serving to this day—as they have for generations—as their burial place. Eamon Duffy's remarkable study, *The Striping of the Altars* (1992), argues that because "building and endowing chantry foundations" was one way of counteracting the pressure to conform to the new religion of the land, only wealthy individuals, families, and guilds could own these chapels and altars. They "lavished money on long-term mortuary provisions" not only to celebrate their dead but also to protect the living.[1] A "chantry" was a kind of insurance policy by means of an investment to pay for priests to pray/chant/sing for the souls of the lord's family.

The original Collegiate Church was founded by Richard, Earl of Arundel and Surrey, the Norfolks' ancestor, under license from Richard II. It was once called the Arundel Priory because it was the spiritual descendent of an eleventh century Benedictine priory, but in organizational terms it was a "college," or order of secular canons, endowed by a lord for the purpose—as was then common—to have mass and prayers said for him and his family. Establishing such a college was similar to another aristocratic act of the era, endowing a Lady Chapel dedicated to the Virgin Mary. In both instances, the architectural structures were either *added on* or constructed *as part of* the fabric of a church or cathedral. They were regarded in law as the property of the lord who endowed them and were not open to the parish laity.[2]

During the Reformation both the Collegiate Church and the Lady Chapel were confiscated by Henry VIII in 1544 when the priory was dissolved, in keeping with the royal "logic" of the times, i.e., that seizing property was a way to make money for the crown and for the loyal "greater and lesser lords of the land," as Hilaire Belloc characterized the other beneficiaries of Henry's fiat.[3]

The king therefore granted both the collegiate church and the parish church back to Henry Fitzalan, the twelfth Earl of Arundel, the same year. In keeping with tradition, both had their own choirs, emphasizing their separate governance.[4]

Fifty years later the twelfth earl's descendants' control of the property was "forfeited by attainder" to Queen Elizabeth I in 1595 in consequence of her anti–Roman Catholic campaign, but "regranted" to Thomas Howard, Earl of Arundel, by the Catholic King James VI of Scotland (James I of England) in 1604 after Queen Elizabeth died in 1603. King Charles, after coming to the throne in 1625, eventually solidified the control of the property by making it "in tail male" in 1628 to the Earl of Arundel, and therefore securing it for the earl's male descendants for all time.[5]

These ownership maneuvers reflected Henry VIII's financial needs (wars with Scotland and France, for example) and Queen Elizabeth's idiosyncratic preferences rather than sheer religious conviction, as scholars have estimated that nearly two-thirds of the confiscated properties were sold, mostly to rich landlords or aristocratic cronies. As for the ten thousand monks, canons, friars, and nuns that inhabited these properties in 1536 when the Dissolution of the Monasteries act was passed, by 1541 there were no longer any of them, or, at least, no publicly professed ones, since select brave souls went into hiding or were tortured and/or executed.

The intriguing tomb of Richard FitzAlan, the 10th Earl of Arundel, who died in 1376, and his wife Eleanor of Lancaster, were celebrated in the evocative poem by Philip Larkin quoted at the head of this chapter. Their tomb was also the victim of the dissolution of the monasteries, since it was banished from the Lewes Priory, where it had been for

13. The Catholic Lord and the Protestant Vicar... 155

two centuries, to Chichester Cathedral, when the Lewes Priory was dissolved in 1537. Eleanor's right hand rests on his right hand, her feet, like his, lightly touch a sleeping dog. These distant relatives of the Norfolk line would have had better luck if they had managed to find their rest in the Fitzalan Chapel, their family's namesake. King Henry VIII was responsible, in a sense, for one of Larkin's concluding lines about them: "Time has transfigured them into Untruth, and only poetry has rescued them." (The poem was read at Larkin's own memorial service.)

Arundel Castle, in the Arun River Valley in West Sussex, continued to be the ancestral seat of the dukes of Norfolk, who with a few notable exceptions kept their faith—if not their lives—throughout the most difficult times of the Reformation. They were the direct descendants of the Howards, two of whom—the cousins Lady Anne Boleyn and Catherine Howard—were wives of Henry VIII and subsequently beheaded. Anne Boleyn's posthumous consolation (assuming she had one) was that she was the mother of the future queen, Elizabeth I. The two female Howards generated a long and continuous line from Sir John Howard, the first Duke of Norfolk, despite the childlessness of Queen Elizabeth and Catherine Howard.

During and after Elizabeth's reign, the Howards once again suffered greatly. Both the fourth Duke of Norfolk and his father, the Earl of Surrey, were beheaded; the fourth duke's son, Philip Howard, died in the Tower but was subsequently canonized by the Roman Catholic Church. Another Howard was beheaded at the end of the seventeenth century during the so-called Popish Plot of Titus Oates. Two Howards became cardinals, one in the seventeenth century and the other at the end of the nineteenth century, while two other Howards in the same eras converted to Protestantism.

Among the defining features of the Fitzalan Chapel was "iron lattice-work or grille" that filled the entire "chancel arch" (as it would normally be called), separating the two sections of the church; it had been in place since the construction of the building in the late fourteenth century. The grill included a wooden door, the key to which was in the hands of the duke's staff who therefore controlled access to the Fitzalan Chapel. In 1872 Gilbert Scott restored the church and positioned the altar and reredos (altar screens or decorations) near the grill work, creating the sanctuary as the space between the north and south transepts. In the accompanying illustration the arrow marks the approximate location of the original wooden door, located to the right of the newly placed altar.[6]

Perhaps out of pique, perhaps simply as an exercise of his ducal prerogatives of ownership in the face (or rather the back) of the new altar,

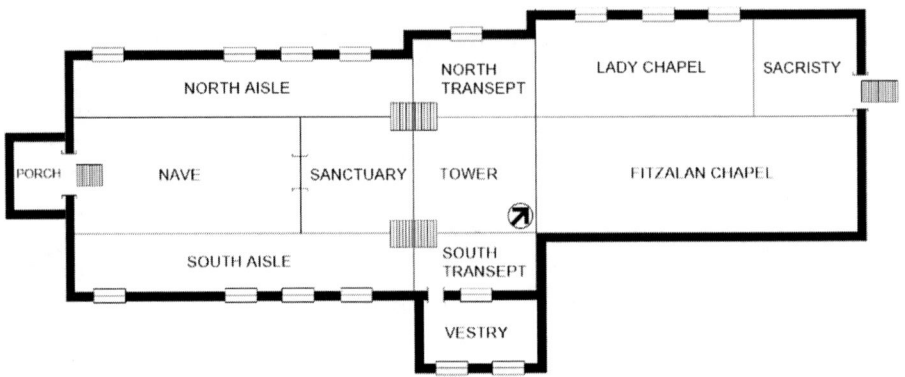

St. Nicholas Church and Fitzalan Chapel, with arrow marking location of original doorway, currently locked, next to the high altar of the parish church (designed by Emily Taylor).

the fifteenth Duke of Norfolk constructed the brick wall on the chapel side of the grill two years later, in 1874. Four years later, George Arbuthnot, the vicar of St. Nicolas Church, precipitated one of the most dramatic Victorian challenges to a divided church by "tearing" down the wall, what the editor of the *Sussex Archaeological Collections* described as "knocking a hole in the brick wall."[7] Lord Coleridge, who was the judge in the case, wrote in his private letters, "The Vicar of Arundel had pulled down and destroyed the wall."[8] Regardless of the severity of his blows, he certainly removed a number of bricks in a symbolic act of asserting his right to enter the chapel that he claimed as the chancel of his parish church. The spectacle of an Anglican minister literally undermining an ancient church barrier no doubt accounted for the numerous articles about the scandal that appeared in the *London Times* in 1878–79.

Very soon after the incursion in the brick wall, the Duke of Norfolk initiated an action of trespass against Arbuthnot in the Common Pleas Division before Lord Chief Justice John Duke Coleridge, who heard the case without a jury. The duke claimed, Arbuthnot's lead attorney stated, that he had a right to "treat" the Fitzalan Chapel "as if it were a room in Arundel Castle."[9] For his part, Arbuthnot asserted that the chapel was in fact a chancel of the parish church and that he and his parishioners were being denied access to their own building and were also deprived of the light and air that should pass from the chapel to the sanctuary.

The trial itself lasted less than a week in March 1879, although a substantial amount of time had been spent earlier by both sides and the judge in researching the convoluted political history of the church buildings and their architectural heritage. The *London Times* asserted

St. Nicholas Church, Arundel, interior view of metal and glass walls separating the church from the Fitzalan Chapel, point-of-view of arrow in the previous illustration (photograph by the author).

that the action raised "a question which it was understood had never before been submitted to judicial decision"[10] (although we know from chapter 3, about Mapledurham, that this assertion was simply not true). Chief Justice Coleridge spent almost six weeks deliberating upon the case, announcing his ruling on May 19.

The brief trial itself was marked by a number of revelations, most of which supported the duke's ownership of the property but called into question the quality of his family's stewardship of the chapel. On a number of occasions, the chapel fell into disrepair, a roof caved in, and it was even used as a storehouse for lumber. Arbuthnot's attorneys argued that the Fitzalan Chapel was therefore not used for religious services and in fact had been neglected by the duke. The chapel was architecturally the chancel of St. Nicholas parish church, and the entire building had been dedicated to the public service at one time. The duke's assertion of "his right to the freehold" came only when Gilbert Scott renovated the church in 1872.

Arbuthnot's witnesses were primarily elderly members of the Arundel parish, with one exception: architect William Butterfield, whom Arbuthnot regarded as his ace in the hole. Butterfield testified, "There was nothing in the church or chancel which architecturally suggested that the Fitzalan Chapel was anything else but the chancel." The iron grill was very unusual only because of its "openness." He acknowledged the presence of an altar in the south transept *before* Scott's restoration moved it to the position in front of the grill, but suggested that it could have been historically one of a number of altars.[11] Years later, Coleridge acknowledged that he did not accept Butterfield's argument that this was a "parochial" altar, not a "high" altar, which would reserve the latter term for the supposed chancel of the parish church that was—in Butterfield's view—Norfolk's chapel. Butterfield was a very great church architect but not a very good church historian.

Although Butterfield would have expected his testimony to carry the day for the vicar, he was actually about to enter a verbal duel with another formidable "witness" (in effect): the historian Edward A. Freeman—who was never called by the duke, but whose widely published research on divided churches had been so thorough and well-circulated among the intellectual aristocracy that he could say after the trial concluded, "with perfect confidence that the claim made by the Duke of Norfolk was in strict analogy with a great number of undoubted historical examples" that he had discussed in numerous essays, especially those published for the antiquarian and church history community.

His essay about a case similar to the Fitzalan Chapel was nonetheless entered into the evidence for the duke. In this definitive essay for the *Archaeological Journal* in 1880, Freeman surveyed numerous examples of divided churches across the land, pointing out that when any given monastery was dissolved, its church often became disused and was torn down (illegally) or "allowed to fall into ruin by [the] lay rectors," giving the parish church the reality as well as the appearance of single standing building. Ironically, the same status was also achieved by other parishes in a remarkable reversal of the usual pattern: the parish church was instead allowed to decay, and the parishioners used the abbey church as their new parish church. Only rarely, as in the idiosyncratic case of the church of Dunster at Minehead (Somerset), did the dispute between monastic and parish churches come out in the open, as the two churches needed arbitration in 1498 and their dispute was settled in a kind of treaty of coexistence, with two distinct choirs in place.[12] (St. Helens Bishopsgate in London had a similar resolution—see chapter 17, below.)

Although the vicar's lawyers tried to prevent the parallel with Arundel by blocking the placement into evidence of another Freeman essay that had appeared in 1856 in the proceedings of the Somersetshire Archaeological and Natural History Society about the Dunster parallel, they were not successful. The Arundel case for Freeman simply

13. The Catholic Lord and the Protestant Vicar... 159

recapitulated all of his numerous other examples of divided churches, except of course the Duke of Norfolk's family never ultimately lost their property rights in the collegiate church that became the Fitzalan Chapel.

Studies of divided churches were only a small part of Freeman's extensive research and teaching interests at Oxford University, which he casually supplemented with activism against the Ottoman Empire, a political radicalism he shared with his tutee (and eventual son-in-law), Arthur Evans, who went on to discover and excavate the Palace of Knossos in Crete in 1894, just two years after Freeman died.

Given his credentials and reputation it is easy to see why Freeman had been so sure about the Arundel case. He had "looked specially to this class of churches for five and twenty years and more; perhaps they have a special charm for me, because nobody seemed to understand them." And although he had "no satisfaction" in seeing a part of a church in private hands, it was plain, he said, that two acts of the parliaments of Henry VIII and Edward VI permitted "the property of colleges and chantries" to "pass into lay hands." Freeman offered one minor and one major addendum to his judgment: he believed the use of "Fitzalan" as the title of the chapel had no historical support, although a number of obituaries of deceased dukes of Norfolk indicated that it was in use—at least possibly—for centuries. But more emphatically, Freeman objected to architect Gilbert Scott's movement of the altar from the south transept to the position "under the central tower," i.e., up against the Duke of Norfolk's partitioning wall. This "so-called restoration ... as usual destroys the history of the building" and has led to the "confusion of the whole story" in the trial.[13] If Freeman had testified in these words at the trial itself, the vicar's case would have collapsed even sooner than it did, as the movement of the altar during the restoration seemed to serve rhetorical, not religious, grounds for the vicar.

Butterfield's testimony stressed that the parish church had a "lesser altar" in the south transept, to be sure, but "it was only suitable for a very small congregation," with their access to the "great altar in the chancel of a collegiate church like Arundel" not always at their ready command.[14]

This revealing testimony from Butterfield was followed by a number of local men, but three of these witnesses are of particular interest, as they focused on the kinds of religious services performed and who controlled the door to the grill. Richard Holmes was not only a churchwarden (and therefore a Protestant) but also the town clerk, the solicitor of Arundel village, and even the local solicitor for the Duke of Norfolk. William Harwood was a woodcutter. Both men testified to attending the funeral services of the last four dukes as well as other funerals which resulted in interments in the Fitzalan Chapel. A third witness, Henry

Hartnell, had been a choir member of the church. He distinctly remembered the funeral of Canon Tierney, the twelfth duke's private Catholic priest, who was buried in the Fitzalan Chapel after a service therein at which the Protestant vicar of Arundel was not present. The duke's solicitor stated that these testimonies proved the chapel was private property because "it would have been illegal for a burial to be made in consecrated grounds without an [Anglican] service" in the parish church.[15]

In the following days, Chief Justice Coleridge may have tipped his hand when he noted that when Arbuthnot's witnesses observed a Church of England service being performed, that act "did not prove much." It "was more important to show the absence of [Anglican] services." Furthermore, Coleridge noted, "for Roman Catholics to be buried with another service besides their own was not considered by them humiliating. It was not, for instance, like receiving the Sacrament at the hands of one who was not a priest."[16]

Whether Arbuthnot's attorneys realized it or not, their case had finally collapsed once Coleridge began to review the movement of the coffin during the funeral services of the dukes. Arbuthnot's lawyer asked why the dukes "should have undergone what must have been to them the humiliation of the bodies being carried through the chancel into the chapel and buried with the rites of another Church." Coleridge understood the political necessities of the dukes of Norfolk all too well: the bodies were usually taken into the church first, at which point "the clergyman could only read the services of the Church of England." It did not mean, however, the end of their funeral, since the procession would then usually pass into the chapel for interment.[17] Going "direct to the chapel from the castle" would be possible but not politically or even socially prudent.

Coleridge's decision followed closely the assertion of the duke that the chapel had always been private property, trumping any architectural verities. "Anyone who looks at the Arundel Church would," Coleridge concluded, "simply from what meets his eye, come to the same conclusion as Mr. Butterfield. It does not need his great authority to say that the general look of the building is in favor of the defendant" Arbuthnot. But the "most important question" is "the property in the disputed building," and in that regard there remained only one decision: "That an aisle or a chancel under the same roof with and open to the rest of a church may be shown by evidence to be the property of a private person, is too clear for argument."[18]

The judge noted the irony that the "utter neglect of this beautiful and interesting" chapel in fact supported "the universal belief that it was in fact ducal property," since "access to it which was denied to the vicar and parishioners, was freely granted to the owls and bats." He also observed that the harsh treatment of Roman Catholics throughout the history of the chapel—"a disgrace to a civilized country"—was not sufficient for the parish to usurp the property should they ever have been so inclined.[19]

Coleridge concluded that perhaps the Duke of Norfolk might have reacted differently had he been "approached in a different spirit," suggesting that when Arbuthnot breached the brick wall the duke was moved to assert his right of ownership. Nevertheless, Coleridge found Arbuthnot guilty of the act of trespass and fined him "40 shillings damages and costs." Stubborn to a fault, Arbuthnot's attempt to raise funds for an appeal seemed to fail like a bad kickstarter campaign, with only thirty pounds at first raised to pay for an appeal that would cost five hundred pounds.[20] But he persevered and eventually appealed the decision to the three justices of the Court of Appeals who also gave their "judgment unanimously for the Duke of Norfolk."[21]

Justice Coleridge had nonetheless hoped that perhaps some future accommodation might be organized. In fact, the iron grill remains in place today, although light may pass easily through the glass wall erected next it. Seven years later, in 1886, the fifteenth Duke of Norfolk had completed repairs to the Fitzalan Chapel and on the occasion of the burial of his mother began a policy of open public masses.[22] Perhaps more grandly, in 1977, more than 400 years after the grill was locked, Prince Charles attended an ecumenical service that breached the arch symbolically if not actually.

Coleridge clearly signaled during the trial that the funerals of the dukes of Norfolk revealed the true state of affairs in a divided church. If we look at three of the sixteen burials of Norfolk family members from 1691 to 1880,[23] these burials in the nineteenth century of the twelfth and fourteenth dukes of Norfolk, both Roman Catholics, and the eleventh and thirteenth, Protestant converts, we will see how the Howards successfully maintained a kind of dual allegiance to the Anglican Church as well as to their Roman Catholicism, acting out—in death, as it were—the same political maneuvering their family had managed since the Reformation.

The funerals of these dukes of Norfolk would satisfy every expectation that the outward sign of a rich and holy life was a spectacular public and religious funeral. The twelfth duke, who was one of the first hereditary Catholic lords to regain his seat in the House of Lords after the passage of the Roman Catholic Relief Bill in 1829, died in 1842. His funeral procession, consisting of numerous carriages, began at Norfolk House in St. James's Square, London, and traveled to the parish church of Arundel, whereupon what only could be described as a "double" service was held, since, as the obituary in the *Gentleman's Magazine* pointed out, the Fitzalan Collegiate Chapel was "annexed to the church of Arundel."[24]

The initial Anglican ceremony was held in the parish church chancel, the space between the north and south transepts. "That part preceding the interment being concluded," the mourners resumed their places in the aristocratic precession and "proceeded with the body" to the Fitzalan Chapel, "where the remainder of the service was performed as soon as the body was deposited in the grave."[25]

This "double" service indicates that the parish church and chapel, while regarded as separate entities, were in fact accessible to each other, at least for the duration of this service. The obituary said "no one" was "more attached to his own religious principles [Roman Catholicism]" as the twelfth duke, while "no one contributed more largely by his munificent donations to promote the interests of the Established [Anglican] Church."[26]

Similarly, the fourteenth duke of Norfolk was laid to rest in 1860, at which time the *London Times* noted that he was "a large and liberal supporter of Roman Catholic charities" as well as the holder of "seventeen livings in the Established Church."[27] His death nevertheless caused both fiscal and family crises. Newman's order, the Oratorians, for example, lost the duke's generous support.

His funeral services, even more elaborate than his grandfather's, began with a burial service in the library of the castle. The funeral procession, with "a number of priests ... went in front, walking two-abreast, and each carrying a lighted taper," and approached the Fitzalan Chapel from the east, bypassing St. Nicholas entirely; in fact, the service was completed by the interment of the duke in the Fitzalan Chapel.[28]

The funerals of the eleventh and thirteenth dukes, both Protestant converts, differed in a number of significant ways. The eleventh duke, who opposed the British role in the American War of Independence, nonetheless had the title of earl marshall, one of the highest of the hereditary officers of the state, when he died. We don't know the specific location of the services, but his cortege entered the churchyard of St. Nicholas in 1815, where it was met by Protestant clergy as well as the duke's own Catholic chaplains.[29]

Henry Charles, the thirteenth Duke of Norfolk, very much an Old Catholic, with a chaplain who did not even like the use of holy water and was unhappy with carrying crosses in a procession, all blatant gestures towards a very *Roman* Catholicism, in part led by Cardinal Wiseman and the other "new" Catholics. Furthermore, his wife was a Protestant.

13. *The Catholic Lord and the Protestant Vicar...*   163

So it was not much of a surprise that he joined the Anglican Church, incensed by the announcement of the re-establishment of Roman Catholic bishoprics in England in 1851.[30] He and his family had a private pew in the Presbyterian Scotch Church in Covent Garden.[31] He built a number of Anglican schools on his estates and also presented a peal of eight bells to St. Nicholas Church.[32] His heir, the fourteenth duke, however, became a staunch Roman Catholic, and his second son married a cousin of the Earl of Shrewsbury. On his deathbed in 1856 the thirteenth Duke "was restored ... to that fold which he scandalized by his temporary apostasy" and received Extreme Unction, the final Roman Catholic sacrament. His funeral procession proceeded from the castle to St. Nicholas, where an Anglican service led by the queen's chaplain and the vicar of Arundel (both Protestant clergy) was held in the nave. "At the proper period," according to the *Gentleman's Magazine*, "the coffin was removed into the Fitzalan Chapel and lowered into the family vault."[33] Although there seems to be little doubt that he died a Roman Catholic, his funeral service was primarily Anglican.

Henry Granville Fitzalan-Howard, the fourteenth duke, unlike his father, never left the Catholic Church and became close ally of Father Faber of the London Oratory. His son, Henry, the fifteenth duke, was practically raised by the Oratorians, and he selected Joseph Hansom (inventor of the Hansom cab and a partner of the Pugins at one time) as the architect of the cathedral church of Our Lady and St. Philip Howard (named after the duke's martyred ancestor during the Elizabethan era) in commemoration of the fifteenth duke's coming of age, a magnificent over-statement of a church, just down the road from the Anglican parish church.

When an Anglican vicar contests the lord of the castle, one can understand that the match would be unequal, despite Lord Coleridge's scrupulous desire to keep the proceedings fair and impartial. Even Freeman admitted that the external appearance of a single church might tempt some to think it was not possible that two "churches" can occupy the "same" building. Freeman argued that in fact whether the two churches had a single building or not was of no matter: one part of the building "belonged to the monks or canons," commonly called the collegiate (or abbey or priory) church, and the other part belonged to the parish, and was therefore commonly called the parish church.[34] In brief, what the Dissolution of the Monasteries put asunder, no later vicar can rejoin.

The duke's legal team fought fairly and decisively for their client. Bowen, however, could not resist teaching an Anglican vicar an old trick—a biblical reference. "The Fitzalan Chapel was a Naboth's

Vineyard, which [Arbuthnot] might be pardoned for coveting, but his letters allowed that the only reasoning for his coveting it was that he might have the pleasure of showing it to visitors."[35] Fortunately for Arbuthnot, he did not yield to temptation any further than a lawsuit: in the bible Jezebel conspired for Naboth's assassination.

Details of the Litigation:
The Duke of Norfolk v. Arbuthnot, 1879

The Queen's Bench

Presiding: Lord Chief Justice (John Duke) Coleridge, without jury.

Charge: Act of trespass.

For the Plaintiff, the Duke of Norfolk:	For the Defendant, Rev. George Arbuthnot:
Dr. Archibald Stephens, QC	Mr. Arthur Charles, QC
Mr. Charles Bowen	Mr. Francis Henry Jeune
Dr. Walter Phillimore	

Verdict: Arbuthnot guilty of the act of trespass, fined "40s. damages and costs," and "judgment [given] against the defendant on his statement of defense and counter-claim."

The Court of Appeal

Presiding: Lords justices Bramwell and Baggallay, and Sir Baliol Brett.

Charge: Against the judgment of the Queen's Bench for the Duke of Norfolk.

For the Plaintiff, Rev. George Arbuthnot:	For the Defendant, the Duke of Norfolk:
Mr. Arthur Charles, QC	Dr. Walter Phillimore
Mr. Francis Henry Jeune	Sir John Holker, QC
Mr. Vicary Gibbs	

Verdict: "Judgment unanimously for the Duke of Norfolk."

14

The Archbishop and the Jesuit College Building Fund
Eyre-Eyre v. Eyre, 1883

> Earth, sweet Earth, sweet landscape, with leavés throng
> And louchéd low grass...
> Thy lovely dale down thus and thus bids reel
> Thy river, and o'er gives all to rack or wrong.
> —Gerard Manley Hopkins, from "Ribblesdale"
> (1881–1882)

In the case of *Eyre-Eyre v. Eyre*, all those Eyres were brothers, descended from recusant Catholics of Derbyshire who, despite losing land in government seizures during the English Reformation, remained immensely wealthy. Father William Eyre, a Jesuit priest, and his brother, Thomas Joseph Eyre, were the plaintiffs, suing their brother Charles Eyre, the Roman Catholic archbishop of Glasgow, over the disbursement of their inheritance from their father, John Lewis Eyre, known as Count Eyre, who died in 1880, leaving a breathtaking estate of 400,000 pounds (equivalent to about fifty million pounds, or sixty-five million dollars, in 2021). Three other potential heirs, two brothers and a sister, had predeceased their father: those deceased brothers had also been priests. Because Lord Arundel, one of the trustees of the estate, wrote a letter to *The Manchester Guardian* in January 1883, supporting the Eyre brothers' suit against the third brother, the archbishop, who was also a trustee of the estate, the scandalous case became public knowledge.[1]

Half the estate was left to the archbishop, and the remaining half to be divided between Father William, his brother Thomas, and the latter's wife. Father William announced that his share, approximately 62,000 pounds (equivalent to about eight million pounds or ten million dollars in 2021), would go to the construction projects at Stonyhurst College, where he was rector. Stonyhurst, the prep school ridiculed as immoral by the renegade ex–Dominican priest Giacinto Achilli, in the Cardinal Newman trial (see chapter 8), as well as by the Tichborne imposter (chapter 12), was then undergoing a massive reconstruction effort that had begun in 1877 and would last until 1889. Father William was quite attached to Stonyhurst, having been prefect of the Philosophers (i.e., the university prep students) from 1871 to 1879, a period in which the college was in transition, according to his obituary, from hosting "foreign princes and noblemen who came to learn English ... and sons of the British aristocracy who had been unable to absorb much knowledge when younger" to "those who were pursuing a high course of studies and aiming at University honours."[2]

Jesuit poet Gerard Manley Hopkins was a somewhat controversial appointee to staff in 1882 to help prepare students to enter London University and similar institutions, since Catholics were still forbidden to attend sublime Oxford and lordly Cambridge. (Hopkins himself was an Oxford grad.) Father William Eyre found this creative young man "mad in the Pickwickian sense," quite an "eccentric," since he was observed on one occasion climbing "into his room publicly through the window, in order to save time by not having to go round by the

Stonyhurst College, Lancashire, premiere Jesuit prep school, from postcard, c. 1970 (author's collection).

14. The Archbishop and the Jesuit College Building Fund   167

corridor" and on another occasion "in the bath [swimming pool] ... with his clothes on."[3]

Hopkins for his part celebrated the chaos of new construction at Stonyhurst with enthusiasm, as this letter to Robert Bridges, his friend who later became poet laureate, suggests: "There is always a stirring scene, contractors, builders, masons, bricklayers, carpenters, stonecutters and carvers ... engines of all sorts send their gross and foul smelling smoke all over us."[4] It is clear Hopkins appreciated this spectacle of change and improvement at his new post.

"There are acres of flat roof," Hopkins added, no doubt used to clambering about on them as he celebrated the "noble view of this Lancashire landscape, Pendle Hill, Ribblesdale, the fells, and all round, bleakish but solemn and beautiful" in poems such as "Ribblesdale" as well as in his journals. Hopkins was doing what he had done as a youth, climbing "very tall trees" and "gazing at the sky and surrounding country in a happy trance."[5] Hopkins took enthusiastically to Stonyhurst, not only writing the occasional poem but also pursuing his interests as an amateur scientist, publishing letters in the distinguished British journal *Nature* on atmospheric conditions such as the dramatic sunsets associated with the world-class volcanic explosions of Krakatoa, located between the islands of Java and Sumatra. Although Hopkins was a classicist by Oxford training, he was a token apprentice to his colleague, Stephen Perry, Stonyhurst's indefatigable astronomer, who was in the first rank of British scientists.

Eyre's Stonyhurst therefore included one of the most important British astronomers of the Victorian era as well as the somewhat difficult young man who would go on to be one of the greatest poets of the twentieth century, his public—and poetic—coming-out having been delayed for almost thirty years after his death in 1889. Eyre wanted Stonyhurst to be a great center of learning and the arts, and he had invited the well-known (and somewhat controversial) poet Coventry Patmore for the school's Prize Day celebration.[6] Patmore would go on to become one of Hopkins's most important mentors and epistolary friends. Patmore shared with Hopkins an admiration of Butterfield.[7] Since Eyre would never benefit—could in fact as a Jesuit not benefit—personally from his father's inheritance, Stonyhurst was for him the next logical and best recipient.

The archbishop and Lord Arundel of Wardour, who had been a student at Stonyhurst himself, were the co-executors of Count Eyre's will, which prescribed their unanimity as a condition for monies to be disbursed. The archbishop vetoed any release of money to Father William because he knew the money would go towards Stonyhurst's construction projects. But what *was* the archbishop's real problem? Like his father, he really didn't like Jesuits.

Furthermore, Father William argued, the archbishop "objected to large Colleges," preferring to use the inheritance for charitable work on a smaller scale. Single-sex establishments such as Stonyhurst especially frightened him, ironically agreeing with the Tichborne imposter that there were moral issues in such arenas. He also expected (hoped?) that the college might go bankrupt or be seized by the government to be used as a barracks.[8]

When Lord Arundell published his letter in the *Manchester Guardian* supporting the release of Father William's share, in effect applying pressure on the archbishop to acquiesce and force the release unilaterally, positions on both sides hardened and the case ended up in Chancery, although members of the Roman Catholic hierarchy, including Cardinal Manning, had already tried to resolve the conflict in favor of the archbishop, the latter having even gone to Rome to solidify his position.[9] A potentially scandalous trial began in 1883, with the archbishop suing his brothers and later Lord Arundell of Wardour also.

Mr. Justice Kay of the Chancery Division exposed the open secret of the suit: that "by the rules of the Society of Jesus any member thereof was prevented from enjoying any money or other property for his own use or benefit, but was obliged to hand over such money or property to the Society." In short, Father William would simply serve as the conduit for an immense fortune to go not to him personally but directly into the Jesuits' building fund. Justice Kay stated that a Jesuit, without being enriched by the money, nonetheless could be a party to such an inheritance. But he came down especially hard on Lord Arundel, who "purported by deed pole to release the property from the power" of the trustees. This unilateral deed pole, or promise, would not stand.[10] "The fund," he concluded, "cannot be distributed during the joint lives of the trustees, unless they join in making an irrevocable appointment." Justice Kay also stated in court that the terms of the will would permit disbursements to be made "from time to time"—and had in fact been made—but in the future such disbursements could only be made if the trustees jointly agreed.[11]

Actually, the deceased knew very well what might happen to his money, because in fact he had asked his son "not to become a Jesuit," in a letter many years earlier in 1854:

> You say I ask you not to remain a Jesuit—this is not quite so—I asked you not to become a Jesuit—I did not wish you, I do not wish you to remain among Jesuits—you never asked me about going to them—if you had bound yourself by vows, and had become a Jesuit, I could not have asked you to break your vows, however much against my will and advice it had been taken.[12]

14. The Archbishop and the Jesuit College Building Fund

The father had already not so gently admonished the son that the latter has already been using this inheritance as a Jesuit: "You probably have forgotten that every [hundred pounds] you drew was a payment in advance."

Archbishop Eyre argued that Lord Eyre always desired to achieve two objectives with his inheritance: to prevent the Jesuits from having "any portion of his money and at the same time he did not wish his Jesuit son to be penniless in case the Jesuit order was dissolved or broken up in this country, or his son resolve to leave the Society, or the Superiors require him to leave the Society." For twenty years before his death, the father had been adamant that none of his estate would go to the Jesuits. The idea that any of William's withdrawals were for his personal use only was unacceptable to him. He was heard to repeat this refusal "hundreds of times," according to memos prepared by the archbishop's lawyers and circulated openly.[13] These memos also accused Lord Arundel of consulting with William only and not the archbishop, and of signing "deeds of release" without the archbishop's knowledge. William Eyre "was not, is not, a free man," his brother argued: "He was controlled by the orders of his [Jesuit] Provincial, Rev. E. Purbrick and his General [of the Jesuits] in Florence."[14]

William was inflamed by his brother's remarks: he asserted that the Jesuit Provincial will get the money—"just the kind of thing that an enemy of the Jesuits would have predicted."[15] Proposal and counterproposal flew back and forth between the brothers over how much of the inheritance the Stonyhurst reconstruction would use up compared to money going to "Jesuit charities" and "other charities and dioceses in England and Scotland."[16]

In the end, sick of all the struggles and to avoid "long and painful litigation," Father William settled out of court for 40,000 pounds,[17] three years after he had already left Stonyhurst for another position, although Stonyhurst still retained his significant patronage. Ironically, his exit also relieved him of further supervision of the "eccentric" poet, but Hopkins was the least of his troubles: Father William had hoped that "no one else leaves me any [more] money" because "the constantly recurring troubles connected with the will ... are of a nature to kill some men."[18]

But his fellow Jesuits appreciated his efforts. His obituary in the order's official publication *Letters and Notices* in 1898 stated that it was the "immediate connection of his name and family inheritance with the raising of its material structure, and with the creation of the new Stonyhurst which meets our eye."[19] Part of the reason Stonyhurst was the target of so many anti–Catholic screeds was its strength as a center of Catholic education, many of its students becoming Jesuit leaders and teachers.

Details of the Litigation: Eyre-Eyre v. Eyre, 1883

Chancery

Presiding: Mr. Justice Kay

Charge: The estate being unequally divided among the three brothers, one of them, the plaintiff, William Eyre, intended to give his twenty-five percent share to his Jesuit order, expressly against his father's wishes, as well as in violation of the deed poll that required unanimity of the two trustees: his brother, the Archbishop of Glasgow, who vetoed the share, and Lord Arundell of Wardour, who supported it.

For the Defendants, William Eyre and Thomas Joseph Eyre:
Mr. Graham Hastings
Mr. Wolstenholme
Mr. Ingle Joyce

For the Co-Defendant, Lord Arundell of Wardour:
Mr. Bagshawn

For the Plaintiff Archbishop Charles Eyre:
Mr. Davey, QC
Mr. Bardswell

Verdict: None; suit withdrawn for out-of-court settlement.

15

The Lord Chief Justice and His Anti-Vivisectionist Son-in-Law
Adams v. Coleridge, 1885–1886

> You will, no doubt, remember that in the autumn of 1856 a gentleman of the name of Anderton was arrested on suspicion of having poisoned his wife, and that he committed suicide whilst awaiting the issue of a chemical enquiry into the cause of her death. This enquiry resulted in an acquittal, no traces of the suspected poison being found; and the affair was hushed up as speedily as possible, many of Mr. Anderton's connections being of high standing in society, and naturally anxious for the honour of the family.
> —Charles Felix, *The Notting Hill Mystery* (1862–3)

John Duke Coleridge had one of the most illustrious careers in the Victorian judiciary. He was made solicitor-general in 1868, attorney-general in 1871, and lord chief justice in 1873. Nonetheless, in 1885 the distinguished lord chief justice became a defendant in a series of contentious lawsuits himself, in part because he believed that his own family tree was in danger of succumbing to lower-class blight, the honor of his daughter, Mildred Mary, having been compromised by a cad. He had failed to prevent the courtship and eventual elopement of Mildred Mary to Charles Warren Adams, a man he just *knew* was a fortune-hunter. Adams, Coleridge argued, had no income and had "made no efforts to obtain permanent employment or secure a regular income." Coleridge's son Stephen, on a visit to the United States, gave what was probably an ill-advised interview to an American reporter covering the developing scandal. Stephen said of Adams, "His life has been aimless and unsteady" and that he, "although a widower past fifty, has thus far in his career been unable to earn more than a bare livelihood." Tactless, to be sure, but Adams himself admitted that he was not strong "in respect of pecuniary means."[1]

Although having an unmarried Coleridge daughter of mature years (she was almost forty) pursued by a man of lower status would hardly have been the equivalent of a convent scandal or a defrocked priest, the family honor of the highest judicial officer in the land was clearly at stake here. Adams's extensive contact with Mildred Mary without appropriate parental permission or female chaperonage was clearly an irritant to the lord chief justice, not to mention the norms of upper-class British society. Furthermore, the lord chief justice had been litigating or judging so many religious scandals in the courts in the past that perhaps he believed he was immune to such mischief. Being a defendant himself was arguably unimaginable to him.

Charles Adams and Mildred Mary may have seemed to be an odd couple, especially in class, but they worked together at the London Anti-Vivisection Society office, where he was its paid secretary and she a very active committee member. Two of Mildred Mary's brothers, Stephen and Bernard, were also associated with this society as crusaders against animal cruelty.

Adams, a lawyer, journalist, and "newspaper proprietor,"[2] had also in years past gained control of a small publishing company that eventually went bankrupt, but not until he had it release, under the pseudonym Charles Felix, his own book, *The Notting Hill Mystery* (1862–63),[3] regarded by experts today as the first detective novel in English.[4] In the novel an investigator cannot decide whether the opening deaths are suicides or might in fact be murders. The indeterminacy of the plot precludes a simple solution of the mystery; the presence of the contemporaneous Victorian fad of "mesmeric agency," or the sleep-like trances of suspects, further complicates the matter.

Adams had been married once before, to the granddaughter of one of the most prolific and popular Victorian writers, Charlotte Yonge, and fascinatingly enough, Mildred Mary's friend and a distant (fourth) cousin of Mildred Mary's father. Mildred Mary herself was the great-grand-niece of Romantic poet Samuel Taylor Coleridge.

Charlotte Yonge actively encouraged the "stay at home" daughters of the upper middle classes to read and write: she formed a club of writers, the Goslings, which included Mildred Mary Coleridge, poet Mary Elizabeth Coleridge, and Christabel Coleridge, Derwent Coleridge's daughter, who later became one of Yonge's close collaborators.

Perhaps we should be surprised that their courtship proceeded amidst the gruesome evidence of limitless Victorian animal carnage. But the romance became more and more public, so much so that at one point, Lord Coleridge extracted a promise from his daughter that she would "abstain" (Adams's word) from all anti-vivisectionist activity. Undeterred, in 1882, a year before they were engaged, Adams sent Coleridge one of his books, the anti-vivisectionist *The Coward Science*, with a weaselly letter asking for a dispensation from the abstinence rule: "I hardly think," Adams wrote, "the perusal of the accompanying volume (which has no horrors in it) would come under that designation; but I would rather be on the safe side, and therefore take the liberty of enclosing to you a copy of which I ask her acceptance—in the hope that the 'rule' will be so far 'discharged' as to permit of its reaching her hands."[5] Most of us would take the wager that she never received this volume, especially in the light of that letter which, like most of the letters in this case, was poisoned at the source—not to mention, at least to my ear, sounds pompous and self-serving.

No less surprising was the furious negative reaction of her family to the relationship. Although Adams's first wife had died and left him a child to raise, his second marriage to the daughter of the lord chief justice would be potentially an affair of state. It certainly became the gossip of high society in London. Elizabeth Rigby (Lady Eastlake), a Coleridge family friend and art historian, as well as spouse of one of the most famous painters in England, was shocked at Mildred Mary's behavior toward her father.

Coleridge's close friend, architect William Butterfield, also tried to intervene with Mildred Mary, who was his friend as well. In a letter Butterfield sent to her—typically, one which Adams insisted be shared with the court—was about Mildred Mary's apparent "pleasure" in stating that her father was in financial difficulties, a situation Butterfield, as the family architect, knew was ridiculous. Butterfield wrote that his "sense of propriety" was "shocked" by her "disparagement" of her father and concluded: "I feel that you are not in a state to be reasoned with." "Your conscience must be asleep," Butterfield concluded, for her to pursue this course of action *with* Adams and *against* her father. Other than demonstrating his obsession with letters, it is not clear what Adams could have hoped by insisting that Butterfield read this letter in court, as it would not place Mildred Mary in a very good light.[6]

By spring 1885, matters had grown more strained in the family, as the couple began to see more and more of each other, progressing to such a dramatic and startling moment that when her father was away Mildred Mary left the Coleridge home, fibbed that she was going to visit friends, and instead met Adams and married him shortly thereafter on June 24, 1885.[7] Later in court, Adams offered a different version of events: Mildred Mary left her father's house, intending to return, but she was "peremptorily forbidden to return." The marriage "itself was owing entirely to Lord Coleridge himself, who had made any other course impossible."[8]

During this period, Lord Coleridge's Jesuit brother, Henry James Coleridge, also had a correspondence with Mildred Mary that was submitted to the arbitrator. While Adams complained about this exchange of letters, he did not in this case insist on all of them being read aloud in court, leaving us in partial frustration about their contents. It is fair to assume, however, that the Reverend Coleridge would not have approved of this match: "Let everything be done," one of his letters that was read, stated, "to break the continuity of the exercise of this baleful influence" of Adams over her.[9]

The inevitable legal action, *Adams v. Coleridge*, was a very complicated series of six court cases, all of which transpired after the marriage had occurred. Adams had sued the Lord Chief Justice and Stephen Coleridge, his son and heir, for libel, maintaining that his proper attentions to Mildred Mary had been maligned by Lord Coleridge, who wrote that Adams "had been neglecting to get an honest livelihood while pursuing" her. Adams clearly expected Mildred Mary's father to support both of them. In a letter to Coleridge read in court, Adams admitted "in respect of pecuniary means" an "objection" to his courtship "might fairly be made." He had only "to speak the word" and she would support him, but "delicacy or pride" prevents him from doing so, even though "a man of sensitive temperament and a woman richer than himself" are involved. He closed this astonishing letter by writing that he leaves it to her father, to his "own good feeling and generosity and fairness, above all your regard for her, to decide upon your future course."[10] Carefully written, perhaps, but not subtle.

Although Coleridge's letter in reply—also read aloud in court—emphasized that Adams had violated all socially acceptable norms of conduct in courtship, not to mention his apparent inability or refusal to secure an income so he could provide for a wife, Coleridge was nonetheless willing to settle 300 pounds "a year on my daughter for life." This was a considerable sum, worth more than 30,000 pounds today (approximately $41,000). The inevitable fuss over the proposed dowry of course appeared in the pages of the *London Times*, and whether Adams or Coleridge suffered more in embarrassment is hard to say. In other cases, Lord Coleridge had already established his judicial rulings and opinions in favor of maintaining the woman's point of view in breach-of-promise suits, because of their inherently unequal position in the eyes of society.

Years later he maintained that such laws "were often the only legitimate means of bringing a scoundrel to book."[11] We must wonder if he had anyone particular in mind.

Some of the really terrible comments about Adams at first did not circulate beyond the family, but we can surmise Mildred Mary had heard them even before they were exposed in court. Stephen Coleridge, the *London Times* pointed out, "described him as a man, whose hand no honest man would touch." Coleridge's other son, Bernard, had called him "an utter scamp, a mere adventurer."[12]

It was difficult for Adams to ignore or put behind him the letter Coleridge wrote to him in November 1883, in reply to Adams's announcement sent to him in August, saying, "Your daughter has 'engaged' herself" to him. The contradictions of Adams's personality were apparent in this letter. While he maintained (ludicrously) that "so far as birth and connections are concerned there is no disparity on [his] side," he admitted that "in respect of pecuniary means" his position is one in which, were he "proposing any immediate issues, objection might be fairly made." Mildred Mary is sufficiently "of age to decide for herself after due caution and counsel how far the business of her present position might perhaps, if sacrificed, be compensated to her in other ways."[13]

Coleridge understood clearly what Adams was saying under all the tentativeness: you, Coleridge, must settle this matter with money. Coleridge wrote to "Mr. Adams" in the third person: "Mr. Adams desires to marry my daughter, but he informs me—at least, so I understand him—that he has absolutely no income of his own, nor any present or speedy prospect of obtaining any, even the smallest." He has in fact spent the better part of a year "in my daughter's company in my house and elsewhere, but as far as I am aware has made no efforts to obtain permanent employment or secure a regular income." Later in court, Stephen Coleridge's letter summarizing Adams's career pointed out his age at the time ("past 50"), that he had been in the army and in the Civil Service, is "without income," and "has no means of support." He would marry Mildred Mary only if Lord Coleridge provided "a liberal settlement," certainly more than the three hundred pounds a year currently on the table. After this remarkable declaration of incompetence, Adams testified that while some of the statements were true, the only one he wished to contest was that his marriage to Mildred Mary depended upon the settlement from her father.[14]

Despite the fact that this would be a marriage he "disliked and disapproved of," Coleridge would be willing to accept it and support it if Adams makes any effort over the next year to try "for some definite employment." Furthermore, Coleridge would at once "settle"

300 pounds on his daughter for life. Adams's response was an insulting scrawl across Coleridge's letter that he returned: "Perused. C.W.A. 13–11–83."[15] It is probably a mystery that it took only six court cases to turn this legal matter into history. Adams announced that the correspondence with Coleridge "may now be allowed to cease" and then turned over copies of 305 letters to the arbitrator, many of which were not relevant to the struggle at hand.[16] Elopement and then a father who would never see his daughter again would be inevitable.

Coleridge and his son Stephen won four of the six decisions outright, the judge concluding that there was "no evidence of malice" against Adams. The two trials in which Adams received a partial victory had to do with clarifying the judges' oft-repeated stipulation that although the late Lord Monkswell was the arbitrator of any settlement or dowry, his decisions had become somewhat compromised because negative letters from the Coleridges and others had reached Monkswell, probably in error. In vain, Monkswell tried to convince Adams that the letters would have no effect on his judgment, but Adams was not reassured. Although a highly regarded arbitrator, Monkswell was, as Adams knew, a friend of the Coleridge family and knew Mildred Mary well. Both sides of the case, nevertheless, had originally agreed upon Monkswell as the arbitrator.[17]

Among the letters Monkswell received included one from a cousin of Lord Coleridge: "Don't let him have the run of your house; it will end in his not marrying her." Cryptic and ominous, to be sure, but it was nothing compared to the letter sent by Mrs. Polsen, the mother of Adams's first wife: "If a broken-hearted mother's words are of any avail, pause [i.e., in the marriage]. No tongue can tell the lengths to which he will go. The most frightful things are stated of him, and not without reason, and his antecedents would shock the most unscrupulous." Almost as an afterthought she stated that his daughter was "living on charity" without any financial support from her father.[18]

The Coleridges wanted to settle quietly out of court, of course, but those pesky letters having been sent (accidentally, I have concluded), to the arbitrator, served, Adams contended, to inflame Monkswell against him. Even the judge agreed that the mother-in-law's letter was *"prima facie* libelous." In the end, compensation for Adams and an annual income settlement for Mildred Mary were reached, but for much less than Adams wanted or expected. Lord Coleridge emphatically denied having promised his daughter 17,000 pounds as a settlement: "It is an absolute fabrication, and a very absurd one," Coleridge wrote in a letter to his friend, Sir Farrer-Herschell, the solicitor-general, that was read in court. Curiously, Coleridge testified that he may have discussed such a figure with Mildred Mary, but said it was not "promised." Such a sum was large even then, but now would be the equivalent of 2,000,000 pounds (about 2,500,000 dollars).[19]

As if to compete with his own published Victorian melodramas, Adams had been forbidden to see Mildred Mary, so they subsequently had to run away and elope. Adams said—again unconvincingly—that he was doing the gentlemanly thing by protecting a daughter who was in flight from her father. At one point, Adams asserted that he was the only one brave enough to say "that the idea of marriage had been forced upon" Adams and Mildred Mary "persistently." Furthermore Lord Coleridge, "having kicked down the ladder by which he had risen" (Adams did not specify what this probable metaphorical disparagement meant), could not provide for his daughter "as he had promised her."[20]

Lord Coleridge's protracted struggle with Adams over the marriage settlement would unsettle everyone in the distinguished Coleridge clan. Adams, who affected ignorance of how such matters were handled among the upper classes, seemed to believe (wrongly) that when his wife died, her settlement would come to him. I suspect that Adams knew that embarrassing the lord chief justice would be the surest path to guarantee a settlement to his (Adams's) satisfaction. Reading between the lines, it seems that Mildred Mary as an unmarried daughter was beholden to her father for economic support, of course, but perhaps her "bad health" and the need to develop her "musical talents" would now be the responsibility of Adams, who had relatively few resources, verging on none, of his own. In Adams's straitened circumstances and perhaps with an unsettled conscience, he came to believe that Lord Coleridge really wanted Mildred Mary to marry him in this unregulated and somewhat scandalous manner; that is, Lord Coleridge was actually scheming to get rid of her! In the meantime Adams strenuously asserted, "His object was not profit or vengeance, but the vindication of his character."[21]

Adams appealed the first trial at the Queen's Bench, whose judge ruled that there had been "no evidence of malice" on the part of Coleridge or his son Bernard against Adams. This appeal or second trial ended in a more positive way for Adams, as Baron Huddeston ruled that the family's decision to offer compensation for Adams should be settled by arbitration with Lord Monkwell. The appeal in the third trial was a mixed decision for the parties involved: there would be "no evidence of malice" on the part of the Coleridges against Adams, but the arbitration with Lord Monkwell would now include a proposed settled by Lord Coleridge of 600 pounds a year for Mildred Mary. Clearly, Adams had gained another 300 pounds.

Observers of the third trial, however, would see an Adams obsessed not only with the "vindication of his character" but also how much and how often the settlement would be paid into *his* account *for* his wife. He seemed also to promise—although by now it is obvious he was incapable of sticking to anything he promised—foregoing any further litigation if the terms of the agreement were settled: "I am glad to be able to state publicly that I have not the slightest intention" of "entering into further litigation of any kind."[22] This was either self-delusion or an outrageous fabrication.

Adams bristled at the implication that he would not accept the financial settlement "as if I had been standing out for a provision for myself." The fact is, he wanted assurance from Coleridge's legal team that even after the court received a document signed by Mildred Mary "as authority for the payment of the money into Mr. Adams's bank, such payment be considered as in discharge of Coleridge's liability to that extent," he would still be allowed to continue his proceedings against the Coleridges. If Lord Coleridge had not dilly-dallied about the payment arrangements, Adams implied, he would have had more time to pursue his claim against Bernard Coleridge. One of the judges, Justice A.L. Smith, was not pleased with this direction in his courtroom: "You have been insisting on terms you are not entitled to under the agreement." The appeal in this third trial was then dismissed, and the previous order of the second trial remained in effect.[23]

Of course the more Adams insisted that he would not pursue more litigation, the more likely it appeared that he intended to do so. He defined the "vindication" of his character in both moral and financial terms, as any neutral observer realized. And that is of course what he did, almost immediately, appealing the verdict of the third trial before the Queen's Bench in a fourth trial because he discovered libel "contained in some letters" send to arbitrator Lord Monkswell, who had been working on the settlement.

The London Times called the fourth trial "an action of a novel and, it is believed unprecedented character—an action for sending letters to an arbitrator by which it was suggested that the plaintiff [Adams] was prejudiced." Lord Monkswell, before his death but after he had made his award to Adams, had received a package of letters that the Coleridges said were forwarded to Lord Monkswell by a mistake by a clerk. Adams said he was a journalist, a "newspaper proprietor," and that Lord Coleridge was his "father-in-law." One can only imagine the collective grinding of teeth and concealed frustration when Adams alluded to his new familial relationship with Lord Coleridge. These letters were libelous, Adams argued, and only served to damage him in "the eyes of said arbitrator." Coleridge could only conclude, in a Dickensian vein, that it was all a "muddle."[24]

The letters, quoted in court, truly reflected the deterioration of the Coleridge family's attitude towards Adams. Lord Coleridge said that further legal proceedings would only encourage Adams—not yet married to Mildred Mary—to believe "that anything can be got from a jury with or without reason." The packet, we would learn in the fifth trial, included a damning letter from the mother of Adams's first wife as well as a letter suggesting that Adams had "bribed" the editor of the *West London Advertiser* "to publish matter defamatory" to Lord Coleridge.[25]

Adams testified indignantly that the libel in these letters drove him to legal action. He had no choice. Certainly the biggest blow against his character was Lord Coleridge's remark that "he had been neglecting to get an honest livelihood while pursuing" Mildred Mary. He said he was "more or less a self-made man," despite the fact that his father had been a judge—surely a remarkable announcement and I suspect fanciful— and he, Adams, could only wish that he could be sitting at his father's bench, "not of course to try this case," but "because had he been alive this case would never have been tried." This mysterious allusion to social class only inflamed Adams even more to attack Lord Coleridge, who "had made a large fortune at Bar, of which, of course, he was undisputed master—it was absolutely at his disposal." And although Lord Coleridge had often "protested against primogeniture and ... hereditary peerage," soon "a peerage came his way." Adams, perhaps not realizing how damaging it would be to his case at this point, stated that he had instructed his solicitor to inform Coleridge that should Mildred Mary predecease him, he wanted it stated in the final agreement that he would still receive "further benefit for himself."[26]

This shocking and naked attack on the class system drew Judge Denman's controlled anger: "Are we not getting rather wide of the mark? Had you better cone to the matter at issue? If we go on this way the case will never end." (Judge Denman had obviously read about *Jarndyce v. Jarndyce* in *Bleak House*.) Adams said that his remarks were relevant because once Coleridge became a peer, he had to worry about providing his son with more money and that action would scant his daughter's dowry. Adams fell afoul of the judge once more when he called the Bishop of Oxford, Lord Coleridge's brother-in-law, to the stand to testify about a letter he had sent to Mildred Mary, his niece. The letter was not quoted because apparently it was for her eyes only, and Lord Coleridge never saw it. Adams at this point must have seemed desperate to use any aristocrat he could find who would somehow expose Coleridge's duplicity. Adams even referred to Mildred Mary as a "Cinderella," no doubt as if she were imprisoned in Lord Coleridge's house.[27]

The fifth trial brought out in great detail the moment when Lord Coleridge had had enough and demanded that the relationship cease. Not surprisingly, there are two versions of the culminating incident, which originated in the anti-vivisection society of which Adams was a paid secretary and Mildred Mary an active committee member. They worked together and produced jointly three volumes of discussion and argument, one of which involved fifteen authors in three languages. Miss Frances Power Cobbe, the honorary secretary, decided to introduce Mildred Mary to the editor of the *Malthusian Review*, which had reviewed or excerpted a book whose publisher had been "prosecuted and sentenced" for his opinions. Apparently, vivisection is an acceptable topic but population control is not, because Adams took it upon himself through a complicated series of letters to warn Lord Coleridge of this matter. (A cynic might wonder if he was afraid that he was about to lose his own faithful coworker to another writer). Lord Coleridge was so disturbed by Miss Cobbe's report of the incident alleging improprieties on Adams's part that he "accused Adams of bringing scandal upon his daughter." Adams agreed to stay away from her, but of course soon reneged and "from one step to another, through the persecution on Miss Coleridge, they were driven first to an engagement and then into marriage."[28]

Lord Coleridge eventually learned that Miss Cobbe had never made such accusations and the incident was mostly of Adams's fabrication to create a rift between father and daughter, a task Adams accomplished. One cannot be surprised that Lord Coleridge would be suspicious of an unemployed suitor who spends all of his time with his "father-in-law," negotiating the marriage settlement. The last straw was Adams's assertion, Coleridge wrote in a letter read aloud in court, that "Miss Cobbe was actuated, among other bad motives, by an unqualified passion for" Adams. When Judge Denman asked if Adams wanted his rebuttal letter to Coleridge read, Adams refused, but that he did want the court to know that Coleridge had written to him that she was "peremptorily forbidden to return" to her father's house. For Adams the final insult was that Coleridge "had declined to be present at his daughter's wedding, and the whole of his side of the family 'cut' her."[29]

Although the trials caused unending rifts in the Coleridge family, any reader sympathetic to tweaking the noses of the pompous elite would acknowledge that Adams enjoyed hounding the lord chief justice in the courtroom, its ironies too delicious to ignore and perhaps too tempting for a middle-class writer without portfolio (or an estate) who enjoyed representing himself in court against the highest judicial figure in the realm and, in the first two trials, jousting with Coleridge's *six* defense attorneys.

Nonetheless, Adams wore his commoner's heart on his sleeve. At one point in the testimony, denying he ever sought any part of the settlement for himself—a point Lord Coleridge insisted he had requested—he admitted that he did sign a memorandum of agreement specifying only Mildred Mary's settlement, trusting that Lord Coleridge's solicitor and he were "conferring together as gentlemen." It is especially clear from a letter Adams sent Lord Coleridge in August 1883, before the marriage, that Adams had primarily one thing on his mind, given he wrote that there was a "delicacy or pride ... which must needs stand between a man of sensitive temperament and a woman richer than himself." In brief, Coleridge will have to exhibit his "own good feeling and generosity and fairness" and arrange for a satisfactory monetary settlement on his daughter. Coleridge's offer of 300 pounds a year was obviously not enough for such "a man of sensitive temperament." Adams made clear he was thinking more of a one-time settlement of 17,000 pounds, a figure Coleridge said never came up in the discussions with Adams.[30]

Some slights are never forgiven: twenty years later Mildred Mary refused to see her cousin, the poet Mary Elizabeth Coleridge, an early feminist and teacher, who came to apologize for obeying the family's demand to shun her socially. Mildred Mary was fourteen years older than Mary Elizabeth, then her best friend. Mildred Mary had taught the younger girl Italian so that they could study Dante together. Mary Elizabeth's attempt at reconciliation failed when she was turned away from Mildred's door in Somerset. Her poignant poem "Broken Friendship" (from *The Collected Poems of Mary Coleridge*), was autobiographical:

> Give me no gift! Less than thyself were nought.
> It was thyself, alas! not thine I sought.
> Once reigned I as a monarch in this heart,
> Now from the doors a stranger I depart.[31]

Although Mary Elizabeth moved in a quite active circle of poets and friends, all her correspondence and personal papers were burned by her family after she died.[32] Since this remarkable circle included the Jesuit poet Gerard Manley Hopkins, Robert Bridges, Hopkins's posthumous editor and poet laureate, and Canon R.W. Dixon, an Anglican divine and poet, also Hopkins's friend, this auto-da-fe was quite a loss. Mary Elizabeth herself had been an early admirer of Hopkins, noting that this "young Oxford student of brilliantly original power" had loved

Canon Dixon's poems "with such devotion that, when he entered the ranks of the Jesuits and was forbidden to take any books with him, he copied out almost all those in his possession."[33]

The Coleridges never really took the measure of Mildred Mary's resolve. The couple had no children. As for Adams: this despised husband of the first-born child of the lord chief justice was included in the family tree in her brother Bernard's history of the family, but not in the biography of her father written by her distant cousin, Ernest Hartley (from the Highgate branch of the family), also a close friend of Hopkins. A reminder, perhaps, that no family tree is safe from pruning.

Mildred Mary's brother, Stephen, fifteen years after the seemingly endless court cases split the family, made a conciliatory gesture of his own by attacking the neglect of important anti-vivisection legislation in his essay, *The Administration of Cruelty of Animals Act of 1876*: "The law, as now administered, affords no protection whatever to animals, and at present only protects the vivisector."[34] It was, alas, too little too late: Mildred Mary remained irrevocably estranged from her illustrious family.

Adams never returned to court. It was probably just as well, as his last moment in the final trial in November 1886 was marked by a testy exchange with the judge, Justice Denman. The latter had already begun his summing-up when Adams interrupted him with a request that still another letter "should be laid before the jury." The judge remarked peremptorily that it was not already "in the evidence" and added: "Then it is far too late now to add to the evidence on either side." Adams could not, however, resist reading still another letter in which Adams asserted that Coleridge had created a "mass of petty slander which has been raked out of every gutter from the Mediterranean to the slums of Hammersmith." Denman had endeavored in vain to keep Adams from reading said letter.[35]

The judge at this point was clearly exasperated. He might have added: there have been too many letters already submitted by both sides, hundreds and hundreds by Adams alone, who was clearly obsessed about what you could do to letters—number them, catalogue them, copy them, transmit them between solicitors' offices, and—most important of all—somehow *get them into evidence* ... whether or not they were relevant to the court's matter at hand. It is almost as if he had a talismanic belief in his ability to provide the court with written evidence. Even the judge wondered why Adams dwelt so much on his discovering that on the Monkswell letters there were "six different series of machine-numberings—four of lithograph, one of ink, and one of pencil."³⁶ The significance of these enumerations was never cleared up. Justice Denman was not amused.

Henry James, one of Coleridge's solicitors, asserted that Adams had a tendency to benefit from his appearing as his own attorney ("in person") because it gave him more latitude to introduce matters that his counsel (had he one) would never do. Two of James's examples of such matters Adams raised do seem irregular, if not irrelevant: (1) "the terms of the settlement made on Lord Coleridge's first marriage" and (2) his son Stephen's salary (he was Coleridge's secretary).³⁷ What would the jury make of such information, except to find Adams inevitably drawn to discussions of money? And the marital history of the Coleridge family which, by the way, was mostly common knowledge?

To be fair to Adams, this jury seemed to appreciate his feistiness. When they came back with their verdict against him in the final trial, they nevertheless tried to read a statement absolving him of the costs for the trial, which the loser usually shoulders. The judge let them read their recommendation even though it was "immaterial." He was appalled: "You have nothing to do with the costs. I give judgment for the defendants [the Coleridges], with costs."³⁸

Coleridge's rare meetings with his daughter at the time of the engagement did not bode well for future contact after the noise of the cases diminished. Before their marriage, Mildred Mary and Adams once visited Coleridge at his home. Adams asked "if he had anything to say about him," given that he been seen escorting his daughter arm-in-arm in a park. "No, nothing," Coleridge replied. Adams quipped: "Then it is a case of Dr. Fell?" referring to the well-known comic translation of lines from Martial, the Roman poet: "I do not like thee, Dr. Fell, / The reason why, I cannot tell." The lord chief justice replied in form: "No, it is not so."³⁹

The next meeting of all three was also remarkable for what did *not* happen. Coleridge offered to speak to Prime Minister Gladstone about a possible position for Adams, presumably in the government. The couple turned him down.⁴⁰ Why? They did not say. What Adams did say later in court (again, perhaps not relevant to the suit at hand) indicated that the couple were set on an absolute separation from the Coleridges, all of whom had "cut" Mildred Mary socially. And her own father did not, of course, attend her "wedding."⁴¹

Adams died in 1903, Mildred Mary twenty-five years later. Her brother Stephen remembered how she had once presided over Lord Coleridge's domestic establishment after his first wife died, the "cherished daughter of the house," but there is no record of another meeting between father and daughter.

Details of the Litigation:
Adams v. Lord Coleridge; Adams v. Coleridge, 1885–1886

Adams v. Lord *[John Duke]* Coleridge; Adams v. *[Bernard]* Coleridge, *June 1885*

Queen's Bench: Common Pleas Division

Presiding: Mr. Justice Manisty, with jury.

Charge: Action of libel.

For the Plaintiff, C. Warren Adams	*For the Defendants*, Lord Coleridge and Hon. Bernard Coleridge
C. Warren Adams ("in person")	Sir Henry James, QC, MP
	Sir Charles Russell, QC, MP
	Mr. Arthur Charles, QC
	Mr. Charles Matthews
	Mr. Lockwood, QC, MP
	Mr. R. Wallace

Verdict: For the defendants: No evidence of malice.

Adams v. Lord Coleridge; Adams v. Coleridge, *June 1885*

Court of Appeal

Presiding: Mr. Baron John Walter Huddeston

Appeal: Judgment for defendants challenged.

For the Plaintiff, C. Warren Adams	*For the Defendants*, Lord Coleridge and Hon. Bernard Coleridge
C. Warren Adams ("in person")	Sir Henry James, QC, MP
	Sir Charles Russell, QC, MP
	Mr. Arthur Charles, QC
	Mr. Charles Mathews
	Mr. Lockwood, QC, MP
	Mr. R. Wallace

Verdict: *Adams v. Lord Coleridge*: "Action to be stayed [suspended]"; *Adams v. [Bernard] Coleridge*: "No judgment to be delivered and action to be stayed"; compensation for Adams to be settled by arbitration with Lord Monkswell.

Adams v. Lord Coleridge; Adams v. [Bernard] Coleridge, *November 1885*

Queen's Bench

Presiding: Mr. Baron Frederick Pollock, Mr. Justice Manisty, and Mr. Justice A.L. Smith

Charge: That the actions of the appeal before Baron Huddeston (#2 above) should not be "considered as stayed" because the terms of settlement have not been reached and "the plaintiff was at liberty to go on with them."

For the Plaintiff, C. Warren Adams *For the Defendants*, Lord Coleridge and Hon. Bernard Coleridge

C. Warren Adams ("in person") Sir Henry James

Verdict: "Appeal against Mr. Baron Huddeston's order [in trial #2] staying the action was dismissed and the order stands, the parties being left to proceed in the arbitration before Lord Monkswell [proposed settlement 600 pounds per annum for Mildred Mary Coleridge]."

Adams v. Lord Coleridge and the Hon. Bernard Coleridge, *November 1885*

Court of Appeal

Presiding: Master of the Rolls

Appeal: "Against a decision" of the Queen's Bench (#3 above) "refusing to set aside an order" staying the actions of libel until the settlement could be reached.

For the Plaintiff, C. Warren Adams *For the Defendants*, Lord Coleridge and Hon. Bernard Coleridge

C. Warren Adams ("in person") Mr. Arthur Charles, QC

Verdict: Appeal denied.

Adams v. Lord Coleridge, *November 1886*

Queen's Bench

Presiding: Mr. Justice Mathew and Mr. Justice Cave

Charge: Libel "contained in some letters" (sent to Lord Monkswell; see #6 below).

For the Plaintiff, C. Warren Adams

C. Warren Adams ["in person"]

For the Defendant, John Duke Lord Coleridge

Mr. Arthur Charles, QC

Mr. Charles Mathews

Verdict: For defendant.

Adams v. Lord Coleridge and Another *[Bernard Coleridge], November 1886*

Queen's Bench

Presiding: Mr. Justice Denman, with a special jury.

Charge: "An action for sending letters to an arbitrator [Lord Monkswell in #3 above] by which it was suggested that the plaintiff was prejudiced."

For the Plaintiff, C. Warren Adams

C. Warren Adams ["in person"]

For the Defendants, Lord Coleridge and Bernard Coleridge

Sir Henry James, QC, MP

Sir Charles Russell, QC, MP

Mr. Arthur Charles, QC

Mr. Charles Mathews

Mr. Lockwood, QC, MP

Mr. R. Wallace

Verdict: For the defendants: "No ground for the charge of malicious and fraudulent publication."

16

The Deathbed Letter and the Secret Codicil of the Perfidious Jesuit
Jerningham v. Caddell, 1888

> Not, I'll not, carrion comfort, Despair, nor feast on thee;
> Not untwist—slack they may be—these last strands of man
> In me or, most weary, cry I can no more. I can;
> Can something, hope, wish day come, not choose not to be.
> —Gerard Manley Hopkins, "Carrion Comfort"
> (c. 1885–7)

That sibling rivalries persist after a parent's death should surprise no one, but *Jerningham v. Caddell* (1881) adds a death-bed scene to such rivalry that anticipated by only a year, and in no less sensational a manner, the climactic moment in Wilkie Collins's *Black Robe* (1882), an intellectual thriller about the possession of a man's soul and his fortune. The anti–Jesuit novel caused a sensation because the plot, in every sense of the word, is resolved only when a dying man allows his son to throw his will into the fireplace, an act that blocks his ancestral Catholic estate from falling into the clutches of scheming Jesuits. Like other Gothic classics of Collins's career, such as *The Woman in White* (1859) and *The Moonstone* (1868), the lesser known *Black Robe* delights in such sensational events as a fatal duel, mysterious strangers, a priest in disguise, a cry for vengeance from beyond the grave, and schemes to steal an inheritance from rightful heirs using a last-minute codicil to a will.

The nexus of the fortune pursued in the *Black Robe* originates in a Roman Catholic monastery and its considerable estate in Yorkshire, confiscated by Henry VIII during the Reformation's suppression of the monasteries and turned over to the Romayne family, friends of the king, who went on to create the magnificent Vange Abbey literally from the fallen stones of the monastery. The Jesuit plot three hundred years later is launched to recover the property that in fact was rightfully "theirs," since "arbitrary confiscation ... even on the part of a king, cannot overrule the law. What the Church once lawfully possessed, the Church has a right to recover."[1] If only Henry VIII and his reign could be so easily finessed. The Jesuits do recover the original deeds proving the Church's ownership from a hidden receptacle in a statue thrown in to Vange Abbey's fishpond before the monks were driven away. Only in a Wilkie Collins melodrama would the crucial document rise up from a fishpond.

In *Black Robe*, Lewis Romayne is the current possessor of Vange Abbey who, by a twist of fate, found himself killing a young man in a duel in France. Ever since he has been haunted by the dead man's younger brother, who had called out to him, "Assassin, assassin, where are you?"[2] The Jesuits will use Romayne's guilt, his brooding personality, and the friendship with a Jesuit in disguise to convert him to Catholicism and to make themselves the beneficiaries of Vange Abbey in his will.

Romayne defies his class and friends by both marrying and converting. His will, however, seems problematical: the Jesuits want him to sign a last-minute codicil that affirms his bequest to them as he lies on his deathbed. He chooses instead to have his playful toddler of a son toss this will into the fire to protect the inheritance for the young boy and his mother.[3]

A vintage Collins plot, to be sure, but what of real life? The unlikely model for such scheming Jesuits turned out to be Peter Gallwey, who, before becoming a Jesuit priest, was a Stonyhurst College student in 1829, "the well-remembered year," he recalled, "of Catholic Emancipation,"[4] the popular name of the long process of granting Roman Catholics the same civil rights afforded their fellow Protestants. Officially it was the *Act for the Relief of His Majesty's Roman Catholic Subjects* that gave Roman Catholics the right to be elected to the British parliament.

Robert Caddell was a few years ahead of Gallwey at Stonyhurst, and there seemed to have been no bonds of friendship between them. Gallway would not see him again for fifty years. In the sermon Gallwey preached at Caddell's funeral service in 1887, Gallwey recalled him as "the only son of affluent and indulgent parents, [one who] led the life of a young gentleman: was always ready to take a part in sports and domestic amusements; was a genial and popular companion, and travelled abroad to see the world,"[5] in short, he led the unfettered, free-wheeling life of a rich English gentleman. His ancestors had settled in Ireland in the twelfth century and had established vast estates, with the largest, 4,816 acres, in County Galway. Caddell sold the Galway holdings but retained ownership of other lots that totaled 6,000 additional acres in counties Roscommon and Sligo, property that would later become part of his contested estate.[6] When he died, unmarried and childless, the male line of the Caddells ended.

Gallwey became a Jesuit priest after his years as a Stonyhurst College student. He returned to the college at mid-century to become Prefect of Studies, with a brief to reform the curriculum to make the students more competitive at the examinations for advanced degrees at the University of London and elsewhere. His simple innovation was to reduce the amount of reading in each class so that the students could study a limited number of texts more intensely.[7] His tenure there was marked, perhaps fortuitously, by the Tichborne Imposter, who "remembered" him there as a professor.[8]

But among the Stonyhurst students his real claim to fame was their division into two opposing camps, the Romans and the Carthaginians, who would then compete in academic contests. That ancient struggle no doubt created spirited pedagogical battles among the students. When he was promoted to the rector of Farm Street Church, the English Jesuits' home church, his parting speech to his students was climaxed by the cry, "Beat the Protestants!"[9] He meant, of course, beat them on the exams for university slots. He went on to become the Father Provincial, or leader, of the English Jesuits.

Only in the last ten years of Caddel's life did Gallwey and Caddell renew their contact, and clearly Gallwey became his spiritual mentor, for their "intimacy," Gallwey said, "has been very much made up of a preparation for [Caddell's] happy death." His "constant aim was in a practical and business-like way to set his house in order." He had begun daily attendance at mass, made "frequent and humble confessions and multiplied acts of contrition to purify his soul from every sin" and did long recitals of prayer and the Rosary.[10] In short, he had made a virtually total transformation from an aristocrat without a care in the world to a humble but attentive penitent.

It is possible that his family was not comfortable with this display of what seemed to them a display of religiosity. Caddell's personal model was a famous convert by Jesus, Zacchaeus the Penitent Publican, who said, "Half of my goods I give to the poor; and if I have wronged any one I give back four-fold." Caddell offered masses for his relatives and alms for anyone he had wronged.[11]

Gallwey was confident that his account of Caddell's afterlife would be consoling, at least to orthodox Catholics. After death came judgment ,which inevitably meant a penitent sinner like Caddell would pass into purgatory, a state of punishment whose pains are only tempered by the knowledge that heaven is guaranteed the sinner after undergoing the torments of this stage of the afterlife. One of the only ways the punishment of purgatory is relieved is by "friends on earth" who "have an unlimited power of relieving, of shortening this most cruel distress" for the sufferer in purgatory. The "charity of survivors" is that power.[12] Only through the "earnest charity of friends on earth" is the "thick night of" purgatory "changed into the twilight of nearer hope, and the huge oppressive load of debt has dwindled down to a little."[13]

It is a paradox, perhaps, but all this talk of debt and alms was clearly not consoling for Caddell's relatives, because they believed that his preparation for death could involve a will that would transform a major proportion of Caddell's estates into substantial bequests to the Jesuits. Rumors circulated through Caddell's family and circle of friends that Caddell had entrusted Gallwey with a letter detailing a secret codicil to his will that named the Jesuits as the beneficiary of an immense fortune of a hundred thousand pounds, today the equivalent of more than ten million pounds. It was *The Black Robe* come to life.

The dying man's sisters, Pauline (a nun) and Sophia, married to Admiral Arthur William Jerningham, were to be left a pittance, only five thousand pounds each, and the Reverend Gallwey himself half that much. Sophia's husband charged that in the end "the poor man could barely sign his name," much less formulate a legacy or write a letter.[14]

Not quite understanding the potential scandal they were heading for, the sisters could only imagine scheming Jesuits all about them. They were aware that Gallwey's leadership in the church included his rectorship of England's leading Jesuit church, the Church of the Immaculate Conception in Farm Street, serving Mayfair, one of the wealthiest districts of London. Society ladies, both Catholic and not, attended services there, and "well-born" converts were numerous. It had "a partially unfair reputation," according to Robert Bernard Martin, one of Gerard Manley Hopkins's biographers, "for keeping an eye out for parishioners more conspicuous for wealth and social position than for humble piety."[15] Although Gallwey had recruited Gerard Manley Hopkins to Farm Street in an attempt to take advantage of the poet's verbal gifts, when Hopkins, in a sermon, presumably to a congregation of those Mayfair ladies, compared the Church to a cow with seven teats from which the flow of milk represented the seven sacraments, it proved to be Hopkins's exit sermon.[16] Gallwey probably never knew that Hopkins wrestled with severe religious dilemmas, as did Caddell, as Hopkins's poem "Carrion Comfort" indicates that he had.

The Caddell sisters assumed that their brother would never have left such a substantial estate to the Jesuits. Perhaps a trifle less principled than she should have been, Sophia believed that the Jesuits would not want the case to go to court. The Jesuits would certainly agree to a compromise settlement of the estate to avoid scandal.

The sisters had some reason to be concerned. Before Caddell died, Sophia learned from Lord Justice Naish, a "personal friend and connection by marriage," that Father Gallwey had announced that Caddell "will write a letter to Pauline." Sophia at first "thought it was sent by post, but [later] believed it was a secret letter Father Gallwey was to keep and give her after my poor brother's death."[17] Pauline was perhaps more hesitant, asking how their brother could "have ever supposed that his own sisters" would make the "effort to prevent his will from being carried out?"[18] If fact, Gallwey had noted exactly that possibility: "If Mr. Caddell could have known or suspected during [his] life that the two sisters to whom he was [devoted?] ... would combine to frustrate and upset his plan," he "would no doubt have provided us" with a document to forestall their blocking his will.[19]

The Jesuit archives in London, however, do have such a letter, clearly from Caddell, dated May 9, 1887, but unsigned:

> Whatever property or money may come to the Society of Jesus by virtue of my will and the letter of instructions which I leave to my sister Pauline I wish to be devoted to the education of Jesuit students in the English Province. The property can be sold if necessary for this purpose. I leave it to the English Jesuits because I dread and very much dislike the spirit of nationalism that prevails in Ireland.[20]

Did the dying man craft this letter under Gallwey's control? Apparently not. Gallwey was never at the final death-bed, seemed to have had nothing to do with any such letter, and was the victim of continuing anti-Jesuit suspicions even among fellow Catholics.

Sophia and her husband hastened to make amends. Austin J. King, the Jerninghams' solicitor, stated, "All imputations against Father Gallwey are unreservedly withdrawn, and I am sure that my clients will take every opportunity of removing any idea of misconduct on his part they may have suggested," including publication of their final decision in *The Tablet*, the official British Catholic weekly newspaper sponsored by the archbishop of Westminster, if Gallwey's Jesuit superiors wished to do so. The "third codicil" of the will "was made without the knowledge of Father Gallwey and therefore without his interference."[21] The potential lawsuit was then withdrawn (or possibly never fully filed).

This will had been drawn up by Caddell's "ordinary solicitor" in 1885, two years before Caddell's death, with its first codicil added that same year, and the second and third codicils entered the year Caddell died. Apparently in the end, the disposition of the estate was more than satisfactory to Sophia, who seemed to be the main engine of discontent all along. In addition to her five thousand pounds, she was to receive 5 percent annual interest on any remaining equity after the death of her sister Joanna. Her behavior in attacking Gallwey may in part be explained by her remark, "My brother did not communicate his wish[es] to me during his lifetime" but clearly consulted Gallwey, she believed.[22]

The Jesuit English Province was bequeathed Caddell's real estate, valued at perhaps ninety thousand pounds, a very considerable sum (almost twelve million dollars today), while Gallwey himself received twenty-five hundred pounds, as did Pauline Caddell (Sister Mary Ann), who turned over this sum to her convent, an act that Sophia seemed to accept. Even Sophia's husband received an annuity of six hundred pounds. In the end Sophia was tortuously placated: "I am however desirous of giving effect to what I believe as aforesaid to have been the wish of my said brother."[23]

Gallwey's reputation was intact. The Jesuit who drew crowds of Londoners for his sermons, considered by his peers to be one of "the leading Catholics" of his day[24] and "perhaps the best-known Jesuit of the day in England,"[25] wore his black robe without disguise when he preached his sermon for Robert Caddell, *A Discourse Over His Remains*, at the Oratory of the Sacred Heart, Bournemouth, on November 17, 1887.

Details of the Litigation:
   Jerningham v. Caddell, 1888

Chancery

Plaintiff: Sophia Jerningham   *Defendant*: Estate of Robert Caddell

Charge: Interference with the estate and will of Robert Caddell by Peter Gallwey.

Resolution: Suit withdrawn before court was seated, plaintiff having determined that defendant was innocent of any interference.

Part III

The Unbuilt Victorian Church

17

Divided Churches, Divided Souls

> There are those who hold there are no unbuildable buildings, only unbuilt ones. ... Perhaps one cannot separate true architectural impossibility from the social will to build.
> —Robert Harbison, *The Built, the Unbuilt, and the Unbuildable* (1991)

More than half of the ten scandalous cases in part II involved the difficulties of reconciling Roman Catholics and Anglicans in the early and mid–Victorian eras. Surprisingly many of the difficulties were architectural as well, especially in the divided churches. Perhaps only the magnanimous and compromising style of the very rich, such as the dukes of Norfolk, could persevere successfully in such a difficult dialectic. Given all the religious tensions, it may come as a surprise that almost all the dukes of Norfolk gave generously to both faiths, seeming to require only one concession in the end: pray over my corpse in Anglican discourse all that you wish, but just make sure you drop my mortal remains in the tomb on the Roman Catholic side of the church. Similar attitudes prevailed among the Catholic lords of the private aisles in the Anglican churches at Mapledurham and Titchborne.

Despite the absence of any absolute correlation among class status, religious conversion, and Victorian church architecture, I would argue that many Victorian religious leaders, architects, and lay activists believed that the key to converting the British working and middle classes from one faith to another (or from no faith to a faith) lay in selecting just the right church architecture. Historical precedent, contemporary artistic trends, occasional theological analysis, and just plain envy informed those who—whether serving on church building

17. Divided Churches, Divided Souls

committees or writing about the power of colored brickwork to sustain religious fervor—sought to proselytize by architecture.

In the end, the variety of models for those who built to convert was quite remarkable. Anglican activists went so far as to build a church for the conversion of the Jews not in the East End (traditional home of London's Jews) but south of the Thames in Camberwell. (Were they to move up in class as they converted?) This Cold Harbour Lane Chapel for Converted Jews resembled a synagogue, but it in turn used a similar gothic element—the rose window—that its architect, G.A. Audsley, had already incorporated in his Toxteth, Liverpool, synagogue on Prince's Road, which also had a Byzantine interior and a mosque-like entranceway.

The careers of the neo-classical architects such as William and Henry Inwood overlapped the arrival of Queen Victoria to the throne in 1837. They celebrated the Greek Revival style in the St. Pancras New Church (1822) on Upper Woburn Place on the cusp of the boroughs of Bloomsbury and St. Pancras in London, creating an Anglican church like no other in London. For the temple-like vestibule of the new church, the builders painstakingly recreated the portico of caryatids—beautiful and powerful female figures—from the 5th century BCE Erechtheum on the Acropolis. Their octagonal vestibule ceiling was also an imitation

The Portico of Caryatids on St. Pancras New Church on Upper Woburn Place, London (photograph by the author).

The Portico of Caryatids of the Erechtheum on the Acropolis, 5th century BCE, from postcard c. 1960 (author's collection).

of the first-century Tower of the Winds, the world's first meteorological building, located in the Roman Agora of Athens.

The Inwoods were also responsible for another Greek Revival church in nearby Camden, the Anglican All Saints Church at the intersection of Camden and Pratt streets. (It is now the Greek Orthodox All Saints Cathedral.) All Saints uses the Corinthian order of columns that originated in the 4th century BCE Choragic Monument of Lysicrates in Athens, a tower celebrating choral performances.

Only the Newmanite celebration of the classicism of Roman basilicas comes close to the Inwoods' divergence from Gothic orthodoxy. For the Oratorians, classical meant a Roman basilica. We have also seen how enthusiastically Anglo-Catholics turned to the architect William Butterfield, the most Pre-Raphaelite and gaudy of Gothicizers, while Roman Catholics remained torn between Puginesque neo-gothic cathedrals and Romanesque basilicas.

In some cases, proponents of conversion by architecture argued historically for their approach—that true "Catholicism" lay in the medieval era (before Henry the VIII's Reformation), or that the working and middle classes preferred Roman temples to Greek ones (or vice versa). Such arguments mixed mostly class bias and theological obsessions, especially when the controversies turned to various class-bound

17. Divided Churches, Divided Souls

traditions, such as the fourteenth-century "lady chapels" dedicated to the Virgin Mary, erected by Roman Catholic aristocrats, maintained in some cases as their private property but usually secured for post–Reformation Anglican churches.

Only three major (and still extant) instances of divided Victorian churches—Arundel, Tichborne, and Mapledurham—retained their Roman Catholic aisles or chapels even after legal challenges, persisting as Roman Catholic islands in Anglican churches. More Roman Catholic cathedrals and churches than monasteries and convents survived the Reformation, although "lady chapels" and other private spaces were serious losses to their Catholic owners.

St. Helen's Bishopsgate survived, in a unique fashion, the Reformation's purge of monasteries and convents in still another variation of the "divided" church. Today St. Helen's appears to have a unified interior space for worship, but originally there were two separate churches on the site, the Church of St. Helen on the south side and the Priory Church of the Benedictine Nuns of St. Helen of the north side. The two doorways on the western end of the undivided church remained in place.

St. Helen's Bishopsgate, showing dual entranceways to the original Church of St. Helen and the Priory Church of the Benedictine nuns of St. Helen (photograph by the author).

Externally, the western wall with two separate doorways to the building has clearly been formed from two separate and "parallel" churches. The convent was suppressed in 1538 and the nave of the Priory Church was "opened" up as one church, now known as St. Helen's Bishopsgate. The former naves of the two churches can be clearly seen as separated by the four great arches added in the fifteenth century. Before the nunnery was suppressed, the nuns were able to listen to the service in St. Helen's Church in their former nave behind a screen and use the still-extant Night Staircase to return to their dormitory. When the nuns were finally pensioned off in 1538, an undivided church in both name and deed remained.

Seemingly nonreligious buildings are a special case because they eschew obvious denominational allegiance. The Rushton Triangular Lodge near Northampton, for example, is one remarkable building that has survived, perhaps because of an almost mystical architectural style that would not seem traditionally Roman Catholic to many contemporaries. And of course it was a private building not open for public worship, Catholic or otherwise. Owner Thomas Tresham, who had

Interior of St. Helen's Bishopsgate, London, showing original four-part archway dividing the two churches (photograph by the author).

conformed to the Elizabethan settlement in the sixteenth century, reconverted to the "old religion" (with the help of a Jesuit missionary). Tresham's contemporary genealogist, Mary E. Finch, has called him an "enigmatic Northamptonshire recusant," his county and background particularly important because he "belonged to a rank only one degree below the peerage," although peers were rare on the ground in his locale.[1] He husbanded his wealth, minded his accounts, and spent his fortune on the buildings that expressed his mystical Catholicism.

Punished for his Roman Catholic views with fifteen years in prison, Tresham designed and constructed the building that is now called Rushton Triangular Lodge (1593–7), but it was also called the Triangular Warrener's Lodge[2]; its decorative features punned on his name (*Tresh*am = Three Am I), the trefoil which was his heraldic sign, and the Holy Trinity, a safe enough religious obsession shared by Catholics and Protestants alike. All these symbolic and literal three's were the unique decorative elements of the building Tresham considered the residence and work-space of his rabbit business, as the lodge was also the home of his warrener, or rabbit supervisor, near the site of numerous semi-underground rabbit warrens.

Outwardly built in a contemporary style, replete with esoteric devices common to other whimsical aristocratic builders, and, perhaps most touching, dedicated to raising bunny families, Tresham's vernacular stone ode to the Trinity complemented at least three other idiosyncratic buildings he erected elsewhere in Northamptonshire. The Market House at Rothwell was decorated with heraldic insignia and trefoils as well as his family shield; his unfinished residential lodge at New Bield at Lyveden was designed in the shape of a cross, obviously symbolizing the passion of Christ; and the hexagonal Hawkfield Lodge may have had a deceptive name, because it may have been too small for hunting or hawking.[3] Somewhat like Rushton in deflecting its avowed purpose, the Hawkfield Lodge is the only building of the four no longer in existence in any form and possibly the only one that was strictly dedicated to the oneness of God. We can assume that Tresham was drawn to his fantastic architectural conceits to deflect, like his rabbits at Rushton, the authorities from his Catholicism, for which he had suffered in the past.

And although Tresham himself was loyal to both Queen Elizabeth and her successor, King James, his son, Francis Tresham, made the mistake of having Guy Fawkes as a friend and was caught up in the Gunpowder Plot against King James. Francis may have had second thoughts, warning his father's brother-in-law, Lord Monteagle, of the plot in an anonymous letter, but it did not keep him from being imprisoned in the

Tower. Although many believed he died there of natural causes before he could be executed, he may have secretly escaped to France.[4]

His disappearance was just one of many freakish moments in this byzantine story. Catholic historians such as Francis Edwards maintain that the Gunpowder Plot was a classic agent provocateur's trap: King James's secretary, Lord Salisbury, stage-managed this Roman Catholic conspiracy that would, in failing, build support for the King's Protestantism and incidentally result in the confiscation of Catholic property and money in the tradition of Henry VIII. The celebration of Guy Fawkes Day (November 5), which really became popular in the Victorian era, used fireworks to represent the explosion from the caskets of gunpowder the conspirators had stowed under the House of Lords to kill James and most of his court and government during his intended state visit to Parliament. The day often featured anti–Catholic costumes: monks, priests, and bishops were mocked by celebrants in religious drag in the streets.

Although many Victorian Roman Catholics, especially those from wealthy families, had maintained accommodations with wealthy and influential Protestants, they could not deter their church—and especially militant missionaries like the Jesuits—from creating a culture of local recruitment. Of course, it helped that there was massive Irish immigration during this period, and one cannot help but speculate that many of the successes in developing expanded congregations had more to do with proximity to the poor and immigrant populations than with architectural decoration.

The medievalism of Ruskin and Pugin—especially evident in the latter's bombshell of a book, *Contrasts; or, A Parallel Between the Noble Edifices of the Fourteenth and Fifteenth Centuries, and Similar Buildings of the Present Day* (1841)—stressed an organic (if not utopian) community of the church and its churchgoers from all classes and stations in life. How to capture the successes of eras past in bringing poor people to worship became an architectural rather than a theological or practical guideline. The Anglican bishop of Exeter, Henry Phillpotts, had this opinion: "When the congregation consists mainly of the poorer orders," it is both the high ritual and the elaborate decorative architecture that wins their hearts. "They recognize ... their own high privilege as Christians, and rejoice to find themselves equal participants with their richest neighbors in the homage thus paid to the common Lord and Father of us all." Phillpotts was writing in the High Church journal, *The Ecclesiologist*, in 1851, at the moment that the greatest Anglo-Catholic triumph, William Butterfield's All Saints Margaret Street church, was being built. Of course the bishop had no intention of fostering illusions

17. Divided Churches, Divided Souls

in his admiring flock: the experience of the church spectacle would give them "solace [for] that poverty to which the providence of God had consigned them."[5]

A.J.B. Beresford-Hope, the president of the Ecclesiological Society, which sponsored so many of the Anglo-Catholic churches like Butterfield's, wanted to opt whenever possible for missionary churches, to go into neighborhoods in which the masses were ripe for conversion if not engulfment: "We must really make our Church a Model Church" with "a boundless area of nave to hold as many as possible of the adjacent all but heathen population." If necessary, it must be high enough "to domineer by its elevation over the haughty and Protestantized shopocracy."[6]

An even more obvious modernist (un–Ruskinian) version of Gothic was considered for a neighboring building in the Woodstock Road, the Anglican Holy Trinity Convent (now St. Antony's College), for which Charles Buckeridge was appointed architect. We do not know if Butterfield competed for this commission, but he had already designed numerous buildings for Anglican sisterhoods, a reflection of his Anglo-Catholic leanings and a fairly controversial practice, since to many mainstream Anglicans the idea of "sisterhoods" and similar practices smacked of obvious "popery," not to mention echoes of Maria Monk.

Buckeridge's proposed design was audacious in structure, as it sited the convent as a modernist version of the medieval spherical triangle or trilobed design, so common in Gothic manuscripts churches as an emblem of the Trinity and its mystery. But the precedent for its radical design of three persons in the Trinity—the Father, Son, and Holy Ghost—go back to the esoteric buildings such as the Rushton Triangular Lodge near Northampton.

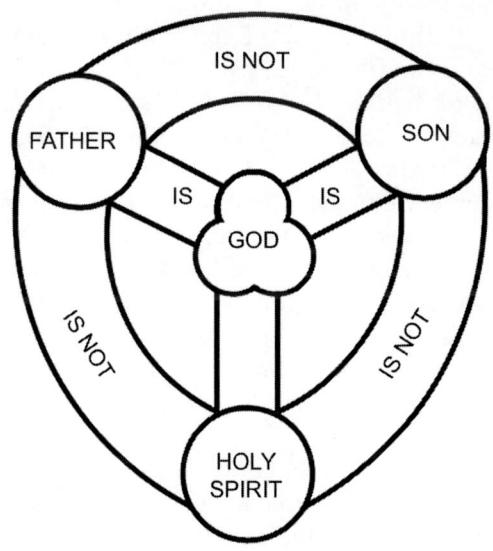

Version of the medieval image of the Trinity, originally proposed for the unbuilt Anglican Holy Trinity Convent (now St. Antony's College) by architect Charles Buckeridge (designed by Emily Taylor).

The central spherical triangle of Buckeridge's design is the chapel representing God, while each of the three circular rooms marking the corners is reached by a staircase from the central chapel. Each of the three outlying rooms is connected to the others by an outer, arcing cloister. Each cloister is a spiritual connection (representing "is not") among the persons of the Godhead, symbolizing that the Father is not the Son, the Son is not the Holy Ghost, and the Holy Ghost is not the Father. The inner cloisters or passageways (each representing "is") connect each person directly with God, so that God *is* the Father, God *is* the Son, and God *is* the Holy Ghost. (The mind boggles at what could have been chanted as one passed through these cloisters.) From the outside the convent was to look like a contemporary Victorian Gothic building, albeit with an "unusual pattern of wings and a central chapel with ... pyramidal roof and spire."[7] But this remarkable building was not to be: instead Butterfield received the commission for the chapel and created a Gothic—but for him somewhat conventional—structure.[8]

St. Etheldreda's Church in London's Ely Place was another conventional medieval building with an unconventional history. The principal early Victorian benefactor of the church was Sergeant Edward Bellasis, whose role as a trustee of Alton Towers properties had been controversial. St. Etheldreda's Church, however, was transformed from medieval Catholic to post–Reformation Anglican and then from a more or less unwanted property to Victorian Catholic. The church is, according to the *Blue Guide*, "a rare survivor in London of work in the Decorated Style from the end of the thirteenth century, comparable with the famous decorated chapel of Prior Crauden which survives at Ely [Cathedral] itself." This "typical two-story medieval private chapel" was for the use of the London residence of the bishop of Ely, situated on Ely Place in the City of London, a settlement or precinct of the "private property" of the bishop of Ely himself.[9] William Lockhart, Newman's friend, was the rector of the English province of the Institute of Charity, popularly known as the Rosminians, for whom Lockhart purchased the building. The order was named after Antonio Rosmini, its Italian founder.

Rosmini was a controversial figure in Italy, often feuding with the Jesuits and in trouble with Rome for some of his writings. However, his order's presence in England after the Catholic Emancipation Act of 1829 was especially important symbolically because his priests reintroduced the wearing of a religious habit and the "Roman collar" in public. Lockhart had been received into the Catholic faith by Luigi Gentili, a Rosminian missionary who arrived in England in 1835. Lockhart's reception preceded Newman's by two years and occasioned Newman's famous

17. Divided Churches, Divided Souls

St. Elthedreda's Church, 13th century, Ely Place, London (photograph by the author).

sermon "On the Parting of Friends," written before Newman had himself converted.[10]

Lockhart was more than a bit disingenuous when he described the moment in 1879 when at a mass celebrated before the Duke of Norfolk and other notables, "Ely Chapel surrendered itself once again to Roman obedience," because in fact Lockhart had purchased the entire chapel at an auction in 1874. More properly and equally remarkable, perhaps, is that it was the first pre–Reformation church to be restored to Roman Catholic worship, discounting of course the divided churches of Arundel, Mapledurham, and Tichborne, whose chapels or aisles represent a true continuity of Catholic worship from pre–Reformation days to the Victorian era. Nonetheless, Ely Chapel was by all definitions reconceived as a Catholic church, a remarkable combination of thirteenth century architecture and nineteenth century Roman Catholic decoration and refurbishing.[11]

St. Etheldreda herself is immortalized in Ely Place with a relic, a fragment of her pale but uncorrupted white hand, that is kept in a reliquary—a bejeweled chest—next to the altar of the church. During the post–Reformation persecution of Catholics, the hand was hidden at the Duke of Norfolk's Arundel Castle. St. Etheldreda, formerly the queen of Northumbria, had been the legendary founder of a seventh century monastery in Ely, upon whose foundation work began on what became the remarkable Ely Cathedral, universally admired, but especially

Prior Crauden's Chapel, part of the original monastic complex on the Ely Cathedral grounds (photograph by the author).

celebrated by Pugin, who called it "one of the most interesting churches in existence."[12]

Gerard Manley Hopkins singled out Prior Crauden's Chapel, as most visitors do, as it was part of the original monastic complex next to the cathedral, but also the Galilee, the porch for penitents, known for its foliage carvings and lancet doorway.

The Galilee had been photographed by Maria Rosina Giberne, Newman's close friend and Hopkins's aunt by marriage. Hopkins, who had been tutored in photography by the Giberne family, called the chapel "beautiful in proportion and even in detail" and the Galilee "full of good detail."[13]

Gallilee Porch entrance for penitents of Ely Cathedral, known for its Gothic carving (photograph by the author).

Perhaps Catholic in spirit but not in fact, *The Lives of the English Saints*, co-authored by Newman with W.A. Faber, was a contentious project also sharing in recognizing the spirit of pre-medieval Catholicism that led to the great cathedrals like Ely. *The Lives* purported to celebrate England as a medieval "Christian nation" and "an Isle of Saints." These saints "framed" their "services and doctrines after the Catholic model." "Where," *The Lives* concludes, "are those services now? There remains but a ruin of what once existed in beauty and honour."[14]

St. Etheldreda is not in *The Lives of the English Saints*. She persists, nonetheless, in a divided Victorian religious culture as a medieval symbol of the contention between the saints and sinners of the Victorian courts. The legacy of Ely Cathedral and St. Etheldreda's in Ely Place typify the dichotomy in so many of the trials and tribulations outlined in the litigated culture that pervades this book: two buildings named Ely, one in possession of the Anglican Church, the other by the Catholic Church, in spiritual terms as divided as the parish churches of Arundel, Mapledurham, and Tichborne.

Chapter Notes

Chapter 1

1. Maria Monk, *Awful Disclosures of Maria Monk*, 200, 204, 248.
2. Mike Mariani, "Nativism, Violence, and the Origins of the Paranoid Style."
3. Monk, *Awful*, 97, 132–33.
4. Monk, *Awful*, 165–8.
5. D.G. Paz, *Popular Anti-Catholicism in Mid-Victorian England*, 13.
6. Monk, *Awful*, 37.
7. Monk, *Awful*, 36.
8. Monk, *Awful*, 44.
9. Monk, *Awful*, 16–17.

Chapter 2

1. Lawrence Stone, *The Crisis of the Aristocracy, 1558–1641*, 731; see also George Andrew Beck, ed., *The English Catholics: 1850–1950*, 223–6.
2. *Rome's Recruits*, 5.
3. Sara Coleridge, *Memoir and Letters of Sara Coleridge*, 468.
4. Ben Weinreb and Christopher Hibbert, eds. *The London Encyclopedia*, 693.
5. Owen Chadwick, *The Victorian Church*, vol. 2, 302.
6. Charles Eastlake, *A History of the Gothic Revival*, 248–49.
7. Chadwick, *Victorian*, vol. 2, 302, 352.
8. "St. Barnabas Church," 5.
9. Ernest Hartley Coleridge, *Life and Correspondence of John Duke Lord Coleridge*, vol. 2, 292–3.
10. Chadwick, *Victorian*, vol. 2, 310.
11. "E.A.T.," *Alexander Heriot Mackonochie: A Memoir*, xiii.
12. E.R. Norman, *Anti-Catholicism in Victorian England*, 107.
13. Maureen Moran, *Catholic Sensationalism and Victorian Literature*, 197–98.
14. "E.A.T.," *Alexander*, 286–9.
15. Richard F. Clarke, "Alexander Heriot MacKonochie," 65–73, 71.
16. Chadwick, *Victorian*, vol. 2, 296.
17. "A Novel Importation," *London Times*, November 13, 1850, 5.
18. "The Priesthood in France," *London Times*, December 5, 1850, 8.
19. "The Fifth of November," *London Times*, November 6, 1850, 6.
20. "Oratory Funeral," *London Times*, November 15, 1850, 5.
21. Wilfrid Ward, *Life of John Henry Cardinal Newman*, vol. 2, 352.
22. Vincent F. Blehl, "Newman on Trial," *The Month*, n.s., 27 (February 1962): 69–80, 78.
23. Winefride Elwes, *The Feilding Album*, 44–5.
24. Elwes, *Feiding*, 62.
25. "Papistical Cauistry," *London Times*, November 15, 1850, 5.
26. "The Murphy Riots," *London Times*, May 28, 1868, 11; May 29, 1868, 5.
27. "Religious Riots in Lancashire," *London Times*, May 28, 1868, 11.
28. "Religious Riots in Lancashire," *London Times*, May 29, 1868, 5.
29. Donald C. Richter, *Riotous Victorians*, 4.
30. "Murphy Riots," *London Times*, May 28, 1868, 11.

Chapter 3

1. Charles Dickens, *Bleak House*, 14–16.
2. Dickens, *Bleak House*, 974–5.
3. William S. Holdsworth, *A History of English Law*, passim.

Chapter 4

1. J.B. Atlay, *The Victorian Chancellors*, vol. 1, 117.
2. Anthony Richard Wagner, *English Genealogy*, 339–40, 350.
3. Howard Gruber, *Darwin on Man: A Psychological Study of Scientific Creativity*, 14.
4. James A. Secord, "Nature's Fancy: Charles Darwin and the Breeding of Pigeons," *Isis* 72, no. 2 (January 1981): 180.
5. Francis Galton, *Hereditary Genius*, 368–70.
6. Francis Galton, "The Identiscope," *Nature*, October 30, 1884, 637.
7. Galton, *Hereditary*, 338–39.
8. Galton, *Hereditary*, 1.
9. Galton, *Hereditary*, 14.
10. Galton, *Hereditary*, 52–53.
11. Galton, *Hereditary*, 189–90.
12. Galton, *Hereditary*, 314–15.
13. Galton, *Hereditary*, 91, 230.
14. D.W. Forrest, *Francis Galton: The Life and Work of a Victorian Genius*, 94.
15. Galton, *Hereditary*, 87.
16. Galton, *Hereditary*, 65.
17. Galton, *Hereditary*, 227.
18. Galton, "Identiscope," 638.

Chapter 5

1. Galton, *Hereditary*, 69.
2. Noel Annan, "The Intellectual Aristocracy," 243–4.
3. Arthur Coleridge, *Reminiscences*, 89.
4. Arthur Coleridge, *Reminiscences*, 6.
5. John Duke Coleridge, "The Late Herbert Coleridge," *MacMillan's Magazine* 5 (November 1861): 59.
6. David McCracken, *Wordsworth and the Lake District*, 116–17.
7. Ernest Hartley Coleridge, *Life*, vol. 2, 57.
8. Arthur Coleridge, *Reminiscences*, 5.
9. Sara Coleridge, *Memoir*, 351.
10. Sara Coleridge, *Memoir*, 470, 485.
11. Ernest Hartley Coleridge, *Life*, vol. 1, 144–5.
12. Wilfrid Woollen, *Father Faber*, 14.
13. Henry James Coleridge, *Father*, 157.
14. John Henry Newman, *The Letters and Diaries of John Henry Newman*, vol. 22, 306–7.
15. John Henry Newman, *Letters*, vol. 23, 182.
16. Joyce Sugg, *Ever Yours Affly*, 281.
17. John Henry Newman, *Letters*, vol. 29, 209.
18. Newman, *Letters*, vol. 30, 438.
19. Newman, *Letters*, vol. 31, 4.
20. Newman, *Letters*, vol. 30, 443.
21. Newman, *Letters*, vol. 31, 197.
22. Newman, *Letters*, vol. 29, 357.
23. Henry James Coleridge, *Father*, 157.
24. Clarke, "Recollections," 164–5.
25. Clarke, 159.
26. Clarke, 172.
27. Frank McDonald, "Forgotten Nun Back to Hold Up Her Corner."
28. Clark, "Recollections," 176.
29. Mary Elizabeth Coleridge, *Gathered Leaves*, 21.
30. Henry Nelson Coleridge, "The Poetical Works of S.T. Coleridge," *Quarterly Review* 52 (August 1834): 38.
31. Henry Russell Hitchcock, *Early Victorian Architecture in Britain*, 571.
32. Paul Thompson, *William Butterfield*, 30–33.
33. Galton, *Hereditary*, 230.

Chapter 6

1. John Summerson, *Heavenly Mansions*, 160–61, 163.
2. Hitchcock, *Early*, 571.
3. Ernest Hartley Coleridge, *Life*, vol. 2, 219.
4. Thompson, *William*, 235.
5. Hersey, *High*, 108.
6. Gerard Manley Hopkins, *Poems*, 22.
7. Thompson, *William*, 323–4.
8. Hopkins, *Journals*, 254–5.
9. Robert Bernard Martin, *Gerard Manley Hopkins*, 400.

10. Hersey, *High*, 96.
11. Ruskin, *Works*, vol. 19, 28.
12. Thompson, *William*, 30.
13. Tyron Landau, *William Butterfield*, 4.
14. Hitchcock, *Early*, 580.
15. Hersey, *High*, 108.
16. Hersey, *High*, 114.
17. Ernest Hartley Coleridge, *Life*, vol. 2, 381.

Chapter 7

1. Annette Dawson, *Cornelia Connelly*, 2.
2. Juliana Wadham, *Case of Cornelia Connelly*, 58.
3. Marie Therese, *Cornelia Connelly*, 61.
4. Dawson, *Cornelia*, 13.
5. *The Life of Cornelia Connelly, 1809–1879*, 135.
6. *The Life*, 180.
7. Wadham, *The Case*, 78.
8. Sugg, *Ever*, 65.
9. *The Life*, 320.
10. A Religious of the Society of the Holy Child Jesus, *A Daughter of Coventry Patmore*, 188.
11. Newman, *Letters*, vol. 2, 334.
12. "Cornelia Connelly: Founder, Society of the Holy Child Jesus, 1809–1879."
13. *The Life*, 155.
14. *The Life*, 155–56.
15. Wadham, *Life*, 127–8.
16. Therese, *Cornelia*, 100.
17. *The Life*, 165–6.
18. Sheila Kaye-Smith, *Quartet in Heaven*, 102–3.
19. "Connelly v. Connelly," *London Times*, March 25, 1850, 6.
20. "Connelly v. Connelly," *London Times*, June 28, 1851, 7.
21. Wadham, *Life*, 130–31.
22. "Connelly v. Connelly," *London Times*, June 28, 1851, 7.
23. "Connelly v. Connelly," *London Times*, June 30, 1851, 7.
24. "Connelly v. Connelly," *London Times*, June 28, 1851, 7.
25. *Reports of Cases Argued and Determined in the English Ecclesiastical Courts*, 291–93.
26. "Connelly v. Connelly," *London Times*, June 28, 1851, 7.
27. "Connelly v. Connelly," *London Times*, June 30, 1851, 7.
28. Marie Therese, *Cornelia*, 108.
29. Marie Therese, *Cornelia*, 101–02.
30. "Convents—Petition of Rev. Pierce Connelly."
31. Marie Therese, *Cornelia*, 146–48; 152.
32. Marie Therese, *Cornelia*, 104.
33. Newman, *Letters*, vol. 14, 280–81.
34. Newman, *Letters*, vol. 15, 487, 515.
35. Newman, *Letters*, vol. 7, 445.
36. Dawson, *Cornelia*, 23.
37. Teresa Huffman Traver, "Losing a Family, Gaining a Church: Catholic Conversion and English Domesticity," *Victorian Review* 37, no. 1 (Spring 2011): 127, 130–31.
38. Traver, "Losing," 127.
39. Henry James Coleridge, "Reflections on a Late Scandal," *The Month* 10 (March 1870): 215.
40. Traver, "Losing," 140.
41. Wadham, *Life*, 142.
42. Marie Therese, *Cornelia*, 113.
43. Wadham, *Life*, 146.
44. Marie Therese, *Cornelia*, 183.
45. Marie Therese, *Cornelia*, 126.
46. Wadham, *Life*, 221–2.
47. *The Life*, 176, 182.

Chapter 8

1. Newman, *Letters*, vol. 8, 59–61.
2. Lance Sieveking, "Remembering Gerard Manley Hopkins," *Listener* 57 (January 1957): 152.
3. Meriol Trevor, *Newman [I]: The Pillar of the Cloud*, 72; Lance Sieveking, *The Eye of the Beholder*, 278.
4. Trevor, *Newman [I]*, 318–19.
5. Trevor, *Newman [I]*, 68.
6. Newman, *Letters*, vol. 19, 14; vol. 28, 127.
7. Sieveking, *Eye of the Beholder*, 223–4.
8. Galton, *Hereditary*, 257–8.
9. Robert Milburn, "The Newman Brothers: Free Choice or Fate?" *Contemporary Review* 258 (May 1991): 267.
10. Sieveking, *Eye*, 217.
11. Meriol Trevor, *Newman [II]: Light in Winter*, 614–5.
12. Sugg, *Ever Yours*, 78–9.

13. Meriol Trevor, *Newman's Journey*, 154.
14. Newman, *Letters*, vol. 19, 220.
15. T. Mozley, *Reminiscences Chiefly of Oriel College and the Oxford Movement*, vol. I, 42–5.
16. Newman, *Letters*, vol. 19, 263–4; Sugg, *Ever Yours*, 82.
17. Newman, *Letters*, vol. 12, 209.
18. Newman, *Letters*, vol. 12, 204.
19. Newman, *Letters*, vol. 18, 124.
20. Newman, *Letters*, vol. 19, 188.
21. Sugg, *Ever Yours*, 215, 220–1; Newman, *Letters*, vol. 13, 433–4; 20, 565–6.
22. Matthew C. Mirow, "Roman Catholicism on Trial: The Libel Case of John Henry Newman and Dr. Achilli," *Catholic Lawyer* 36 (1996): 405.
23. Cardinal Nicholas Wiseman, "Dr. Achilli," *Dublin Review* 28 (June 1850): 485, 511.
24. Trevor, *Newman [I]*, 66.
25. John Henry Newman, *Lectures on the Present Position of Catholics in England*, 198.
26. Wilfrid Ward, *Life of John Henry Cardinal Newman*, vol. I, 252.
27. Trevor, *Newman [I]*, 554–55.
28. Newman, *Letters*, vol. 14, 508.
29. John Henry Newman, *Sermon Notes of John Henry Cardinal Newman 1849–1878*, 103.
30. Trevor, *Newman [I]*, 556.
31. W.F. Finlason, *Report on the Trial and Preliminary Proceedings in the Case of the Queen on the Prosecution of G. Achilli v. Dr. Newman*, 33.
32. Vincent F. Blehl, "Newman on Trial," *The Month*, n.s., 27 (February 1962): 75.
33. Sugg, *Ever Yours*, 90–91, 96.
34. Newman, *Letters*, vol. 14, 511.
35. Mirow, "Roman," 417.
36. Mirow, "Roman," 415.
37. Finlason, *Report*, 54–5.
38. Finlason, *Report*, 69.
39. Finlason, *Report*, 22–3.
40. Finlason, *Report*, 59–60.
41. Finlason, *Report*, 78–9.
42. Finlason, *Report*, 84.
43. Finlason, *Report*, 85.
44. Finlason, *Report*, 83; 125.
45. Finlason, *Report*, 101.
46. Finlason, *Report*, 22, 74.
47. Finlason, *Report*, 49.
48. Finlason, *Report*, 120, 133, 125.
49. Finlason, *Report*, 130, 134, 140–41.
50. Finlason, *Report*, 132.
51. Finlason, *Report*, 144.
52. Finlason, *Report*, 64.
53. Newman, *Lectures*, 199.
54. Newman, *Lectures*, 204.
55. Finlason, *Report*, 25.
56. Finlason, *Report*, 152.
57. Finlason, *Report*, 154, 174–5.
58. Finlason, *Report*, 111.
59. Finlason, *Report*, 112.
60. Finlason, *Report*, 181, 200.
61. Finlason, *Report*, 190.
62. Finlason, *Report*, 210.
63. Finlason, *Report*, 210.
64. Newman, *Letters*, vol. 15, 525.
65. Newman, *Letters*, vol. 15, 278.
66. Newman, *Letters*, vol. 15, 278–79, 284.
67. Newman, *Letters*, vol. 15, 278.
68. Blehl, "Newman on Trial," 77.
69. S. Gilley, "Achilli (Giovanni) Giacinto (b. c. 1803)," *Oxford Dictionary of National Biography*, passim.
70. Finlason, *Report*, 204–05.
71. Newman, *Letters*, vol. 15, 287.
72. Newman, *Letters*, vol. 15, 389.
73. Newman, *Letters*, vol. 26, 60.
74. John Hungerford Pollen, "Newman in Dublin," *The Month*, September 1906, 319.
75. Newman, *Letters*, vol. 31, 103.
76. Newman, *Letters*, vol. 31, 299.
77. Newman, *Letters*, vol. 15, 233.
78. James Patrick, "Newman, Pugin, and Gothic," *Victorian Studies* 24 (Winter 1981): 199.
79. Patrick, "Newman," 199.
80. Stephen C. Humphrey, ed. *Blue Guide to Churches and Chapels of Northern England*, 395.
81. Patrick, "Newman, Pugin," 197.
82. Newman, *Letters*, vol. 13, 460.
83. Phoebe Stanton, *Pugin*, 151, 171.
84. Michael Napier and Alistair Laing, *The London Oratory: Centenary 1884–1984*, 23.
85. Newman, *Letters*, vol. 12, 220–22.
86. Napier and Laing, *London Oratory*, 23.
87. Ambrose Phillipps de Lisle, *The Life and Letters of Ambrose Phillipps de Lisle*, vol. I, 314–15.
88. Napier and Liang, *London Oratory*, 87.
89. Rosemary Hill, *God's Architect:*

Pugin and the Building of Romantic Britain, 1.

Chapter 9

1. Tony Hadland, *Thames Valley Papists: From Reformation to Emancipation, 1534–1829*, 84.
2. Hadland, *Thames*, 60.
3. Hadland, *Thames*, 115.
4. Maynard Mack, *Alexander Pope: A Life*, 248.
5. Mack, *Alexander*, 257, 31.
6. Nigel Cawthorne, *Sex Lives of the Kings and Queens of England*, 155.
7. Claire Tomalin, *Mrs. Jordan's Profession: The Actress and the Prince*, 301.
8. Cawthorne, *Sex Lives*, 155.
9. Tomalin, *Mrs. Jordan's*, 318.
10. Tomalin, *Mrs. Jordan's*, 318.
11. Tomalin *Mrs. Jordan's*, 318.
12. Tomalin, *Mrs. Jordan's*, 5.
13. Tomalin, *Mrs. Jordan's*, 6.
14. Tomalin, *Mrs. Jordan's*, 318.
15. Tomalin, *Mrs. Jordan's*, 318.
16. Tomalin, *Mrs. Jordan's*, 319.
17. Tomalin, *Mrs. Jordan's*, 310.
18. Tomalin, *Mrs. Jordan's*, 313.
19. A.H. Cooke, *The Early History of Mapledurham*, 176.
20. Cooke, *Early*, 140.
21. Cooke, *Early*, 120.
22. "Arundel Church," *London Times*, April 14, 1879, 3.
23. "Mapledurham Church," *London Times*, April 16, 1879, 11.
24. Cooke, *Early*, 176.
25. Nikolaus Pevsner and Jennifer Sherwood, *Oxfordshire*, 694.
26. William Butterfield, "Arundel Church," *London Times*, April 15, 1879, 5.

Chapter 10

1. Michael Fisher, *Alton Towers: A Gothic Wonderland*, 57, 167.
2. Wilkie Collins, *The Dead Secret*, 56.
3. Fisher, *Alton*, 134.
4. William Schupbach, "Visiting the Stigmatics of the South Tyrol—I. Maria Domenica Lazzari."
5. Simon Jenkins, *England's Thousand Best Churches*, 627.
6. Denis Gwynn, *Lord Shrewsbury, Pugin, and the Catholic Revival*, 122.
7. Stanton, *Pugin*, 138–40.
8. Fisher, *Alton*, 54.
9. Fisher, *Alton*, 58.
10. Fisher, *Alton*, 74.
11. Fisher, *Alton*, 90.
12. Fisher, *Alton*, 89–90.
13. Fisher, *Alton*, 97.
14. Fisher, *Alton*, 25.
15. Fisher, *Alton*, 259.
16. Gwynn, *Lord Shrewsbury*, 140.
17. Rosemary Hill, *God's Architect: Pugin and the Building of Romantic Britain*, 266.
18. Henry James Coleridge, "A Memorial" [James Robert Hope-Scott], *The Month* 19 (1873): 278, 285.
19. Henry James Coleridge, "A Memorial," 289.
20. Robert Ornsby, *Memoirs of James Robert Hope-Scott of Abbotsford*, vol. 2, 215.
21. Edward Belassis, *Memorials of Mr. Serjeant Belassis*, 42.
22. Earl of Shrewsbury Papers, Special Collections, Georgetown University.
23. Fisher, *Alton*, 159.
24. Gwynn, *Lord Shrewsbury*, 2.
25. Henry Wharton, *Reports of Cases Argued*, vol. 95, 218–220.
26. Wharton, *Reports*, 218–220.
27. Wharton, *Reports*, 218–220.
28. "The Shrewsbury Estates," *London Times*, August 5, 1859, 10.
29. "The Earl of Shrewsbury on His Title and the Estates," *London Times*, October 5, 1859, 9.
30. Earl of Shrewsbury Papers, Special Collections, Georgetown University.
31. Fisher, *Alton*, 16.

Chapter 11

1. Martineau, *Sister Anna's Probation*, April 12, 1862, 426.
2. Susan P. Casteris, "Virgin Vows: The Early Victorian Artists' Portrayal of Nuns and Novices," *Victorian Studies* 24 (Winter 1981): 76–78.
3. "Saurin v. Star and Kennedy," *London Times*, February 4, 1869, 10.
4. Newman, *Letters*, vol. 14, 229.
5. Chadwick, *Victorian Church*, vol. 2, 509.

6. Mary Scholastica Joseph, *The Great Convent Case: Saurin v. Star and Kennedy*, 52.
7. "Saurin v. Star," February 4, 1869, 10.
8. Mary Scholastica Joseph, 86.
9. Mary Scholastica Joseph, 53.
10. Mary Scholastica Joseph, 121.
11. "Saurin v. Star," February 26, 1869, 8.
12. Mary Scholastica Joseph, 113.
13. Mary Scholastica Joseph, 87.
14. Mary Scholastica Joseph, 23; "Saurin v. Star," February 4, 1869, 10.
15. Mary Scholastica Joseph, 133.
16. Mary Scholastica Joseph, 66.
17. "Saurin v. Star," February 5, 1869, 8.
18. "Saurin v. Star," February 4, 1869, 10.
19. Mary Scholastica Joseph, 15; "Saurin v. Star," February 6, 1869, 8.
20. "Saurin v. Star," February 6, 1869, 8.
21. "Saurin v. Star," February 4, 1869, 10.
22. Mary Scholastica Joseph, 66; "Saurin v. Star," February 6, 1869, 8.
23. Mary Scholastica Joseph, 79.
24. Mary Scholastica Joseph, 27.
25. Mary Scholastica Joseph, 81.
26. Mary Scholastica Joseph, 98.
27. Mary Scholastica Joseph, 30.
28. Mary Scholastica Joseph, 88.
29. Mary Scholastica Joseph, 73.
30. Mary Scholastica Joseph, 127.
31. Mary Scholastica Joseph, 102.
32. Mary Scholastica Joseph, 77.
33. Mary Scholastica Joseph, 37.
34. Mary Scholastica Joseph, 73.
35. "Saurin v. Star," February 26, 1869, 8.
36. "Saurin v. Star," February 26, 1869, 8.
37. "Saurin v. Star," February 26, 1869, 8.
38. Mary Scholastica Joseph, 156.
39. Mary Scholastica Joseph, 144.
40. Mary Scholastica Joseph, 157.
41. Mary Scholastica Joseph, 174.
42. Mary Scholastica Joseph, 157.
43. Mary Scholastica Joseph, 158; "Saurin v. Star," February 27, 1869, 11.
44. Mary Scholastica Joseph, 158–9.
45. Mary Scholastica Joseph, 161.
46. "Saurin v. Star," February 4, 1869, 10.
47. Mary Scholastica Joseph, 7.
48. Mary Scholastica Joseph, 158.
49. Mary Scholastica Joseph, 158.
50. Mary Scholastica Joseph, 159.
51. Mary Scholastica Joseph, 167.
52. Mary Scholastica Joseph, 171.
53. "Saurin v. Star," February 27, 1869, 11.
54. Mary Scholastica Joseph, 171.
55. "Saurin v. Star," February 10, 1869, 9; January 12, 1870, 10; April 21, 1870, 9.

Chapter 12

1. Douglas Woodruff, *Tichborne Claimant*, 5.
2. William Hamper, "Church Notes from Tichborne, Hants," *Gentlemen's Magazine* 80, n.s. 3 (1810): 306.
3. Woodruff, *Tichborne*, 4.
4. Bram Stoker, "Arthur Orton."
5. "The Great Imposter," *London Times*, March 2, 1874, 10.
6. J.B. Atley, "The Tichborne Trial," *Famous Trials of the Century*, 166.
7. "Great Imposter," 10.
8. Atlay, *Tichborne*, 176.
9. Lord Maugham, *The Tichborne Case*, 86.
10. "The Tichborne Case," *London Times*, January 15, 1872, 4; "Great Imposter," 10.
11. Ernest Hartley Coleridge, *Life*, vol. 2, 181.
12. Geddes MacGregor, *The Tichborne Imposter*, 195.
13. "Great Imposter," 10; Atlay, *Tichborne*, 279.
14. Atlay, *Tichborne*, 221–2.
15. Atlay, *Tichborne*, 231.
16. Atlay, *Tichborne*, 216.
17. McWilliam, *Tichborne Claimant*, 83–4.
18. Robyn Annear, *The Man Who Lost Himself: The Unbelievable Story of the Tichborne Claimant*, 127.
19. Annear, *The Man*, 238.
20. Woodruff, *Tichborne*, 123.
21. "The Tichborne Case," *London Times*, July 25, 1873, 11.
22. Atlay, *Tichborne*, 360.
23. "The Tichborne Case," *London Times*, July 25, 1873, 11.
24. Atlay, *Tichborne*, 291.
25. "The Tichborne Case," *London Times*, June 5, 1873, 10.
26. Atlay, *Tichborne*, 291.

27. Woodruff, *Tichborne*, 66.
28. "The Tichborne Case," *London Times*, April 1, 1872, 8.
29. Hopkins, *Journals*, 410.
30. Ernest Hartley Coleridge, *Life*, vol. 2, 188.
31. Atlay, *Tichborne*, 287.
32. Ernest Hartley Coleridge, *Life*, vol. 2, 178.
33. Rohan McWilliam, *Tichborne Claimant: A Victorian Sensation*, 71.
34. McWiliam, *Tichborne Claimant*, 81–2.
35. McWilliam, *Tichborne Claimant*, 77.
36. Arthur Coleridge, *Reminiscences*, 5–6.
37. Maugham, *Tichborne*, 284–6.
38. Atlay, *Tichborne*, 323.
39. Maugham, *Tichborne*, 274.
40. Ernest Hartley Coleridge, *Life*, vol. 2, 195.
41. Ernest Hartley Coleridge, *Life*, vol. 2, 196.
42. Maugham, *Tichborne*, 313.
43. Maugham, *Tichborne*, 313–4.
44. Maugham, *Tichborne*, 313–4.
45. Maugham, *Tichborne*, 318–9.
46. Maugham, *Tichborne*, 318–9.
47. Maugham, *Tichborne*, 320–21.
48. Atlay, *Tichborne*, 351.
49. Maugham, *Tichborne*, 323.
50. Maugham, *Tichborne*, 331.
51. "The Tichborne Case," *London Times*, August 22, 1873, 8.
52. "The Tichborne Case," *London Times*, August 22, 1873, 8.
53. Michael Gilbert, *Claimant*, 217.
54. "The Tichborne Case," *London Times*, April 27, 1872, 12.
55. Maugham, *Tichborne*, 352.
56. Maugham, *Tichborne*, 352–6.
57. Atlay, *Tichborne*, 362.
58. "The Tichborne Case," *London Times*, June 7, 1873, 10.
59. "The Tichborne Case," *London Times*, June 7, 1873, 10.
60. "The Tichborne Case," *London Times*, July 25, 1873, 11.
61. Annear, *The Man*, 343.
62. "The Tichborne Case," *London Times*, July 25, 1873, 11.
63. Woodruff, *Tichborne*, 364.
64. Annear, *The Man*, 369.
65. Annear, *The Man*, 352–4; Woodruff, *Tichborne*, 138–9, 361.
66. Maugham, *Tichborne*, 365.
67. Maugham, *Tichborne*, 366.
68. Woodruff, *Tichborne*, 377.
69. Ernest Hartley Coleridge, *Life*, vol. 2, 416.
70. "The Tichborne Case," *London Times*, August 22, 1873, 8.
71. Mark Twain, *Following the Equator*, 108–09.
72. "The End of Roger Tichborne," *London Times*, November 18, 1874, 5.

Chapter 13

1. Eamon Duffy, *The Stripping of the Altars: Traditional Religion in England c. 1400–c. 1580*, 139–402.
2. E.A. Freeman, "The Case of the Collegiate Church of Arundel," *Archaeological Journal* 37 (1880): 245.
3. Hilaire Belloc, *Elizabeth: Creature of Circumstance*, 83.
4. Freeman, "The Case," 261–4.
5. John Martin Robinson, *The Dukes of Norfolk: A Quincentennial History*, 100.
6. "[Duke of] Norfolk v. Arbuthnot," *London Times*, March 26, 1879, 6.
7. "The Arundel Chancel Case," *Sussex Archaeological Collections* 30 (1880): 33.
8. Earnest Hartley Coleridge, *Life*, vol. 2, 237.
9. "[Duke of] Norfolk v. Arbuthnot," *London Times*, March 28, 1879, 4.
10. "[Duke of] Norfolk v. Arbuthnot," *London Times*, March 26, 1879, 6.
11. "[Duke of] Norfolk v. Arbuthnot," *London Times*, March 27, 1879, 4; "Arundel Chancel," 36.
12. Freeman, "The Case," 253, 256, 257–59.
13. Freeman, "The Case," 269.
14. "Arundel Chancel," 36.
15. "[Duke of] Norfolk v. Arbuthnot," *London Times*, March 26, 1879, 6.
16. "[Duke of] Norfolk v. Arbuthnot," *London Times*, March 27, 1879, 4.
17. "[Duke of] Norfolk v. Arbuthnot," *London Times*, March 27, 1879, 4.
18. "[Duke of] Norfolk v. Arbuthnot," *London Times*, May 19, 1879, 6; see also Elvins, *Arundel Priory*, 100–01.
19. Elvins, *Arundel Priory*, 96, 99.
20. "Arundel Chancel," 50.

21. "[Duke of] Norfolk v. Arbuthnot," *London Times*, May 19, 1879, 6.
22. Elvins, "Arundel," 73.
23. "Arundel Chancel," 46.
24. "Obituary" [12th Duke of Norfolk], *Gentlemen's Magazine* 171, n.s. 17 (1842): 542–543.
25. "Obituary" [12th Duke of Norfolk], 542–3.
26. "Obituary" [12th Duke of Norfolk], 542–3.
27. "Death of the [14th] Duke of Norfolk," *London Times*, November 27, 1860, 4.
28. "Obituary" [14th Duke of Norfolk], *Gentlemen's Magazine* 210, n.s. 56 (1861): 99–100.
29. "The Late [11th] Duke of Norfolk," *Gentlemen's Magazine* 85, n.s. 8 (1815): 631–632.
30. Napier and Laing, "London Oratory," 53; Gwynn, "Lord Shrewsbury," 131.
31. "Obituary" [13th Duke of Norfolk], *Gentlemen's Magazine* 199, n.s. 45 (1856): 419.
32. Robinson, *Dukes*, 202.
33. "Obituary" [13th Duke of Norfolk], 419, 421.
34. Freeman, "The Case," 245–46.
35. *London Times*, March 29, 1879, 6.

Chapter 14

1. Gerald Roberts, "Living with Fr. Eyre: Hopkins at Stonyhurst College 1882–84," *Hopkins Quarterly* 39 (Summer–Fall 2012): 79.
2. Roberts, "Living," 80.
3. Roberts, "Living," 82.
4. Stephen C. Humphrey, *The Letters of Gerard Manley Hopkins to Robert Bridges*, 151–2.
5. Humphrey, *Letters*, 151–2.
6. Roberts, "Living," 84.
7. Coventry Patmore, "Walls and Wall-Painting at Oxford," *Saturday Review*, December 26, 1857, 583.
8. Roberts, "Living," 79.
9. "William Eyre," *Weekly Register*, May 5, 1883, Archivum Britannicum Societatis Iesu (ABSI), London.
10. "Release of Powers" [Eyre v. Eyre-Eyre], *The Law Times*, February 1, 1896, 308.
11. "Eyre-Eyre v. Eyre," *London Times*, July 31, 1883, 3.
12. Eyre Case Legacy, Letter to William Eyre from Count Eyre, October 30, 1854 (Box OA, Archivum Britannicum Societatis Iesu, London).
13. Eyre Case Legacy, Box OA, Archbishop Eyre, memo, n.d., ABSI.
14. Eyre Case Legacy, Box OA, Archbishop Eyre, memo, n.d., ABSI.
15. Eyre Case Legacy, Box OA, William Eyre, memo, September 20, 1882, ABSI.
16. Eyre Case Legacy, Box OA, William Eyre, memo, September 20, 1882, ABSI.
17. Roberts, "Living," 80.
18. Roberts, "Living," 79.
19. Eyre Case Legacy, Box OA, Miscellaneous Memos, *Letters and Notices* #121, April 1898, 429, ABSI.

Chapter 15

1. "Adams v. Lord Coleridge," *London Times*, November 19, 1886, 3.
2. "Adams v. Lord Coleridge," *London Times*, November 25, 1886, 3.
3. Charles Felix, *The Notting Hill Mystery*.
4. Paul Collins, "Before Hercule or Sherlock, There Was Ralph," *New York Times Book Review*, January 9, 2011, 23.
5. "Adams v. Lord Coleridge," *London Times*, November 22, 1886, 3.
6. "Adams v. Lord Coleridge," *London Times*, November 19, 1886, 3.
7. "Adams v. Lord Coleridge," *London Times*, November 19, 1886, 3.
8. "Adams v. Lord Coleridge," *London Times*, November 20, 1886, 5.
9. "Adams v. Lord Coleridge," *London Times*, November 18, 1886, 3.
10. "Adams v. Lord Coleridge," *London Times*, November 18, 1886, 3.
11. "Adams v. Lord Coleridge," *London Times*, November 19, 1886, 3; Ginger Frost, *Promises Broken: Courtship, Class, and Gender in Victorian England*, 15.
12. "Adams v. Lord Coleridge," *London Times*, November 18, 1886, 3.
13. "Adams v. Lord Coleridge," *London Times*, November 18, 1886, 3.
14. "Adams v. Lord Coleridge," *London Times*, November 19, 1886, 3.

15. "Adams v. Lord Coleridge," *London Times*, November 23, 1886, 3.
16. "Adams v. Lord Coleridge," *London Times*, November 23, 1886, 3.
17. "Adams v. Lord Coleridge," *London Times*, November 23, 1886, 3.
18. "Adams v. Lord Coleridge," *London Times*, November 23, 1886, 3.
19. "Adams v. Lord Coleridge," *London Times*, November 23, 1886, 3.
20. "Adams v. Lord Coleridge," *London Times*, November 23, 1886, 4.
21. "Adams v. Lord Coleridge," *London Times*, November 17, 1885, 3.
22. "Adams v. Lord Coleridge," *London Times*, November 17, 1885, 3.
23. "Adams v. Lord Coleridge," *London Times*, November 17, 1885, 3.
24. "Adams v. Lord Coleridge," *London Times*, November 18, 1886, 3.
25. "Adams v. Lord Coleridge," *London Times*, November 18, 1886, 3.
26. "Adams v. Lord Coleridge," *London Times*, November 18, 1886, 3.
27. "Adams v. Lord Coleridge," *London Times*, November 18, 1886, 3.
28. "Adams v. Lord Coleridge," *London Times*, November 18, 1886, 3; November 19, 1886, 3.
29. "Adams v. Lord Coleridge," *London Times*, November 20, 1886, 5.
30. "Adams v. Lord Coleridge," *London Times*, November 19, 1886, 31.
31. Mary Elizabeth Coleridge, *The Collected Poems of Mary Elizabeth Coleridge*, 51.
32. Mary Elizabeth Coleridge, *Collected Poems*, 51.
33. Richard Watson Dixon, *The Last Poems of Richard Watson Dixon*, v.
34. Stephen Coleridge, "The Administration of the Cruelty to Animals Act of 1876," *Fortnightly Review*, n.s., 7309 (March 1900): 392–398.
35. "Adams v. Lord Coleridge," *London Times*, November 18, 1886, 3; November 26, 1886, 3.
36. "Adams v. Lord Coleridge," *London Times*, November 20, 1886, 5.
37. "Adams v. Lord Coleridge," *London Times*, November 22, 1886, 3.
38. "Adams v. Lord Coleridge," *London Times*, November 24, 1886, 3.
39. "Adams v. Lord Coleridge," *London Times*, November 20, 1886, 4.
40. "Adams v. Lord Coleridge," *London Times*, November 20, 1886, 4.
41. "Adams v. Lord Coleridge," *London Times*, November 20, 1886, 5.

Chapter 16

1. Wilkie Collins, *The Black Robe*, 35.
2. Collins, *Black Robe*, 12.
3. Collins, *Black Robe*, 233–4.
4. Peter Gallwey, *Salvage from the Wreck: A Few Memories of Friends Departed, Preserved in Funeral Discourses*, 324.
5. Gallwey, *Salvage*, 324–5.
6. "Estate: Caddell," *Landed Estate Database*.
7. M. Gavin, *Memoirs of Father P. Gallwey, S.J.*, 3.
8. "The Tichborne Case," *London Times*, May 31, 1873, 10.
9. Gavin, *Memoirs*, 6.
10. Gallwey, *Salvage*, 325.
11. Gallwey, *Salvage*, 327.
12. Gallwey, *Salvage*, 335.
13. Gallwey, *Salvage*, 339.
14. Robert Caddell, Box D/4, memo May 22, 1888, ABSI.
15. Robert Bernard Martin, *Gerard Manley Hopkins*, 280–81.
16. Martin, *Gerard*, 282.
17. Robert Caddell, Box D/4, memo May 22, 1888, ABSI.
18. Robert Caddell, Box D/4, Statuary Declaration of Mrs. P. Caddell, 1887, ABSI.
19. Robert Caddell, Box D/4, Draft Nores, Point 19, ABSI.
20. Robert Caddell, Box D/4, unsigned letter of Caddell, May 9, 1887, ABSI.
21. Robert Caddell, Box D/4, notes of Austin AS. King, June 16, 1888, ABSI.
22. Robert Caddell, Box D/4, memo of Sophia Jerningham, May 22, 1888, ABSI.
23. Robert Caddell, Box D/4, memo of Sophia Jerningham, May 22, 1888, ABSI.
24. Gavin, *Memoirs*, 7–8.
25. Martin, *Gerard*, 279.

Chapter 17

1. Mary E. Finch, *Wealth of Five Northamptonshire Families: 1540–1640*, 66.

2. Finch, *Wealth*, 182.
3. Finch, *Wealth*, 182.
4. Alan Haynes, *The Gunpowder Plot: Faith in Rebellion*, 96.
5. Hersey, *High Victorian Gothic*, 96.
6. Thompson, *Butterfield*, 321.
7. Howard Colvin, *Unbuilt Oxford*, 113–5.
8. Thompson, *Butterfield*, 391.
9. Humphrey, *Blue Guide to Churches and Chapels of Southern England*, 356.
10. Gwynn, *Lord Shrewsbury*, 100.
11. Humphrey, *Blue Guide*, 356–7.
12. Hill, *God's Architect*, 157.
13. Hopkins, *Journals*, 187.
14. John Henry Newman and James Toovey, *The Lives of the English Saints*, 370–76.

Bibliography

NOTE: All trials covered in the *London Times* are referenced below by the *title of the case*—in the same way that the indices of the *Times* reference them—and *not* by the heading of the actually published article, usually the name of the court. Thus "Duke of Norfolk v. Arbuthnot" appears below, but not "Court of Common Pleas" (as it actually appeared in newsprint). In a similar way, any letters to the editor are cited by the subject heading, e.g., "Arundel Church." I have used the *Times* as well as any published transcripts of the trials, in part to double-check for accuracy, but it is not universally known that—in the words of the lord chief justice in *Saurin v. Star and Kennedy*—it was "common not to take shorthand notes of the speeches of counsel." As a result—quite a surprise, I would say—the judge would sometimes actually read aloud the morning's newspaper report of the speeches of counsel from the court session of the day before.

"Adams v. Lord Coleridge." *London Times*, November 17, 1885, 3; June 11, 1886, 3; November 18, 1886, 3; November 19, 1886, 3; November 20, 1886, 4–5; November 22, 1886, 3; November 23, 1886, 3–4; November 24, 1886, 3–4; November 25, 1886, 3; November 26, 1886, 3.
Aldrich, Megan. *Gothic Revival*. London: Phaidon, 1994.
Allies, T.W. *Journal in France in 1845 and 1848 with Letters from Italy in 1847*. London: Longman, Brown, Green, and Longmans, 1849.
Allitt, Patrick. *Catholic Converts*. Ithaca: Cornell University Press, 2000.
Amherst, W.J. "Frederick Lucas." *Dublin Review* 16, 3rd series (1886): 392–428.
Andrews, Anne. *A History of Tixall: Tixall's Churches*. Tixall: Hanyards, 1995.
Annan, Noel. "The Intellectual Aristocracy." In *Studies in a Social History*, ed. J.H. Plumb, 231–287. London: Longmans, Green, 1955.
Annear, Robyn. *The Man Who Lost Himself: The Unbelievable Story of the Tichborne Claimant*. London: Constable and Robinson, 2002.
Archivum Britannicum Societatis Iesu (ABSI). The Archives of the English Province of the Society of Jesus. London.
Arnstein, Walter L. *Protestant Versus Catholic in Mid-Victorian England: Mr. Newdegate and the Nuns*. Columbia: University of Missouri Press, 1982.
Arundel Cathedral. Norfolk: Cathedral of Our Lady and St. Philip, n.d.
"The Arundel Chancel Case." *Sussex Archaeological Collections* 30 (1880): 31–51.
"Arundel Church." *London Times*, April 2, 1879, 12; April 10, 1879, 11; April 14, 1879, 3; April 15, 1879, 4.

Bibliography

Arundel Parish Church, 1780–1880. Norfolk: St. Nicholas Community Programmes Team, 1986.

Atley, J.B. "The Tichborne Trial." In *Famous Trials of the Century.* London: Grant Richards, 1899, 160–392.

———. *The Victorian Chancellors.* 2 vols. London: Smith, Elder, 1906/1908.

Baker, Joseph Ellis. *The Victorian Novel and the Oxford Movement* (1932). Reprint, New York: Russell and Russell, 1965.

Ballantine, William [Serjeant]. *Some Experiences of a Barrister's Life.* New York: Henry Holt, 1882.

Beck, George Andrew, ed. *The English Catholics: 1850–1950.* London: Burns and Oates, 1950.

Belassis, Edward. *Memorials of Mr. Serjeant Belassis.* London: Burns and Oates, 1895.

Belloc, Hilaire. *Elizabeth: Creature of Circumstance.* London: Harper, 1942.

Bennett, F. *The Story of W.J.E. Bennett.* London: Longmans, Green, 1909.

Berman, Cassandra N. *Wayward Nuns, Randy Priests, and Women's Autonomy: "Convent Abuse" and the Threat to Protestant Patriarchy in Victorian England.* Religious Studies Honors Projects: DigitalCommons@Macalester College. https://digitalcommons.macalester.edu/cgi/viewcontent.cgi?referer=https://www.google.com/&httpsredir=1&article=1000&context=reli_honors.

Bisgood, Marie Therese. *Cornelia Connelly: A Study in Fidelity.* Westminster, MD: Newman, 1963.

Blacker, C.P. *Eugenics: Galton and After.* Cambridge: Harvard University Press, 1952.

Blehl, Vincent F. "Newman on Trial." *The Month,* n.s., 27 (February 1962): 69–80.

Bloomfield, Paul. *Uncommon People: A Study of England's Elite.* London: Hamish Hamilton, 1955.

Brampton, Henry Hawkins. *The Reminiscences of Sir Henry Hawkins, Baron Brampton.* 2 vols. London: E. Arnold, 1904.

Brown, Daniel. *Hopkins's Idealism: Philosophy, Physics, Poetry.* New York: Oxford University Press, 1997.

Butterfield, William. "Arundel Church." *London Times,* April 15, 1879, 4.

Cameron, A.T. *Religious Communities of the Church of England.* London: Faith, 1918.

Cannadine, David. *Aspects of Aristocracy: Grandeur and Decline in Modern Britain.* New Haven: Yale University Press, 1994.

Capper, Elizabeth, et al. *St. Helen's Church.* Norfolk: Heritage House Media, 2009.

Carlyle, Thomas. "Jesuitism" (1850). In *Latter-Day Pamphlets* (1853). Reprint, Freeport: Books for Libraries, 1972.

Casteris, Susan P. "Virgin Vows: The Early Victorian Artists' Portrayal of Nuns and Novices." *Victorian Studies* 24 (Winter 1981): 157–184.

"Catholics and Catholics." *London Times,* October 21, 1872, 10.

Cawthorne, Nigel. *Sex Lives of the Kings and Queens of England.* London: Prion, 1994.

Chadwick, Owen. *The Spirit of the Oxford Movement: Tractarian Essays.* Cambridge: Cambridge University Press, 1990.

———. *The Victorian Church.* 2 vols. New York: Oxford University Press, 1966 and 1970.

"Church Notes from Tichborne, Hants." *Gentlemen's Magazine* 80, n.s. 3 (1810): 305–306.

Clarke, Richard F. "Alexander Heriot MacKonochie." *The Month* 70 (September 1890): 65–73.

———. "Recollections of Henry James Coleridge." *The Month* 78 (June 1893): 167–181.

Cobbett, William. *A History of the Protestant Reformation in England and Ireland, 1824–25.* New York: John Hoyle, 1832.

Coburn, Kathleen. *In Pursuit of Coleridge.* London: Bodley Head, 1977.

Coleridge, Arthur. *Reminiscences.* Ed. J.A. Fuller-Maitland. New York: E.P. Dutton, 1921.

Coleridge, Bernard John Seymour (Lord). *The Story of a Devonshire House.* London: T. Fisher Unwin, 1905.

Coleridge, Edith. *Memoir and Letters of Sara Coleridge.* New York: Harper, 1874.

Coleridge, Ernest Hartley. *Life and Correspondence of John Duke Lord Coleridge, Lord Chief Justice of England.* 2 vols. London: William Heinemann, 1904.

Coleridge, Henry James. *Among the Prophets*. Published serially in *The Month* 17 (1872), 1–32, 268–296, 476–498; 19 (1873), 1167–1238, 292–310, 436–450; 29 (1874), 86–96.

———. *Anemone: A Tale*. Published serially in seventeen groups of three chapters each in *The Month* beginning with chapters 1–3 in vol. 33 (August 1877) and ending with chapters 49–51 in vol. 37 (December 1879).

———. *The Dialogues of Lydney*. Published serially in *The Month* beginning in vol. 10 (1869) and concluding in vol. 13 (1870).

———. "A Father of Souls." *The Month* 70 (October 1870): 153–164.

———. "A Memorial" [for James Robert Hope-Scott]. *The Month* 19 (1873): 274–291.

———. "Reflections on a Late Scandal." *The Month* 10 (March 1870): 201–216.

———. *Wafted Seeds*. Published serially in *The Month* beginning with chapter 1 in vol. 12 (1870) and concluding with chapter 50 in vol. 14 (1871).

Coleridge, Henry Nelson. "The Poetical Works of S.T. Coleridge." *Quarterly Review* 52 (August 1834): 1–38.

Coleridge, John Duke. "The Late Herbert Coleridge." *MacMillan's Magazine* 5 (November 1861): 56–60

———. "The Nineteenth Century Defenders of Vivisection." *Fortnightly Review*, n.s., 37 (February 1882): 225–238

Coleridge, John Taylor. *A Memoir of the Rev. John Keble*. 2 vols. Oxford and London: James Parker, 1870.

Coleridge, Mary Elizabeth. *The Collected Poems of Mary Elizabeth Coleridge*. Ed. Theresa Whistler. London: Rupert Hart-Davis, 1954.

———. *Gathered Leaves*. London: Constable, 1910.

———. *Non Sequitur*. London: James Nisbet, 1900.

Coleridge, Sara. *Memoir and Letters of Sara Coleridge*. Ed. Edith Coleridge. New York: Harper, 1874.

———. *Sara Coleridge and Henry Reed*. Ed. Leslie Nathan Broughton Ithaca: Cornell University Press, 1937.

Coleridge, Stephen. "The Administration of the Cruelty to Animals Act of 1876." *Fortnightly Review*, n.s., 7309 (March 1900): 392–398.

———. *Memories*. London: John Lane, 1913.

Collins, Paul. "Before Hercule or Sherlock, There Was Ralph." *New York Times Book Review*, January 9, 2011, 23.

Collins, Wilkie. *The Black Robe* (1881). Reprint, Stroud: Sutton, 1994.

———. *The Dead Secret* (1856). Reprint, New York: Harper and Row, 1874.

Colvin, Howard. *Unbuilt Oxford*. New Haven: Yale University Press, 1983.

"Common Pleas Division." *London Times*, May 19, 1879, 6.

Connelly, Pierce. *Reasons for Abjuring Allegiance to the See of Rome: A Letter to the Earl of Shrewsbury*. Philadelphia: Herman Hooker, 1852.

"Connelly v. Connelly." *London Times*, March 25, 1850, 6; June 28, 1851, 7; June 30, 1851, 7.

"Convents—Petition of the Rev. Pierce Connelly." Hansard. HC deb, vol. 116, cc931–5. May 12, 1851. https://api.parliament.uk/historic-hansard/commons/1851/may/12/convents-petition-of-the-rev-pierce.

Cooke, A.H. *The Early History of Mapledurham*. Oxford: Oxfordshire Records Society, 1925.

"Cornelia Connelly: Founder, Society of the Holy Child Jesus, 1809–1879." Society of the Holy Child Jesus. April 2014. http://vzsl938fcge1a49db1un9ih1.wpengine.netdna-cdn.com/wp-content/uploads/2014/04/here.pdf.

Crook. J. Mordaunt. *Victorian Architecture: A Visual Anthology*. New York: Johnson Reprint, 1971.

Curl, James Stevens. *English Heritage Book of Victorian Churches*. London: B.T. Batsford/English Heritage, 1995.

Darwin, Charles. *The Descent of Man*. London: John Murray, 1871.

———. *On the Origin of Species*. London: John Murray, 1859.

———. *The Variation of Animals and Plants Under Domestication.* London: John Murray, 1868.
Darwin, Francis, ed. *The Life and Letters of Charles Darwin.* 2 vols. New York: D. Appleton, 1887.
Dawson, Annette. *Cornelia Connelly: Three Characteristics.* London: Catholic Truth Society, 1979.
"Death of the [14th] Duke of Norfolk." *London Times*, November 27, 1860, 4.
Dickens, Charles. *Bleak House* (1853). Ed. Nicola Bradbury. Reprint, London: Penguin, 1996.
Disraeli, Benjamin. *Lothair.* New York: D. Appleton, 1881.
Dixon, Richard Watson. *The Last Poems of Richard Watson Dixon, D.D.* Ed. Robert Bridges. London: Henry Froude, 1905.
Dole, Carol M. "Mary Coleridge." *DLB* 19: 77–80.
Duffy, Eamon. *The Stripping of the Altars: Traditional Religion in England c. 1400–c. 1580.* New Haven: Yale University Press, 1992.
"The Duke of Norfolk vs Arbuthnot." *London Times*, March 26–29, 1879, and May 19, 1879.
"[Duke of] Norfolk v. Arbuthnot." *London Times*, March 26, 1879, 6; March 27, 1879, 4; March 28, 1879, 4; March 29, 1879, 6; March 31, 1879, 9; May 19, 1879, 6.
Earl of Shrewsbury. *Letter from the Earl of Shrewsbury to Ambrose Lisle Phillipps Esq. Descriptive of the Estatica of Caldaro and the Addolorata of Capriana,* London: Charles Dolman, 1841.
"The Earl of Shrewsbury on His Title and the Estates." *London Times*, October 5, 1859, 9.
The Earl of Shrewsbury Papers. Special Collections, Georgetown University. https://findingaids.library.georgetown.edu/repositories/15/resources/10582.
Eastlake, Charles. *A History of the Gothic Revival* (1872). Reprint, Whitefish, MT: Kessinger, 2007.
"E.A.T." *Alexander Heriot Mackonochie: A Memoir.* Ed. Edward Francis Russell. London: Kegan Paul, 1890.
"Editorial" [*Norfolk v. Arbuthnot*]. *London Times*, March 31, 1879, 9.
Edwards, Francis O. "The Archives of the English Province of the Society of Jesus at Farm Street, London." *Society of Archivists Journal* 3 (1966): 107–115.
———. *The Enigma of Gunpowder Plot, 1605: The Third Solution.* London: Four Courts, 2008.
———. *Guy Fawkes: The Real Story of the Gunpowder Plot.* London: Rupert Hart-Davis, 1969.
Elvins, Mark Turnham. *Arundel Priory, 1380–1980: The College of the Holy Trinity.* London: Phillimore, 1981.
Elwes, Winefride. *The Feilding Album.* London: Geoffrey Bles, 1950.
"The End of Roger Tichborne." *London Times*, November 18, 1874, 5.
"Estate: Caddell." *Landed Estate Database.* NUI Galway of Gaillimh. http://landedestates.nuigalway.ie/LandedEstates/jsp/estate-show.jsp?id=696.
"Eyre-Eyre v. Eyre." *London Times*, July 31, 1883, 3.
Faber, Geoffrey, *Oxford Apostles* (1936). Reprint, Harmondsworth: Penguin, 1954.
"Father William Eyre Obituary." *Letters and Notices* 131 (April 1898): 424–430.
Felix, Charles [Charles Warren Adams]. *The Notting Hill Mystery, Once a Week,* November 1862–January 1863. https://www.gutenberg.org/files/46153/46153-h/46153-h.htm.
"The Fifth of November." *London Times*, November 6, 1850, 6.
Finch, Mary E. *The Wealth of Five Northamptonshire Families: 1540–1640.* Oxford: Northamptonshire Record Society/Oxford University Press, 1956.
Finlason, W.F. *Report on the Trial and Preliminary Proceedings in the Case of the Queen on the Prosecution of* G. Achilli v. Dr. Newman. London: C. Dolman, 1852.
Fisher, Michael. *Alton Towers: A Gothic Wonderland.* Stafford: M.J. Fisher, 1999.
———. *Staffordshire and the Gothic Revival.* London: Landmark, 2006.
Fitzgerald, Percy. *Father Gallwey.* London: Burns and Oates, 1906.

Fitzsimons, John, ed. *Manning: Anglican and Catholic* (1951). Reprint, Westport, CT: Greenwood, 1979.
Foister, Susan. *Cardinal Newman, 1801–90: A Centenary Exhibition*. London: National Portrait Gallery, 1990.
Forrest, D.W. *Francis Galton: The Life and Work of a Victorian Genius*. London: Elek, 1974.
Frank, Ellen Eve. *Literary Architecture: Essays Towards a Tradition*. Berkeley: University of California Press, 1979.
Freeman, E.A. "The Case of the Collegiate Church of Arundel." *Archaeological Journal* 37 (1880): 244–270.
Frost, Ginger. *Promises Broken: Courtship, Class, and Gender in Victorian England*. Charlottesville and London: University Press of Virginia, 1995.
Gallwey, Peter. *Salvage from the Wreck: A Few Memories of Friends Departed, Preserved in Funeral Discourses*. London: Burns and Oates, 1889.
Galton, Francis. *Hereditary Genius* (1870). 2nd ed. New York: Appleton, 1875.
_____. "The Identiscope." *Nature*, October 30, 1884, 637–638.
_____. *Inquiries into Human Faculty and Its Development*. London: Macmillan, 1883.
_____. "Pangenesis." *Nature*, May 4, 1871, 5–6.
Gavin, M. *Memoirs of Father P. Gallwey, S.J.* London: Burns and Oates, 1913.
Gerard, John. "A Notable Convent Scandal." *The Month* 109 (1907): 428–429.
Gilbert, Michael. *The Claimant*. London: Constable, 1957.
Gilbert and Sullivan Archive. *Trial by Jury: Plot Summary*. https://gsarchive.net/trial/html/trial_plot_summary.html.
Gilley, S. "Achilli (Giovanni) Giacinto (b. c. 1803)." *Oxford Dictionary of National Biography*. Oxford: Oxford University Press, 2004.
Girouard, Mark. *Rushton Triangular Lodge*. London: English Heritage, 2004.
Gompertz, Mary Catherine. *The Life of Cornelia Connelly 1809–1879*. London: Longmans, Green, 1922.
Gorman, W. Gordon. *Converts to Rome*. London: Sands, 1910.
Grant, Neil. *The Howards of Norfolk*. London: Franklin Watts, 1972.
"The Great Imposter." *London Times*, March 2, 1874, 9–10.
Griffin, Susan M. "Revising the Popish Plot: Frances Trollope's 'The Abbess and Father Eustace.'" *Victorian Literature and Culture* 31 (2003): 279–293.
Griggs, Earl Leslie. *Coleridge Fille: A Biography of Sara Coleridge*. London: Oxford University Press, 1940.
_____. *Hartley Coleridge: His Life and Work*. London: University of London Press, 1929.
Grosart, Alexander B. *The Prose Works of William Wordsworth*. Vol. 3. London: Edward Moxon, 1876.
Gruber, Howard. *Darwin on Man: A Psychological Study of Scientific Creativity*. New York: E.P. Dutton, 1974.
Gwynn, Denis. *Cardinal Wiseman* (1929). Reprint, Dublin: Browne and Nolan, 1950.
_____. *Father Dominic Barberi*. Buffalo: Desmon and Stapleton, 1948.
_____. *A Hundred Years of Catholic Emancipation (1829–1929)*. London: Longman, Green, 1929.
_____. *Lord Shrewsbury, Pugin, and the Catholic Revival*. London: Hollis and Carter, 1946.
Hadland, Tony. *Thames Valley Papists: From Reformation to Emancipation, 1534–1829*. Mapledurham: Tony Hadland, 1995.
Hainton, Raymonde, and Godfrey Hainton. *The Unknown Coleridge: The Life and Times of Derwent Coleridge 1800–1883*. London: Janus, 1996.
Hamper, William. Harbison, Robert. *The Built, the Unbuilt, and the Unbuildable*. Cambridge: MIT Press, 1991.
Harris, Elizabeth Furlong Shipton. *From Oxford to Rome*. London: Longman, Brown, Green, and Longmans, 1847.
Harvey, John. *English Cathedrals*. London: P.T. Batsford, 1956.
Haynes, Alan. *The Gunpowder Plot: Faith in Rebellion*. London: Grange, 1994.

"Hearsay Evidence." *London Times*, November 25, 1871, 6.
Hersey, George. *High Victorian Gothic*. Baltimore: Johns Hopkins University Press, 1972.
Hibbert, Christopher. *King Mob: The London Riots of 1780*. London: Longmans, Green, 1958.
Hill, Rosemary. *God's Architect: Pugin and the Building of Romantic Britain*. New Haven: Yale University Press, 2007.
"Historical Chronicle" [11th Duke of Norfolk]. *Gentleman's Magazine* 86, n.s. 9 (1816): 64–66.
Hitchcock, Henry Russell. *Early Victorian Architecture in Britain*. New Haven: Yale University Press, 1954.
Holdsworth, William S. *A History of English Law*. 3 vols. 2nd ed. London: Methuen, 1903.
Holmes, J. Derek. *More Roman Than Rome: English Catholicism in the Nineteenth Century*. London: Burns and Oates, 1978.
_____. "Newman's Reputation and the Lives of the English Saints." *Catholic Historical Review* 51, no. 4 (January 1966): 528–538.
Hopkins, Gerard Manley. *Further Letters of Gerard Manley Hopkins Including His Correspondence with Coventry Patmore*. Ed. Claude Colleer Abbott. 2nd ed. London: Oxford University Press, 1956.
_____. *The Journals and Papers of Gerard Manley Hopkins*. Ed. Humphrey House and Graham Storey. 2nd ed. London: Oxford University Press, 1966.
_____. *The Letters of Gerard Manley Hopkins to Robert Bridges*. Ed. Claude Colleer Abbott. London: Oxford University Press, 1955.
_____. *Poems*. Ed. Robert Bridges. London: Humphrey Milford, 1918.
Horne, Abbot. *Relics of Popery*. London: Catholic Truth Society, 1949.
Howard, Henry. *Earl of Surrey: The Works of Henry Howard Earl of Surrey and of Sir Thomas Wyatt the Elder* (1815–16). University of Toronto Libraries: Representative Poetry Online. https://rpo.library.utoronto.ca/displayHughes.
Humphrey, Stephen C., ed. *Blue Guide to Churches and Chapels of Northern England*. New York: Norton, 1991.
_____. *Blue Guide to Churches and Chapels of Southern England*. London: A. and C. Black, 1991.
Hunt, W. Holman. *The Oxford Union Society*. Oxford: Oxford University Press, 1906.
"Ireland." *London Times*, July 9, 1872, 8; October 21, 1872, 10; December 17, 12.
Isham, Gyles. *Rushton Triangular Lodge*. London: Her Majesty's Stationery Office, 1970.
Jenkins, Simon. *England's Thousand Best Churches*. London: Allen Lane, 1999.
"Justifiable Curiosity." *London Times*, November 25, 1871, 5.
Kaye-Smith, Sheila. *Quartet in Heaven*. New York: Harper, 1952.
Keating, Joseph. "Father John Hungerford Pollen, S.J." *The Month* 145 (1925): 446–448.
Kilde, Jeanne Halgren. *Sacred Power, Sacred Space: An Introduction to Christian Architecture and Worship*. Oxford and New York: Oxford University Press, 2008.
Kingsley, Charles. *The Saint's Tragedy* (1848). In *The Poetical Works of Charles Kingsley*. New York: Thomas Y. Crowell, n.d.
_____. "Why Should We Fear the Romish Priests?" *Fraser's Magazine* 37 (1848): 467–474.
_____. *Yeast* (1851). London: Macmillan, 1893.
Knight, Roger. *King William IV: A King at Sea*. London: Allen Lane, 2011.
Landau, Tyron. *William Butterfield, 1814–1900*. London: Fischer Fine Art Exhibition Catalog, 1982.
Lane, Jane. *Titus Oates*. London: Andrew Dakers, 1949.
Larkin, Philip. *Philip Larkin: The Complete Poems*. Ed. Archie Burnett. New York: Farrar, Straus and Giroux, 2012.
Laskow, Sarah. "The Nun's Story." *Lapham's Quarterly*, April 16, 2015. https://www.laphamsquarterly.org/roundtable/nuns-story.
"The Late [11th] Duke of Norfolk." *Gentlemen's Magazine*, 85, n.s. 8 (1815): 631–632.
Leighton, Angela, and Margaret Reynolds, eds. *Victorian Women Poets: An Anthology*. Oxford: Blackwell, 1995.

The Life of Cornelia Connelly, 1809–1879: Foundress of the Society of the Holy Child Jesus. London: Longmans, Green, 1922.
Lumsden, Joy. "The True and Remarkable History of Andrew Bogle." *Jamaican History Studies* 11, no. 4 (October 1999). https://sites.google.com/site/myjamaicanhistoryarticles/the-true-and-remarkable-history-of-andrew-bogle.
MacGregor, Geddes. *The Tichborne Imposter.* Philadelphia: Lippincott, 1957.
Mack, Maynard. *Alexander Pope: A Life.* New York: W.W. Norton, 1985.
Manning, Henry Edward. *The Vatican Council and Its Definitions: A Pastoral Letter to the Clergy.* New York: D. and J. Sadlier, 1871.
"Mapledurham Church." *London Times,* April 16, 1879, 11.
Marcus, Steven. *Dickens: From Pickwick to Dombey.* New York: Basic, 1965.
Mariani, Mike. "Nativism, Violence, and the Origins of the Paranoid Style." *Slate,* March 22, 2017. http://www.slate.com/articles/news_and_politics/history/2017/03/the_awful_disclosures_of_maria_monk_and_the_origins_of_the_paranoid_style.html.
Marie Therese. *Cornelia Connelly: A Study in Fidelity.* Westminster, MD: Newman, 1961.
Martin, Robert Bernard. *Gerard Manley Hopkins: A Very Private Life.* London: HarperCollins, 1991.
Martineau, Harriet. *Sister Anna's Probation. Once a Week*: March 5, 1862, 309–315; March 22, 1862, 337–344; March 29, 1862, 365–373; April 5, 1862, 393–398; April 12, 1862, 421–426.
Mary Scholastica Joseph (Sister). *The Great Convent Case: Saurin v. Star and Kennedy.* London: Ward, Lock, and Tyler, 1869.
Maugham, Lord. *The Tichborne Case.* London: Hodder and Stoughton, 1936.
Mayhew, Henry. *London Labour and the London Poor* (1861–2). Reprint, New York: Dover, 1968.
McAdam, Gloria. "Willing Women and the Rise of Convents in Nineteenth-Century England." *Women's History Review* 8 (1999): 411–441.
McCracken, David. *Wordsworth* and the *Lake District.* Oxford: Oxford University Press, 1984.
McDonald, Frank. "Forgotten Nun Back to Hold Up Her Corner." *Irish Times,* April 1, 1998. https://www.irishtimes.com/news/forgotten-nun-back-to-hold-up-her-corner-1.140150?mode=print&ot=example.AjaxPageLayout.ot.
McWilliam, Rohan. *The Tichborne Claimant: A Victorian Sensation.* London: Continuum UK, 2007.
Midgley, J.B. *Antonio Rosmini: Priest, Founder of the Institutes of Charity.* London: Catholic Truth Society, 2015.
Milburn, Robert. "The Newman Brothers: Free Choice or Fate?" *Contemporary Review* 258, (May 1991): 267–269.
Mirow, Matthew C. "Roman Catholicism on Trial: The Libel Case of John Henry Newman and Dr. Achilli." *Catholic Lawyer* 36 (1996): 401–453.
Monk, Maria. *Awful Disclosures of Maria Monk: The Thrilling Mysteries of a Convent Revealed!* and *Six Months in a Convent* (c. 1836). Reprint, London: Forgotten, 2012.
Moran, Maureen. *Catholic Sensationalism and Victorian Literature.* Liverpool: Liverpool University Press, 2007.
———. "The End of the Beginning: A Reply to Christopher Prendergast." *New Left Review* 41 (2006): 71–85.
Morris, John, ed. *The Life of Mother Henrietta Kerr* (1886). 4th ed. Roehampton: Convent of the Sacred Heart, 1921.
Mozley, T. *Reminiscences Chiefly of Oriel College and the Oxford Movement.* 2 vols. London: Longmans, Green, 1882.
Muratore, Umberto, and Dennis Hare. *Antonio Rosmini: His Life, His Friends, His Works, His Thought.* Genoa: Centro Internazionale di Studi Rosminiani, 1997.
"The Murphy Riots." *London Times,* May 28, 1868, 11; May 29, 1868, 5.
Napier, Michael. *The London Oratory.* Norwich, CT: Jarrold, 1987.
Napier, Michael, and Alistair Laing. *The London Oratory: Centenary 1884–1984.* London: Trefoil, 1984.

Newman, Francis W. *Contributions Chiefly to the Early History of the Late Cardinal Newman.* London: Kegan Paul, Trench, and Trubner, 1891.

———. *Phases of Faith, or Passages from the History of My Creed* (1850). 6th ed., 1860. Reprint, New York: Humanities, 1970.

Newman, John Henry. *Apologia Pro Vita Sua.* Ed. David J. Delaura. New York: W.W. Norton, 1968.

———. *Autobiographical Writings.* Ed. Henry Tristram. New York: Sheed and Ward, 1957.

———. *Callista: A Tale of the Third Century.* London: Burns and Oates, 1855.

———. *Eight Lectures on the Position of Catholics in England.* Ed. W. Barry. London: Catholic Truth Society, 1890. (Omits "Lecture V" of the 1851 edition.)

———. *An Essay on the Development of Christian Doctrine* (1845). Reprint, Garden City: Doubleday, 1960.

———. *Gain and Loss: The Story of a Convert* (1848). 6th ed. London: Burns and Oates, 1874.

———. *Lectures on the Present Position of Catholics in England.* London: Burns and Lambert, 1851.

———. *The Letters and Diaries of John Henry Newman.* 32 vols. Oxford: Clarendon, 1978–1984, vols. 1–4, ed. Ian Ker and Thomas Gornall; vol. 5, ed. Thomas Gornall; vol. 6, ed. Gerard Tracy. London: Nelson, 1961–1972, vols. 11–22, ed. C.S. Dessain, et al. Oxford: Clarendon Press, 1973–1977, vols. 23–31, ed. C.S. Dessain and Thomas Gornall. New York: Oxford University Press, 2009, vol. 32, ed. Francis J. McGrath.

———. *The Letters of John Henry Newman.* Ed. Derek Stanford and Muriel Spark. Westminster, MD: Newman, 1957.

———. *Newman the Oratorian.* Ed. Placid Murray (1968). 2nd ed. Leominster: Fowler Wright, 1980.

———. *A Packet of Letters: A Selection from the Correspondence of John Henry Newman.* Oxford: Clarendon, 1983.

———. *Sermon Notes of John Henry Cardinal Newman 1849–1878.* Ed. Fathers of the Birmingham Oratory. London: Longmans, Green, 1913.

———. *Sermons and Discourses: 1839–57.* New York: Longmans, Green, 1949.

———. *Tract Number Ninety: Remarks on Certain Passages of the Thirty-Nine Articles* (1841). 2nd ed. Reprint, New York: H.B. Durand, 1865.

———. *Tracts Theological and Ecclesiastical.* Reprint, Westminster, MD: Christian Classics, 1974.

———. *Two Essays on Biblical and Ecclesiastical Miracles* (1870). London: Longmans, Green, 1918.

Newman, John Henry, and James Toovey. *The Lives of the English Saints.* 6 vols. 1844–45. Ed. Arthur Wollaston Hutton. London: S.T. Freemantle, 1901.

Nixon, Judd V. *Gerard Manley Hopkins and His Contemporaries: Liddon, Newman, Darwin, and Pater.* New York: Garland, 1993.

———. "The Kindly Light: A Reappraisal of the Influence of Newman on Hopkins." *Texas Studies in Literature and Language* 31 (Spring 1989): 105–142.

Norman, E.R. *Anti-Catholicism in Victorian England.* New York: Barnes and Noble, 1968.

"A Novel Importation." *London Times,* November 13, 1850, 5.

"Obituary" [12th Duke of Norfolk]. *Gentlemen's Magazine* 171, n.s. 17 (1842): 542–543.

"Obituary" [13th Duke of Norfolk]. *Gentlemen's Magazine* 199, n.s. 45 (1856): 419–421.

"Obituary" [14th Duke of Norfolk]. *Gentlemen's Magazine* 210, n.s. 56 (1861): 98–100.

Oliphant, Dave, and Carl Sutton, eds. *Hopkins Lives: An Exhibition and Catalogue.* Austin: Harry Ransom Humanities Research Center, 1989.

Oliver, E.J. *Coventry Patmore.* New York: Sheed and War, 1956.

Ornsby, Robert. *Memoirs of James Robert Hope-Scott of Abbotsford.* 2 vols. London: John Murray, 1884.

"Papistical Casuistry." *London Times,* November 15, 1850, 5.

Parker, John Henry. *An Introduction to the Study of Gothic Architecture* (1849). 8th ed. London, Parker, 1888.

Patmore, Coventry. *The Angel in the House Together with The Victories of Love*. London: George Routledge and Sons, n.d.
_____. *The Poems of Coventry Patmore*. Ed. Frederick Page. London: Oxford University Press, 1949.
_____. "Walls and Wall-Painting at Oxford." *Saturday Review*, December 26, 1857, 583–4.
Patrick, James. "Newman, Pugin, and Gothic." *Victorian Studies* 24 (Winter 1981): 184–207.
Paz, D.G. *Popular Anti-Catholicism in Mid-Victorian England*. Stanford: Stanford University Press, 1992.
_____. *The Priesthoods and Apostasies of Pierce Connelly: A Study of Victorian Conversion and Anticatholicism*. Lewiston: Edwin Mellen, 1986.
Pevsner, Nikolaus, and Jennifer Sherwood. *Oxfordshire*. Harmondsworth: Penguin, 1974.
Phillipps de Lisle, Ambrose. *The Life and Letters of Ambrose Phillipps de Lisle*. 2 vols. Ed. E.S. Purcell. London: Macmillan, 1900.
Pollen, Anne. *John Hungerford Pollen*. London: John Murray, 1912.
Pollen, John Hungerford, II. "The Centenary of the Restoration of the Society of Jesus." *The Month*, vol. 123 (January 1914): 56–71.
_____. *The Life and Letters of Father John Morris of the Society of Jesus*. London: Burns and Oates, 1896.
_____. "Newman in Dublin" (1890). *The Month*, September 1906, 317–320.
_____. "Recollections of Henry James Coleridge." *The Month* 78 (June 1893): 153–181.
_____. "Thomas, Earl of Arundel, and His Catholicism, 1585–1646." *The Month* 138 (November 1921): 385–398.
The Pre-Raphaelites. London: Tate Gallery Exhibition, 1984.
"The Priesthood in France." *London Times*, December 5, 1850, 8.
Reed, John Shelton. *Glorious Battle: The Cultural Politics of Victorian Anti-Catholicism*. Nashville: Vanderbilt University Press, 1996.
Reid, Forrest. *Illustrators of the Eighteen Sixties: An Illustrated Survey* (1928). New York: Dover, 1974.
"Release of Powers" [*Eyre v. Eyre-Eyre*]. *The Law Times*. Vols. 99–100. London: Law Times, 1895–96. February 1, 1896, 308. https://books.google.com/books?id=S_04AQAAMAAJ&pg=RA1-PA308&lpg=RA1-PA308&dq=eyreeyre+v+eyre+law+case+England&source=bl&ots=CS99C2jWos&sig=kMBqNKiFxO9J7Eq1WsFxgCoKyUk&hl=en&sa=X&ved=0ahUKEwih_NSb1ebNAhUBeD4KHTMD6Q4ChDoAQgoMAQ#v=onepage&q=eyreeyre%20v%20eyre%20law%20case%20England&f=false.
A Religious of the Society of the Holy Child Jesus. *A Daughter of Coventry Patmore: Sister Mary Christina, S.H.C.J*. London: Longmans, Green, 1924.
"Religious Riots in Lancashire." *London Times*, May 29, 1868, 5.
Report on Manuscripts in Various Collections. London: His Majesty's Stationary Office, 1904. https://archive.org/stream/variousmanuscripts03greauoft/variousmanuscripts03greauoft_djvu.txt.
Reports of Cases Argued and Determined in the English Courts of Common Law with Tables of the Cases and Principal Matters. Vol. 95. Ed. Henry Wharton. Philadelphia: T. and J.W. Johnson, 1870.
Reports of Cases Argued and Determined in the English Ecclesiastical Courts. Ed. Edward D Ingraham. Vol 2. Philadelphia: P.H. Nicklin and T. Johnson, 1831. https://books.google.com/books?id=no40AAAAIAAJ&pg=PA292&lpg=PA292&dq=mrs+molony+to+ireland&source=bl&ots=HRZFBn9kQx&sig=ACfU3U3W44LuDlgcqw8OS8PV8Z2Is4jQTA&hl=en&sa=X&ved=2ahUKEwittua8rfrlAhWwo1kKHfTkDowQ6AEwAXoECAgQAQ#v=onepage&q=mrs%20molony%20to%20ireland&f=false.
Richter, Donald C. *Riotous Victorians*. Athens: Ohio University Press, 1982.
Rickaby, Joseph. *Index to the Works of John Henry Cardinal Newman* (1914). Reprint, Westminster, MD: Christian Classics, 1977.
_____. "[Mrs. Humphrey Ward's] *Helbeck of Bannisdale*." *The Month* 92 (1898): 1–6.

Robbins, William. *The Newman Brothers: An Essay in Comparative Intellectual Biography.* Cambridge: Harvard University Press, 1966.

Roberts, E., and E. Crockford. *A History of Tichborne.* Tichborne: Church of St. Andrew at Tichborne, n.d.

Roberts, Gerald. "Living with Fr. Eyre: Hopkins at Stonyhurst College 1882–84." *Hopkins Quarterly* 39 (Summer–Fall 2012): 77–87.

Robinson, John Martin. *The Dukes of Norfolk: A Quincentennial History.* Oxford: Oxford University Press, 1982.

Rome's Recruits: A List of Protestants Who Have Become Roman Catholics. Burns and Oates: Oxford and London, 1878. Reprint of *The Whitehall Review,* September 28 and October 5, 12, and 19, 1878.

Rowell, Geoffrey. *The Vision Glorious: Themes and Personalities of the Catholic Revival in Anglicanism.* Oxford: Clarendon, 1983.

Ruggles, Eleanor. *Journey into Faith: The Anglican Life of John Henry Newman.* New York: Norton, 1948.

Ruskin, John. *The Art Criticism of John Ruskin.* Ed. Robert L. Herbert. Garden City, NY: Anchor, 1964.

_____. *The Works of John Ruskin.* Ed. E.T. Cook and A. Wedderburn. 39 vols. London: George Allen, 1903–1912.

"St. Barnabas Church." *London Times,* December 23, 1850, 5.

"St. Etheldreda's Chapel in Ely-Place." *London Times,* March 5, 1875, 6.

St. Etheldreda's Ely Place. London: Scala Arts and Heritage, 2013.

St. Helen's Church. Norfolk: Jarrod, 2009.

St. Ignatius of Loyola. *The Spiritual Exercises* (1548). Trans. Elder Mullan. New York: P.J. Kennedy, 1914.

St. Nicholas Parish Church Arundel: A Short History Guide. Norfolk: St. Nicholas, n.d.

"Saurin v. Star." *London Times,* February 4, 1869, 10; February 5, 1869, 8; February 6, 1869, 8; February 26, 1869, 8–9; February 27, 1869, 8; December 10, 1869, 9; January 12, 1870, 10; April 21, 1870, 9.

Schupbach, William. "Visiting the Stigmatics of the South Tyrol—I. Maria Domenica Lazzari." April 20, 2011. http://blog.wellcomelibrary.org/2011/04/visiting-the-stigmatics-of-the-south-tyrol-i-maria-domenica-lazzari.

_____. "Visiting the Stigmatics of the South Tyrol—II. Maria Domenica Lazzari and Maria von Moehrl." April 20, 2011. http://blog.wellcomelibrary.org/2011/04/visiting-the-stigmatics-of-the-south-tyrol-ii-maria-domenica-lazzari-and-maria-von-moehrl.

Secord, James A. "Nature's Fancy: Charles Darwin and the Breeding of Pigeons." *Isis* 72, no. 2 (January 1981): 162–186.

Seymour, M. Hobart. *Mornings Among the Jesuits at Rome.* New York: Harper, 1855.

Shairp, John Campbell. *John Keble: An Essay on the Author of "The Christian Year."* Edinburgh: Edmonson and Douglas, 1866.

"The Shrewsbury Estates." *London Times,* August 5, 1859, 10.

Siddall, Ruth. "Urban Geology in St. Pancras Church." St. Pancras New Church, 2012. http://www.ucl.ac.uk/~ucfbrxs/Homepage/walks/StPancrasNewChurch.pdf.

Sieveking, Isabel Giberne. *Memoir and Letters of Francis W. Newman.* London: Kegan Paul, Trench, and Trubner, 1909.

Sieveking, Lance. *The Eye of the Beholder.* London: Hulton, 1957.

_____. "Remembering Gerard Manley Hopkins." *Listener* 57 (January 1957): 151–152.

Smart, C.M. *Muscular Churches: Ecclesiastical Architecture of the High Victorian Period.* Fayetteville: University of Arkansas Press, 1989.

Stanton, Phoebe. *Pugin.* New York: Viking, 1971.

Stoker, Bram. "Arthur Orton." *Famous Imposters* (1910). Project Gutenberg. https://www.gutenberg.org/ebooks/51391.

Stone, Lawrence. *The Crisis of the Aristocracy, 1558–1641.* New York: Oxford University Press, 1965.

"The Story of Martin Guerre." *London Times,* December 12, 1871, 5.

Street, G.E. *Brick and Marble in the Middle Ages: Notes of a Tour in the North of Italy* (1855). Reprint, Cambridge: Cambridge University Press, 2012.
Stuart, Janet. "Father Peter Gallwey, S.J." *The Month* 122 (September 1913): 225–233.
Sugg, Joyce. *Ever Yours Affly: John Henry Newman and His Female Circle*. Leominster: Fowler Wright, 1996.
Summerson, John. "Charting the Victorian Building World." In *The Unromantic Castle*. London: Thames and Hudson, 1990.
_____. *Heavenly Mansions and Other Essays on Architecture* (1963). Reprint, New York: W.W. Norton, 1998.
Sutcliffe, Edmund F. *Bibliography of the English Province of the Society of Jesus, 1773–1953*. Roehampton: Manresa, 1957.
Svaglic, Martin J. "Charles Newman and His Brothers." *Publications of the Modern Language Association* 71 (1956): 370–385.
Swaab, Peter. *The Regions of Sara Coleridge's Thought*. New York: Palgrave MacMillan, 2012.
Thompson, Paul. *William Butterfield*. Cambridge: MIT Press, 1971.
Thornton, R.K.R. *All My Eyes See: The Visual World of Gerard Manley Hopkins*. Sunderland: Coelfrith, 1978.
Thurston, Herbert. "Catholic Writers and Elizabethan Readers: IV—Philip Earl of Arundel." *The Month* 86 (January 1896): 32–50.
"The Tichborne Case." *London Times*, April 1, 1872, 8; January 15, 1872, 4; April 27, 1872, 12; July 12, 1872, 9; May 31, 1873, 10; June 5, 1873, 10–11; June 7, 1873, 10; July 25, 1873, 11; July 26, 1873, 10–11; August 22, 1873, 8.
Tomalin, Claire. *Mrs. Jordan's Profession: The Actress and the Prince*. New York: Alfred A. Knopf, 1995.
Traver, Teresa Huffman. "Losing a Family, Gaining a Church: Catholic Conversion and English Domesticity." *Victorian Review* 37, no. 1 (Spring 2011): 127–143.
Trevor, Meriol. *Newman [I]: The Pillar of the Cloud*. Garden City, NY: Doubleday, 1963.
_____. *Newman [II]: Light in Winter*. Garden City, NY: Doubleday, 1963.
_____. *Newman's Journey* (1974). London: Fount Paperbacks, 1996.
Trollope, Frances. *Father Eustace*. London: Henry Colburn, 1847.
Trower, C.F. "The Arundel Chancel Case." *Sussex Archaeological Collections* 30 (1880): 31–51.
Tucker, Melvin J. *The Life of Thomas Howard: Earl of Surrey and Second Duke of Norfolk, 1443–1524*. The Hague: Mouton, 1964.
Tuckwell, William. *Reminiscences of Oxford*. London: Cassell, 1900.
Twain, Mark. *Following the Equator* (1897). Reprint, London: John Beaufoy, 2017.
Wadham, Juliana. *The Case of Cornelia Connelly*. New York: Pantheon, 1957.
Wagner, Anthony Richard. *English Genealogy*. Oxford: Clarendon, 1960.
Walsh, James. *Forty Martyrs of England and Wales*. London: Catholic Truth Society, 1972
Walsh, Walter. *The Secret History of the Oxford Movement*. 3rd ed. London: Swan Sonnenschein, 1898.
Ward, Mrs. Humphrey. *Robert Elsmere*. London: Macmillan, 1888.
Ward, Wilfrid. *The Life of John Henry Cardinal Newman*. 2 vols. London: Longmans, Green, 1912. http://www.newmanreader.org/biography/ward/index.html.
Weinreb, Ben, and Christopher Hibbert, eds. *The London Encyclopedia*. London: Macmillan, 1983.
Wharton, Henry, ed. *Reports of Cases Argued and Determined in the English Courts of Common Law* [Earl of Shrewsbury v. Scott]. Philadelphia: T. and J.W. Johnson, 1870. Vol 95: 1–222. https://books.google.com/books?id=kYcwAAAAIAAJ&pg=PA8&lpg =PA8&dq=jesuit+gilbert+earl+of+shrewsbury&source=bl&ots=afXXn3_7fZ&sig=a OJyNGcLNPbyNgQc1BwHQDIxszo&hl=en&sa=X&ved=0ahUKEwjwz5nE65TNAh UMMSYKHbcyBa4Q6AEIPjAG#v=onepage&q=jesuit%20gilbert%20earl%20of%20 shrewsbury&f=false.
"What Will Be Done with the Ritualists?" *The Spectator*, November 22, 1879, 9.

Williams, Raymond. *The Long Revolution* (1961). Reprint, Harmondsworth: Penguin, 1965.

———. *Marxism and Literature*. Oxford: Oxford University Press, 1977.

Williams, Richard. *Mapledurham House*. Mapledurham: Mapledurham House, 1977.

Wiseman, (Cardinal) Nicholas. "Dr. Achilli." *Dublin Review* 28 (June 1850): 469–511.

Woodruff, Douglas. *The Tichborne Claimant: A Victorian Mystery*. New York: Farrar, Straus, and Cudahy, 1957.

Woolf, Virginia. "Sara Coleridge." *Death of a Moth and Other Essays*. London: Hogarth, 1942.

Woollen, Wilfrid. *Father Faber*. London: Catholic Truth Society, 1962.

Zaniello, Tom. "Another Link Between Hopkins and Newman." *Hopkins Quarterly* 22 (Winter–Spring 1995): 45–50.

———. "The Coleridges: Notes on a Family Associated with Hopkins." *Hopkins Quarterly* 40 (Winter–Spring 2013): 8–18.

———. "The Divided Victorian Church: Butterfield and the Anglo-Catholic Compromise." *Religion and the Arts* 5 (2001): 172–184.

———. *Hopkins in the Age of Darwin*. Iowa City: University of Iowa Press, 1989.

Index

Achilli, Giacinto 19, 64–65, 69–82, 87
Adams, Charles Warren 171–186
Adelaide, Queen 91, 102
All Saints Babbacombe Church 46
All Saints Margaret Street Church 47, 107, 200
Alton Towers 84, 99–112
Annan, Noel 2–3, 26–27
Arbuthnot, the Rev. George 157–161
Arnold, Tom 16
Arundel of Wardour, Lord 134, 165, 167–168
Arundel Castle 152–153, 155, 157
Atlay, J.B. 132, 137, 145, 148

Ballantine, Sergeant William 131
Balliol Chapel 45
Barberi, Dominic 65
Bardolf, Sir Robert 89, 95
Beckham, William Thomas 99–100
Bellasis, Sergeant Edward 55, 62, 106, 109–110, 202
Bennett, W.J.E. 12–13, 47
Beresford-Hope, A.J.B. 201
Blount, Lyster 89
Blount, Martha 90
Blount, Richard 89, 94–98
Bogle, Andrew 130–134, 149
Borges, Jorge Luis 149
Bowles, Emily 55, 58–59, 114
Bradden, Mary Elizabeth 138
Bridges, Robert 1, 3, 41, 167, 181
Brownbill, Father 67
Buckeridge, Charles 201–202
Butterfield, William 3, 13–15, 35, 38, 41–42, 44–48, 85, 90–97, 157–159, 162, 173, 196, 200–201

Caddell, Pauline 190–192
Caddell, Robert 188

Caddell, Sophia 190–192
Calvat, Melanie 40
Campbell, Lord Chief Justice John 72, 74, 78, 80, 87, 144
The Castle of Andalusia 143
Chantrey, Francis 92–93
Church of the Immaculate Conception (Mayfair) 190
Clarke, Richard F. 40
Cobb, Frances Power, 180
Cockburn, Sir Alexander 3, 73, 75–77, 108–109, 117–118, 122, 140, 145, 148–149
Coleridge, Bernard 182, 184–186
Coleridge, Christabel 11, 12, 172
Coleridge, Derwent 41–42
Colerdige, Edward 90, 95–96, 106
Coleridge, Ernest Hartley 1, 49, 136, 145, 174
Coleridge, Henry James 36–40, 42–45, 144–145
Coleridge, Henry Nelson 34, 41–43
Coleridge, Herbert 43
Coleridge, Lady Jane 37, 48
Coleridge, Lord Chief Justice John Duke 3, 13, 32–35, 34–35, 42–43, 48–49, 118–120, 136–139, 160–161, 164, 171
Coleridge, John Taylor 33, 80–82, 87
Coleridge, Mary Elizabeth 40–41, 172, 181–182
Coleridge, Mildred Mary 37, 171–174, 181
Coleridge, Samuel Taylor 3, 32, 28, 93, 172
Coleridge. Sara 10, 12, 25, 35, 42
Coleridge, Stephen 171–172, 174–175, 178, 182–183
Collins, Wilkie 10, 101, 187
Connelly, Adeline 53, 61

229

Index

Connelly, Cornelia 52–63, 68, 114
Connelly, Pierce 52–63, 68
Cornthwaite, Rev. 118
Cumming, Rev. 15
Cundy, Thomas 12
Cusack, Margaret Anna 40

Darwin, Charles 2, 25, 27–28
de Kock, Paul 143–144
de Lisle, Ambrose Phillipps 83
Dennam, Judge 179, 182–183
Dickens, Charles 21, 24, 102
Disraeli, Benjamin 27, 110–11
Dixon, Canon R.W. 40, 181
Doughty, Catherine (Lady Radcliffe) 129, 141, 145, 149
Drummond, Henry 56
Dyce, William 47

Eastlake, Sir Charles 13
Eastlake, Lady Elizabeth Rigby 173
The Ecclesiologist 46–48
Elizabeth I, Queen 154–155, 199
Elizabeth II, Queen 94
Ely Cathedral 104, 206
Erechtheum 196
Evangelical Alliance 69–70
Eyre, Archbishop Charles 165, 169
Eyre, John Lewis 165, 168–169
Eyre, Thomas Joseph 169
Eyre, William 165–166, 168–170

Faber, Frederick Wilfrid 64, 83, 163, 206
Feilding, Rudolph 19
Feilding, Louisa Pennant 19
Finlason, W.F. 72–74, 76, 78–81
Fitzalan Chapel 152, 154, 156–190
Fitzclarence, Augustus, Duke of Clarence 90, 93, 97–98, 102
Fonthill Abbey 99–100
The Fourth Plinth 97–98
Freeman, Edward A. 158–159, 163
Fust, Judge J.H. 56

Gallilee Porch 205
Gallwey, Peter 188
Galton, Francis 2, 27–30, 32, 42, 66–67
Giberne, George 65
Giberne, Maria Rosina (Sister Maria Pia) 2, 36, 66, 81–82, 205
Giffard, Hardinge 139, 150
Gilbert and Sullivan 2, 148–149
Gladstone, W.E. 11
Gregory XVI, Pope 54

Gribble, Herbert 84–85
Guerre, Martin 141–142, 148
The Gunpowder Plot 18, 199
Guy Fawkes Day 18, 199

Harris, Elizabeth Furlong Shipton 60
Hawkfield Lodge 199
Henrietta Maria, Queen 88
Henry VIII, King 10, 15, 78, 113, 154–155, 159, 187–188, 196, 200
Hofstadter, Richard 7
Holy Trinity Convent 201
Hope-Scott, James Robert 106, 109–110
Hopkins, Gerard Manley 1, 3, 11, 15, 36, 38, 41, 45, 46, 69, 81, 165–167, 181, 187, 190, 205
Hopkins, Millicent 46
Howard, Lord Edmund 109
Hubbard, John Gallibrand 40
Huddeston, Baron 177

Inwood, William and Mary, 195–196
The Irvingites 56, 71, 106

James, Sir Henry, 183
Jarndyce v. Jarndyce 21–22
Jordan, Mrs. Dora (Dorothea Bland) 91–94

Kay, Justice 168
Kenealy, Edward Vaughan 133, 141–146, 148–149
Kennedy, Julia (Sister Mary Magdalen) 115, 145–151
Kenworthy, Sister Mary Francis 61–62
Kingsley, Charles 82

L'Addolorata (Maria Domenica Lazzari) 102
Landor, William Savage 90–91
Laprimaudaye, C.J. 42, 53–54
Laprimaudaye, Maria Margaret Theresa 81
Larkin, Philip 152, 155
L'Estatica (Maria von Moehrl) 102
Lewis, Janet 148
Lockhart, William 202
Loder, Mary Ann 134
Lush, Mr.Justice 140, 142
Lushington, Colonel 130, 135

Mackonochie, Alexander 13–15, 47
Manning, Henry, Cardinal 54, 168
Market House @ Rothwell 199

Index

Martineau, Harriet 113–114
Mary Agnes, Sister 6–7
Mayhew, Henry 9
Mellor, Judge 113–116, 140, 145–146
Millais, John Everett 17, 113–114
Monk, Maria 6–8, 16, 39, 70, 76, 113, 115–116, 134, 201
Monkswell, Lord 177–178, 182
Mozley, Thomas 68, 83
Murphy, William 20

New Bield @ Lyveden 100, 105, 199
Newman, Charles 67
Newman, Frank 65–66
Newman, Cardinal John Henry 3, 7, 11, 16, 18–19, 26, 34–35, 37, 45, 48, 58–61, 64, 103, 114, 120, 202–206
Norfolk, 11th Duke 161–162
Norfolk, 12th Duke 17, 161
Norfolk, 13th Duke 161–163
Norfolk, 14th Duke 85, 123, 161–164
Norfolk, 15th Duke 85, 152, 156, 161

oratorians 11, 36, 64, 82–86
Orton, Arthur 30–31, 38, 125, 130–150
Orton, Charles 134

Paddington Old Cemetery (Willesden Land Cemetery) 146
pangenesis 28
The Papal Aggression 15
Patmore, Coventry 54, 167
Patmore, Emily 54
Patteson, John Coleridge 35
Perry, Stephen 167
Phillimore, Dr. R. 94–96
Phillipps, Ambrose 70, 83, 85–86
Phillpotts, Bishop Henry 200
Pollen, John Hungerford 81
Polsen, Mrs. 176
Pope, Alexander 90
Prior Crauden's Chapel 204–205
Pugin, W.E.M. 13, 26, 44, 54, 83–84, 86, 99–106, 111, 200, 205
Pusey, Nathan 35, 36, 45, 85

Rakowitz, Michael 98
Reed, Rebecca Theresa 6
The Rosminians 108, 202
Ruskin, John 1, 3, 44, 200
Rushton Triangular Lodge 100–101, 199

St. Alban's Holborn 14, 47
St. Andrew's Church 127–128

St. Barnabas Church 112–13, 47
St. Etheldreda 204, 206
St. Etheldreda's Church (Ely Place) 108, 202–204, 206
St. Helen's Church Bishopsgate 158, 197–198
St. John, Ambrose 67, 71,
St. Margaret's Church Mapledurham 89–90, 93–97
St. Nicholas Church 152, 155–157, 162–163
St. Pancras New Church 195
St. Paul's Covent Garden Rectory 48
Saurin, Susanna Mary (Sister Scholastica) 113–124
Scott, Gilbert 155, 157, 159
Seymour, Henry 134
Shaftesbury, Earl 55, 78–79
Shrewsbury, 13th Earl 107–109
Shrewsbury, 15th Earl 107, 109
Shrewsbury, 16th Earl 8, 40, 70, 99–100, 102–104, 106–107, 110–111
Shrewsbury, 17th Earl 58–59, 106–108
Shrewsbury, Lady 55
Shrewsbury and Talbot, 18h Earl 108–112
Shrewsbury and Talbot, 19th Earl 110
Shrewsbury and Talbot, 20th Earl 111
Shrigley, David 97–98
Sieveking, Isabel Giberne 36, 65–66
Star, Mary Ann (Sister Mary Joseph) 113–124
stigmatics 102
Stonyhurst College 55, 102, 129, 135, 144–146, 188–189
Stowe, Harriet Beecher 7
"structure of feeling" 2–3, 26–27

Thesiger, Frederic 72, 76–78
Tichborne, Alfred Joseph 130
Tichborne, Arthur Joseph 130
Tichborne, Chidioch 125–126, 139
Tichborne, Henry 126
Tichborne, Henry Alfred Joseph 130
Tichborne, Lady Mabella 126
Tichborne, Robert 126–127
Tichborne, Roger 31, 125
Tichborne Bonds 144
The Tichborne Dole 126
Tichborne-Doughty, Henriette Felicite (Lady Doughty) 130, 148
Tresham, Francis 199
Tresham, Sir James 129
Tresham, Sir Thomas 100, 105, 198–199
Twain, Mark 149

Victoria, Queen 93

Whalley, G.H. 20, 137
Whiteread, Rachel 98
William IV, King 90–97, 102
Williams, Raymond 2, 26

Wiseman, Cardinal Nicholas 17–19, 55, 64, 69, 72, 162
Wollascott, William III 89

Yonge, Charlotte 172